The Church of Stuart Pearce and other stories

Rich Fisher

Foreword by Brian Rice

First published in 2018 through Createspace

ISBN-13: 978-1981701711

ISBN-10: 1981701710

www.facebook.com/churchofstuartpearce

This Facebook page was set up in the run-up to the publication date for this book, and it includes lots of photos and other material relating to some of the tales shared within the 28 chapters.

You can also find the author on Twitter and Instagram, although don't expect him to be massively interesting on either of these mediums!

Twitter - @mrrichfisher

Instagram – mrrichfisher

Dedicated with love to the memory of
Neil Richard Warburton,
4/4/1980 – 6/5/2000

Rich Fisher

Foreword

As a former player of Nottingham Forest from 1985 to 1991, it gives me great pleasure to be asked to write a few words to introduce this book.

It's a book about what it's like to be an avid football fan, travelling the country supporting your chosen team. In today's game it is more important than ever that we remind everyone involved with football that the fans play a massive part in our national sport.

As a player, you love to hear the fans cheering the team on and being the extra man when things are tough. At Forest, during my time the fans certainly inspired the players on the field and gave the club tremendous vocal support. Several decades after it amazes and humbles me that they still sing my name and talk about my goal away at Arsenal in the FA Cup.

I very much hope that you enjoy reading Rich's book. From collecting football stickers, autographs and programmes to long away game journeys, I am sure there will be many stories you'll be able to relate to and look back at with a smile. Whether you are a Forest fan or not this book will bring memories flooding back to every football fan.

Brian Rice

1. 1989 and all that

"Al and I took great delight in pinning the Thatcher pic to the dartboard in order to chuck arrows at her. I guess I was always destined to be a Red..."

The year 1989 seems like a long time ago now – probably because it was!

Stats from those days reveal that the average price of a house in the UK was just £54,000. A pint of lager would've cost you £1.08. And a litre of petrol cost just 38 pence.

Mind you, the average annual salary was just £13,000 – or £17,000 if you lived in London.

1989 was an interesting time too in terms of global politics. Here in the UK, Margaret Thatcher was in her penultimate year as the nation's first ever female Prime Minister. Tensions between the Western and Eastern Blocs had also been rumbling on for many years – and it was the final year of the 80s when Thatcher infamously gave US President George Bush Senior a rigorous handbagging over Cold War diplomacy.

Meanwhile, other major global events during the year included the Tiananmen Square massacre in China, and the fall of the Berlin Wall.

Of course though, being just nine years old, I was largely oblivious to most of these goings on. I only really knew Thatcher as that annoying squeaky woman portrayed on the TV show *Spitting Image* – and also because I had the misfortune of sharing her birthday. This was something my maternal grandfather, a staunch Tory, took great pride in. At one point he even wrote to the milk snatcher just to tell her, like she would've really given a monkey's - although to be fair to her she did send him a reply and included a signed photo.

Sadly for Grandad, this treasured item wasn't quite treated with the reverence he probably hoped for when he ceremoniously handed it over to me. In the house where I grew up with my Mum and Dad and elder brother Al in the Nottingham suburb of Mapperley, we had a dartboard set up in our garage – and within minutes of taking possession of the Thatcher pic, Al and I took great delight in pinning her to the board in order to chuck arrows at her.

I guess I was always destined to be a Red...

So what else was happening in 1989?

Well along with *Spitting Image*, popular programmes on TV included *Blind Date* and *Only Fools and Horses;* while in the world of pop, the acid house movement was in full swing and the Stone Roses released their debut album.

But again, given my age, I was largely oblivious to this. My only real knowledge of music was based on what was on the radio at that time – largely manufactured Stock, Aitken and Waterman pap such as Kylie and Jason - or whatever my Mum and Dad happened to be listening to.

Out of my parents, Dad was the big music lover – and it was sometime around 1989 that he'd signed up for Britannia Music Club, a mail order company popular back in those days who would send you the latest albums through the post. An LP released that year that I remember being played a lot in our house was Tina Turner's 'Foreign Affair', which has some great songs on it – although for years I was convinced that the track 'Steamy Windows' was actually called 'Stevie Windows'!

Along with Tina Turner, I can also remember us being subjected quite a lot during this period to the horrors of Phil Collins and the Eurythmics. But in fairness to Dad, he'd not long acquired a CD player – so not only was he getting his hands on the latest new releases, he'd also begun the process of gradually reacquiring all the albums of his youth in the new format. As such, I got to hear a fair amount of brilliant stuff from the 60s and 70s such as the Beatles and David Bowie.

Not that I appreciated it back then – as a kid, you generally dismiss anything that your parents are into as being deeply uncool. And besides, I had so many other things going on around me at that particular point in time that I didn't really think much about music.

Like most nine-year-olds, my life largely revolved around school and home. As is probably the case for the majority of kids, school was a place I had a love-hate relationship with – however, the house where I spent most of my childhood holds nothing but happy and nostalgic memories. Money was tight - but Mum and Dad both worked hard, and budgeted carefully to ensure that Al and I never went without anything.

Our house was a place where people always seemed to be coming and going. Dad had grown up in a massive family as one of nine brothers and sisters, while my Mum's parents lived practically round the corner - so there were always plenty of grandparents, aunties, uncles and cousins around. And up in my little bedroom, I'd usually be preoccupied with either Lego, my pet guinea pig, making paper aeroplanes, or my large collection of *Dandy* and *Commando* comics.

Like most kids though who grow up in the 80s, much of my leisure time was actually spent 'playing out'. The rectangle-shaped chunk of suburban Nottingham stretching from Mapperley Top in the north down to the Carlton Forum playing fields in the south was pretty much the extent of my universe – and I was free to spend hours on end out on my BMX or my skateboard as long as I didn't roam too far.

All in all, life definitely felt a lot simpler back in 1989 than the modern age that today's children are growing up in. Indeed, an academic called Professor Dan Woodman from the University of Melbourne in Australia gained a lot of media coverage during the summer of 2017, when he labelled all people born between 1977 and 1983 as 'Xennials'. His argument was that we basically had the best of both worlds - in the sense that we were able to enjoy our childhoods during a relatively innocent time, but were still able to harness the benefits of emerging technology by the time we were teenagers.

Having been born within the qualifying six-year timeframe to be a Xennial, I think there's a lot to be said for this theory. I'm certainly glad that I got to spend so much of my childhood out in the fresh air playing with my mates - rather than just gazing vacantly at a tablet or a smartphone for hours on end, which is seemingly the basis of existence for most young people today.

That said, a rudimentary amount of technology was starting to creep into my world as a nine-year-old. By 1989 we'd actually had a computer in our house for a couple of years - a 48k ZX Spectrum that I shared with Al, which had a range of games that you loaded via a cassette tape. Looking back, the capability of that machine was laughably basic – but at the time it felt like the very height of cutting edge. We'd spend many happy hours playing games like

Daley Thompson's Decathalon, which was famous for wrecking joy sticks across the country - while it still haunts me to this day that I could never get past the 'Eugene's Lair' level in *Manic Miner*.

1989 was also a landmark year for me in that I went abroad on holiday for the very first time. Previously during my childhood, family holidays had been chalets and caravans in places like Skegness and Chapel St Leonards. With package trips to the Mediterranean becoming increasingly affordable though, Mum and Dad decided in the summer of 1989 to push the boat out by splashing out on a ten-day break to Menorca. It was a brilliant holiday, and one that I still remember vividly.

All in all, when I look back at that final year of the 80s, I regard my life at the time as a very fulfilled one - and I think I would've continued to get along quite happily if Nottingham Forest Football Club had never muscled in on my consciousness.

But muscle in they did – and it was 1989 when my little world suddenly changed forever…

2. The start of it all

"In the fickle world of the primary school playground, possessing a sponge football guaranteed considerable popularity among your peers..."

Though I'm regarded by most people who know me as a massive Forest fan, I never had the Reds shoved down my throat as a kid.

My Dad had been to a few matches in the 60s when he was a teenager, but he'd never been what you'd call a massive fan. The big Forest fanatic in the family was actually one of his younger brothers, my Uncle Stephen.

Sadly Stephen's no longer with us, but in 1979 he made the trip to Munich to see the Reds win their first of two back-to-back European Cups.

Unfortunately for me though, Forest's glory days of the late 70s and early 80s were slightly before my time – I was only born in 1979. And my earliest memory of having any real awareness of football wasn't until 1985, when I started collecting Panini's *Football 85* stickers.

At that point in my life, aged six, there were few greater thrills than emerging from the newsagents and tearing open the packet of stickers you'd just squandered your pocket money on – especially if it turned out you'd got a 'shiny'. Hours were spent in little huddles on the playground at Mapperley Plains Primary School with fellow collectors, comparing our 'swaps' to the sound of a time-honoured mantra.

"Got got got got got got got. Need..."

Of course, this was a more innocent age for football stickers, before things took a somewhat darker turn a few years later when Panini was bought out by the controversial business tycoon Robert Maxwell – a man well-known to Forest fans in the late 80s and early 90s after he became Chairman of the Reds' local rivals Derby.

But as I was sticking Forest players such as Steve Wigley and Gary Fleming into my album, I'm not sure I even had much concept of the fact that the Reds were my local team. And to be honest, I'm not even sure I knew why I was collecting the stickers at all really – it was probably something I decided to do simply because my older brother Al and his mates were doing it.

In fact, I think the most enjoyment that I derived from my stickers was butchering some of my swaps to make my own mongrel footballers – cutting out Liverpool hardman Graeme Souness' moustache or Stoke City defender George Berry's afro, and sticking them onto some poor Watford journeyman to create something approximating a bad police e-fit.

I never managed to complete my *Football 85* album - and if it hadn't been football stickers, it could've easily been something else. Indeed, after *Football 85* ran its course, I actually went on to try and complete Panini's World Wildlife Fund album. That said, there wasn't a massive amount of difference between the elusive grizzly bear sticker in that and Coventry City's bearded giant of a centre-half, Brian Kilcline.

But a few years on, by the time we'd reached the late 80s, I slowly but surely began to develop a genuine interest in football – not entirely unconnected with the fact Forest were starting to blossom into something special.

For much of the decade, the Reds had been in a relative lull. Brian Clough's side had by no means been terrible – today, most fans would happily sacrifice a limb for the current Forest team to be as 'bad' as the Reds were in the 80s! Nevertheless, league positions in the old First Division of 5th, 7th, 12th, 5th, 3rd, 9th, 8th and 8th from 1980 to 1987 were a bit underwhelming after the achievements of the previous few years. Meanwhile, Liverpool and Everton had had a Scouse monopoly between them on the league title for pretty much the entire decade.

As it happened, football in England was probably about as unfashionable as it's ever been during the mid-to-late 80s – what with the game blighted by violence on the terraces and tragic deaths at Bradford and Heysel. If you go back to the stats for the 1985-86 season, it's telling that Forest - despite finishing in the top half of the old First Division - pulled an average gate of just 16,000.

Despite the low attendances though, Brian Clough was very much in the process of assembling his second great Forest team - built around exciting young players like Stuart Pearce, Neil Webb, Des Walker, and of course his own son Nigel. It was that 1987-88 season when everything really started to click - and Forest shirts suddenly began to appear at school along with all the ubiquitous Everton and Liverpool ones. I remember my mate Kris Walden having the Reds shirt with 'Skol' plastered across the front - this being a period in the club's history when they were going through a series of kit sponsorship deals with dubious beer brands.

It was also around this time I started playing football – mainly for the simple reason that I'd reached that age at school where you actually start doing proper sports in P.E., rather than just made-up games involving lobbing beanbags around.

And I quickly discovered that I loved playing the beautiful game.

As well as P.E. lessons, I began playing footy with my mates during break times – abandoning previous pastimes such as dobby, and wolfing down my sarnies at dinner time in two seconds flat just so I was free to go straight outside and get the absolute maximum amount of game time.

Matches on the school's concrete playground would sometimes end up being as much as 23-a-side, and would usually be chaotic affairs. When attempting a mazy dribble you'd find yourself trying to get past not only the opposition players, but also other obstacles ranging from dinner ladies to girls with skipping ropes.

Play would also rumble on indefinitely, with scores reaching ridiculous figures, until either the end-of-playtime whistle went, or the ball ended up somewhere beyond reach. Anyone guilty of hoofing a shot over the fence or onto the school roof would naturally be treated like a pariah - although our school's long-suffering caretaker Mr Roddis fast achieved legendary status for the endless patience he showed in recovering stray balls and allowing play to continue. There were even times when he was called upon to retrieve footwear – as you'd occasionally get someone swing their leg so hard to kick the ball that their shoe would come flying off and end up on the school roof.

Of course there was no referee to control any of these epic footballing battles, so there'd be endless bickering if anything contentious happened - or sometimes even about what the score was. On those odd occasions when the two sets of players were actually able to agree that a foul had been committed, play would resume with a free-kick or penalty – and if you were the one taking a spot-kick, it was pretty much mandatory to take an elaborate 20-metre run-up before leathering the ball as hard as you could towards the goal. That said, if you ever find any old footage of Forest from the mid-to-late 80s, Stuart Pearce's approach to taking penalties wasn't wholly dissimilar at that time!

All in all, those hours spent playing football at primary school were very happy ones – I certainly recall them far more vividly than anything I actually did in lessons.

Though there was one frustration – the fact that we weren't actually allowed to play with a proper football.

It's funny, but those of us who grew up in the 70s and 80s tend to look back on our formative years as being a golden age before jobsworths came along and ruined childhood by making everything safe. However, the 'health and safety gone mad' tendencies of the modern world were already well and truly underway by the late 80s – as the only type of football we were allowed to use at school back then were those daft sponge ones.

Nevertheless, in the fickle world of the primary school playground, possessing a sponge football guaranteed considerable popularity among your peers. And looking back, those balls were actually years ahead of their time – as they offered a very rudimentary form of goal-line technology during certain weather conditions. Yes, with our playground not having a proper pitch, we had to set up our own goals against the school walls with the classic cliché of jumpers for goalposts – so inevitably, there'd be heated discussions on a regular basis about whether a shot had actually gone in or not. But when it was wet, the sponge balls would soak up several gallons of water and thus leave a telltale wet mark whenever they hit the wall – leaving no-one in any doubt.

But where do Forest come into all this, you might be wondering?

Well when you start playing football as a kid, I think there very quickly comes a point when you decide you want to emulate your heroes – so I think it was only going to be a matter of time before I pinned my loyalties to one team. I shudder now at the thought, but at one point during this period I had a brief flirtation with Manchester United, simply because a well-meaning family friend had noticed my growing interest in football and given me a hand-me-down United shirt – one from the era when their shirts had 'SHARP' splashed across the front.

Fortunately though, I quickly saw the light – and while I can't remember a single 'Road to Damascus' moment where I decided I was definitely a Forest fan, that decision was definitely made sometime in the spring of 1989.

And to be fair, it was a no-brainer. After all the promise shown by Forest in the 1987-88 season, in which they ended up finishing third in the league, the 1988-89 campaign had seen the Reds make a slow start – with Brian Clough's team languishing in mid-table by Christmas. However, in the immediate aftermath of the festive period they went on a 18 match run without defeat in all competitions - including at one point ten successive victories.

As part of this unbeaten run Forest swept aside everyone from Arsenal to Spurs, and were playing a free-flowing brand of passing football that was exciting to watch. There was suddenly a real buzz around Nottingham for what was happening down at the City Ground, and it was a buzz that only grew as the Reds climbed the league table and also reached the latter stages of all the domestic cup competitions – getting to the final of the League Cup and Simod Cup (both of which they'd go on to win); and also the semi-finals of the FA Cup, where they were pitted against Liverpool.

Sadly of course, that FA Cup semi-final is remembered for the horrific events that occurred at Hillsborough, and the needless loss of 96 lives.

But on an infinitely more trivial note, it's also a major marker in my own personal 'journey' as a football fan – because the first Forest match I can actually remember making a point of sitting and watching was the replay of the Hillsborough semi-final, where the Reds ended up losing 3-1 to Liverpool at Old Trafford.

I went to watch the match on TV round at my mate Stewart Green's house. As we all know, the game is one that history will remember as a strange and sombre occasion – although while I was aware of what had happened at Hillsborough, the enormity of it all was a bit lost on me at the time as a mere nine year old. In fact, the one thing recall about the game more than anything else was thinking what a ridiculous name Liverpool's goalkeeper Bruce Grobbelaar had.

In some ways I'd decided to start supporting a team at the worst possible point in the year. That match between Forest and Liverpool took place just a few weeks before the very end of the 1988-89 season. Before I knew it then, the season was over - and I was left having to wait a few months before I could properly immerse myself in my new interest.

It's funny, but when you're an adult, years and even decades seem to pass in the blink of an eye. As a kid though, mere summers seemed to go on forever – and that was certainly the case during that summer 1989 as I waited for the new football season to start. The weeks seemed to drag and drag - and every day I'd pounce on my Dad's copy of the *Nottingham Evening Post* as soon as it came clattering through the letterbox, turning straight to the sports section in the hope of even the smallest morsel of information on Forest.

Still, every cloud has a silver lining. If nothing else, those long summer months did at least give me plenty of time to work on Dad and try and persuade him to take me to my first ever game...

3. First game

"It was nothing less than a revelation to hear five thousand people all singing "The referee's a wanker" in unison..."

Now when you're a football fan, your first ever game is just as important a landmark in your life as your first record if you're a music fan.

And like that guy who's able to smugly boast that the first single he bought was by the Clash or Nirvana, I'm proud to say that my first Forest game was a pretty credible one: Arsenal at home, Saturday 16 September 1989 – with the Gunners arriving at the City Ground just a few months after dramatically snatching the league title from Liverpool with pretty much the final kick of the 1988-89 season.

I'm not sure why my Dad picked that particular game as our first outing to the football. It was the Reds' second Saturday home game of the 1989-90 season, and I guess he could've just as easily taken me to the previous one – the opening game of the season against Aston Villa.

It may have been that Dad didn't really given it much thought. Having asked him about it many years later, he couldn't even remember what the first game was that we'd gone to together!

It's also quite possible that Dad regarded our first trip to see Forest as being no more significant at the time than any other father-son activity that we might have done together. After all, as a kid you tend to give lots of different things a go. It's entirely possible that we could've left the City Ground at full-time with me deeply unmoved by the experience, or just happy to have ticked a box - and that it'd prove to be the first and last time we'd go to the match.

As it turned out, the reality would be anything but.

Whatever his reasons were though, I'm glad Dad chose the game that he did - as the fact that Forest were playing against the reigning league champions gave the occasion a fair amount of gravitas.

Of course, the logistics of my first trip to the City Ground had actually begun a couple of weeks beforehand, when Dad went to buy our tickets. Those tickets were pinned ceremoniously to the corkboard in our kitchen – and all that was left to do was to count the days until matchday.

Back in 1989 at Forest you could buy what was known as a 'tandem' ticket for one adult and one child. I've still got our ticket stubs from that match against Arsenal – and given how much it costs to go and watch football these days, it amazes me really that Dad was able to bag top seats for us to watch two teams that had finished first and third in the top flight the previous season for a total of just £8.50.

Those top seats were in the upper tier of what was then known as the Executive Stand – now renamed the Brian Clough Stand. We went to the game in Dad's trusty red Vauxhall Belmont - and after parking up, I can remember my excitement as the ground lurched into view as we made our way across Lady Bay Bridge.

Having grown up in Nottingham, I'd seen the City Ground on numerous occasions when we'd driven past the place.

But this was the first time I was actually *going there*.

Of course, that first glimpse of the ground might have been altogether more memorable had we arrived via Trent Bridge. This would've allowed me to drink in what surely remains to this day one of the most spectacular settings of any football stadium anywhere in the country – complete with the sight of 'FOREST' spelt out in white seats.

But my Dad is nothing if not a very practical man – and the fact that there was plenty of free street parking available around the industrial estate just off the Colwick Loop Road was always going to win the day.

After a brief stop so I could spend 80p of my precious pocket money on a copy of the matchday programme, Dad and I clanked through the turnstiles – and after climbing what seemed like endless flights of concrete steps, we finally arrived at our red plastic seats.

Looking at those faded ticket stubs, it appears we were sat on row 11 seats 15 and 16 - roughly in line with the edge of the penalty area. I remember Dad was sat on my left, which means I must have sat in seat 15 – and whilst writing this book there were numerous occasions when I had idle thoughts about trying to buy the same seat for a Forest home game, just to see if sitting in the exact same spot brought any memories flooding back.

To be honest though, despite the passing of time and despite the fact that I was still quite young, I actually remember my first visit to the City Ground pretty vividly. Which is interesting, as I've spoken to lots of fellow fans who went to their first game when they were around the same age that I was - and many of them have only hazy recollections, and sometimes of relatively trivial things.

But for me, much of the matchday experience that afternoon has remained imprinted on my memory. It's almost as if I already knew on some subconscious level that it was a day I'd look back upon as a major marker in my life – and that it was therefore important to retain as much detail as possible.

We'd arrived for the game ridiculously early, what with Dad having always been infamous within our family for his zealously punctual nature – although this was fine because I was happy to just take it all in. I remember being amazed at how high up we were, and just how green the pitch looked – while my senses were also filled by the sounds of the chart hits of the day being played over the tinny tannoy, and the heady scent of Bovril and tobacco smoke.

What's more, I also had my copy of the matchday programme to keep me entertained.

Now old football programmes often provide a fascinating snapshot of a particular point in time - and the one from my first ever Forest game is no exception. I still actually have my copy of it, and when I flick through it now the one thing that stands out is the fact that there's an advert for a local car showroom - featuring a photo of Nigel Clough being presented with a Ford Sierra with his name and the name of the dealership plastered all over it. Given that most of today's top footballers drive around in Aston Martins and Ferraris, it seems almost comical now.

Before long I began treating matchday programmes as sacred scriptures, even taking a special folder with me to matches to ensure I kept them in pristine condition. On that day though in September 1989, I committed what is regarded among programme collectors as an unforgivable sin. Yes, when the two teams for the afternoon were read out over the tannoy and it turned out there were a few changes to the line-ups that had been printed on the back cover of the programme, I crossed out the names of the players who weren't playing with a biro, and replaced them with the names of those who were.

For the record, the Forest player who missed out that day was Brian Rice, with Brian Clough having decided to replace him with Terry Wilson.

Probably the most notable thing about the programme from my first game though is that the front cover features an action shot of Stuart Pearce – which seems quite apt in hindsight. While I was new to the world of Forest, I was already well aware that the man known as 'Psycho' was a hugely influential player for the mighty Reds. What I didn't know was just how much he'd go on to become an enduring presence in my life over the next few decades.

Eventually I exhausted the contents of the programme, and there was still a fairly long wait until kick-off time – but by this time the players had emerged from the tunnel to do their pre-match warm-ups. Looking down onto the pitch, I couldn't quite believe the fact that I was actually viewing the Forest team in the flesh. I'd only ever seen them previously on TV – so as far as I was concerned, it was no different to seeing BA Baracus or Michael Knight or any other number of people who'd I'd only ever seen on the small screen.

That said, from our lofty perch up in the Gods of the upper tier of the Executive Stand, the likes of Steve Sutton and Gary Crosby looked no bigger than Subbuteo players.

Actually, thinking about it, Gary Crosby *wasn't* much bigger than a Subbuteo player!

One member of the Forest team who wasn't present on the pitch though as the players warmed up was that man Stuart Pearce – and even though he'd been named in the Reds team that would be playing that afternoon, his absence got my nine-year-old mind whirring with anxiety.

Was he injured?

Was he leaving Forest to sign for another club?

These fears were happily unfounded - and over time, I discovered that the Reds' inspirational captain never actually came out onto the pitch for his pre-match warm-up. I can only assume he must have had a private anteroom just off the dressing room, where he got ready by wrestling a few bears and ripping telephone directories in half!

As kick-off drew closer, the City Ground started to fill up. History records an attendance of 22,216 that day – and from our vantage point, I can remember watching the swarms of fans streaming over Trent Bridge as they made their way to the turnstiles. I'd never seen so many people - except for perhaps trips to Nottingham's famous Goose Fair. This was also the era when bringing inflatables to matches was a national trend, and I particularly remember the sight of hundreds of inflatable 'Forest trees' in the Junior Reds' section directly opposite us.

Finally the players came out of the tunnel – followed by Brian Clough in his famous green sweater - and as soon as the two team's captains had completed the handshakes and coin toss, we were off.

As far as I recall, the game was quite an entertaining one. For much of the proceedings, the two teams were deadlocked at 1-1. Paul Merson had given Arsenal an early lead, though it wasn't long before Forest's permatanned midfielder Garry Parker rifled a spectacular 25-yard shot into the top corner of the Bridgford End net - not only pulling the Reds level, but also giving me my first glimpse of those dancing potato men graphics on the scoreboard.

Alas though, it was the Gunners who ended up taking home the points, winning 2-1 thanks to a late goal from Brian Marwood.

However, far more than anything that happened on the pitch, the one thing that made the biggest impression on me that afternoon was the group of fellow Forest fans crammed into the little cowshed behind the goal to my right. This was my first insight into the legendary Trent End - which at the time was well-established as the place where the Reds' most vocal supporters would congregate on a matchday.

Even before the game actually kicked off, I'd found myself absolutely fascinated by the Trent End. Nowadays at the City Ground, you tend to find the place pretty much empty if you arrive for a match an hour before the start. Back in 1989 though, half the stadium was still made up of terracing – the Trent End at one end, and the old Bridgford End at the other. This meant a large percentage of Forest fans had to get themselves inside the ground in good time if they wanted to bag a decent spot - and those who arrived early to take position in the middle pen of the Trent End would use the time to warm up their voices in readiness for 90 minutes of cheering on the team.

Some of the songs that I heard sung by the Trent End that afternoon as Dad and I counted down the minutes to kick-off have been passed down the generations, and remain part of the Forest songbook to this day. Others, such as 'Let's all have a disco' – always accompanied by enthusiastic mass pogoing - seem to have sadly slipped into the annals of history.

 The best thing though was when the two teams came out onto the pitch to warm up. This saw the Trent End launch into what I soon learned was a long-standing matchday tradition of singing each of the players' names until receiving some sort of acknowledgement.

"Nigel Nigel…"

"Ooh Tommy Gaynor!"

"You'll never beat Des Walker…"

"Woah, Harry Harry – Harry Harry Harry Harry Harry Hodge.."

But the biggest reception of all was for Stuart Pearce, when the teams came out ready for kick-off and Psycho finally decided to grace us with his presence. Indeed, the sight of the entire Trent End chanting "Psycho! Psycho!" in unison, whilst simultaneously pumping their fists in the direction of the Forest captain, was an incredible thing to witness for someone uninitiated as I was in the ritual generally referred to by most Reds fans as 'the Psycho salute'. The respect was mutual too, with Psycho responding by running over to the Trent End with arms raised, muscles bulging like a real life He-Man.

As the match got underway though, I quickly discovered the noise from the Trent End was by no means just adulation – particularly if you happened to be one of the match officials.

Now as a nine-year-old, I was at that age where hearing a swear word was impossibly exciting – even relatively minor swear words. I have vivid memories from when I was about five or six of my Dad playing an LP by the

70s comedy singer Ivor Biggun that featured an uproarious track called 'I've Farted' – which, at the time, seemed like just about the funniest thing in the world to my brother Al and I. Meanwhile, my Uncle Tony – one of my Dad's six brothers - was someone I regarded throughout my childhood as a heroic figure, largely on the strength of being the most gifted exponent of the art of swearing I've ever met.

Needless to say then, it was nothing less than a revelation that afternoon at the City Ground to gaze down upon the Trent End and hear five thousand people all singing "The referee's a wanker" in unison after a particularly iffy decision by the man in black.

And it wasn't just the ref who attracted the derision of the Trent End either. Despite their success the previous season, Arsenal weren't the most attractive of teams to watch at the time - and throughout the game, the Trent End derided them with choruses of "Boring boring Arsenal." A number of the Gunners' individual players were also singled out for special attention. Every time big goalkeeper John Lukic took a goal kick he was subjected to a raucous cry of "You fat bastard" – although I would discover over time that pretty much every opposing keeper received this treatment from the Trent End, even if (like Lukic) they weren't actually a fat bastard.

Meanwhile Arsenal's Tony Adams was serenaded with regular cries of "Ee-aw!", and "Come and get yer carrots!" Which was all a bit harsh really - as far from being a donkey, Adams was undoubtedly one of the finest defenders of his generation. Still, it was all part of the fun - and I guess the Arsenal captain got the last laugh on the day, given that it was his team that trooped off the pitch victorious at full-time.

Following the final whistle then, Dad and I left the ground – and while it was Arsenal who were going away with the three points, I still hadn't reached that stage of rabid fandom where a defeat for the Reds would go some way towards ruining my entire weekend.

However, as we joined the bottleneck of fans all trying to get up the steps onto Lady Bay Bridge, I don't think there was ever any question as to whether we'd do it again.

And that was that really.

Life was never quite the same again…

4. Getting sucked in

"Sutton, Laws, Pearce, Walker, Chettle, Hodge, Crosby, Parker, Clough, Chapman, Rice - all these years later, I can still reel off those eleven names without missing a beat..."

After dipping my toes in the water and going to my first game, it's no exaggeration to say that Forest very quickly started take over my life.

As that 1989-90 football season rumbled on, Dad continued to take me on regular outings to the City Ground. It became something of a fortnightly routine – and we'd always sit in the upper tier of the Executive Stand, which started to feel like a home from home.

Back in those days at Forest, it was actually quite common for kids to sit away from whichever grown-up had brought them to the match - with the child often deposited in the Junior Reds section in the Main Stand, and the adult then watching the game from elsewhere in the ground. I think this worked out cheaper for whoever was paying - with tickets for the Junior Reds section having been available at a heavily discounted rate.

Personally though, I'm glad that Dad never went down this route. Rather than being left to watch the match with a load of kids that I didn't know, I liked the fact that I got to sit in part of the ground where I was surrounded mostly by adults. It all just felt a bit more grown-up – and even in the relatively sedate surrounds of the upper tier of the Executive Stand, it meant the matchday experience had the added excitement of getting to hear the occasional swear word.

But best of all, I just liked sitting with Dad – and going to the match quickly assumed the status of being our 'thing' that we did together.

Quality father-son bonding time, if you like.

Happily it wasn't long before I got my first taste of victory. My first ever trip to the City Ground had ended in defeat for Forest – however during my second visit I got to see the Reds cruise to a comfortable 2-0 win against Charlton Athletic.

Now with all due respect to Charlton, they probably weren't the most impressive scalp for Forest at the time – but for me, witnessing a win against the Londoners afforded some significant bragging rights. This was because my brother Al and I had been attending judo classes for a number of years on Saturday mornings that were run by a chap called Dave Lawrence – and he just so happened to be the brother of Lennie Lawrence, who was Charlton's manager at the time!

When I look back on that game against Charlton, there are two things that stick in my mind the most. The first of these was the fact that Charlton won the toss before kick-off and chose to swap ends - which meant Forest were attacking the Trent End in the first half rather than the second.

I've never really been able to understand why football teams think it gives them some sort of psychological edge to make the home team swap ends – and even as a nine-year-old, I remember thinking it was a bit weird.

Meanwhile, the other thing I remember is how the game made me realise the full extent of Stuart Pearce's importance to the Forest team at the time. That day the Reds' inspirational captain was out injured, which meant Brett Williams taking his place at left back – and with all due respect to the moustachioed reserve defender, it was apparent as I watched the match that a Forest team without 'Psycho' was a Forest team without its beating heart.

The impact of Psycho's absence even stretched to the crowd. At my first Forest game against Arsenal, I'd quickly noticed that Stuart Pearce doing pretty much anything was something that could always be guaranteed to get the fans going – be it a raised fist to the Trent End, a rampaging run into the opposition half, or unceremoniously dumping an unsuspecting winger on his backside.

Without Psycho's swashbuckling antics though, the atmosphere that afternoon against Charlton felt noticeably flat.

And I'm pretty sure Psycho would've won the toss too!

Thankfully Psycho's injury was only a brief one, and he was back in the team by the time Dad and I made our next trip to the City Ground, where we saw

Forest draw 2-2 with QPR.

That said, it wasn't just about the skipper - the Forest team from that season generally had a lot going for it. Sutton, Laws, Pearce, Walker, Chettle, Hodge, Crosby, Parker, Clough, Chapman, Rice - all these years later, I can still reel off those eleven names without missing a beat. It just trips off the tongue, in the same way as John, Paul, George and Ringo, or Hannibal, Face, BA and Murdoch.

Of course, there would be the occasional game back in those days when there might be the odd change to the line-up – maybe Franz Carr in for Gary Crosby, or perhaps Terry Wilson for Steve Chettle.

But like most managers at that time, Brian Clough had a tendency to decide on his best eleven and stick to it – the advent of 'squad rotation' still a long way into the future.

Meanwhile, the next Forest game that Dad and I went to was a League Cup tie against Everton – my first midweek match. Not only did this provide me with my first experience of seeing the City Ground looking slightly otherworldly and ethereal under the glow of the floodlights, it also meant I got to stay up far later than my usual bedtime on a school night.

Fortunately my teacher at the time, Mr Mason, was a big football fan himself – so he didn't give me too much grief in class the next day when I turned up clearly still half asleep!

One thing I also remember from that game against Everton was Dad taking me before kick-off on my first ever visit to the Forest club shop – as I'd turned ten only a few weeks earlier, so it seemed a good place to go and spend my birthday money.

Back in those days though, the club shop wasn't the modern emporium that fans are familiar with today. No, to buy whatever item of Forest-related tat that was tickling your fancy, you had to muscle your way into a dingy cubby hole at the back of the Main Stand. All the goods were kept behind thick glass much like a Liverpudlian off licence, and you had to shout your order through a tiny serving hatch. If I remember rightly, I ended up blowing my cash that evening on a 'Psycho' T-shirt.

Further trips to the City Ground followed for games against Norwich and

Southampton – and by the time Dad and I had been to half a dozen or so Forest matches, I think it's fair to say that I was fully hooked.

I was also starting to develop an understanding of other teams and Forest's place in the grand scheme of English football. I began to feel proud of the fact that the club I supported was actually a relatively small provincial one - but one which had nonetheless achieved massive success over the last few decades thanks to the mercurial management of Brian Clough.

I also felt proud of the fact that the Reds had a long tradition of playing the beautiful game 'the way it's supposed to be played', with Cloughie's philosophy being all about attractive passing football and showing respect to both the opponents and the referee. This was a far cry from quite a few of the other teams plying their trade in the top flight at the time, with the likes of Millwall, Wimbledon, Crystal Palace and Arsenal being all about hoofing the ball in the air, doing their best to intimidate the match officials at every opportunity, and kicking their opponents off the pitch. I began to find it particularly satisfying when Forest managed to bag a victory against any of those sides – it always felt like a genuine triumph of good against evil.

Beyond Forest meanwhile, my new love of football was such that I also began spending more and more of my spare time playing the beautiful game. My brother Al and I would often play out in the street – either taking it in turns to leather shots at each other, or partaking in the classic street games of 'kerbie' and 'wall-y'.

There would sometimes be days when I had no-one to play with – but that still didn't stop me. In fact, on those occasions I'd spend hours on my own kicking a ball against the wall in front of my house with my left foot, just because I wanted to be like Stuart Pearce. And it wasn't a bad investment of time – as all these years later I still have a pretty decent left peg, even though it's not my natural foot.

Looking back, most of our neighbours were amazingly tolerant, given that I'd often end up wading into their gardens to retrieve wayward shots.

That said, the majority of my footballing exploits actually took place over on the Carlton Forum playing fields, just down the road from where we lived. Brilliantly, the local powers-that-be had decided not long after I got into football to install some state-of-the-art astroturf pitches there, with proper goals and even floodlights. Of course, you were only officially allowed to play on these facilities if you'd paid whatever the hourly rate was – however, the gates generally weren't manned, so if there was a pitch free Al and I and our mates would generally sneak on and claim it.

We spent hours playing for free on those astroturf pitches - and had the skinned knees to prove it. Often there'd be enough other local kids around to get a bit of a match going. Otherwise we'd play 'three and in', or a particularly brutal game that was popular at the time called 'headers and volleys' – where, if you ran out of lives, you were subjected to the punishment of standing facing the back of the goal while all the other players took it in turns to try and blast the ball as hard as possible at the back of your head!

Occasionally someone from the Carlton Forum Leisure Centre would come along to chase off the freeloaders such as ourselves – but that was all part of the fun. There also came a point when access to our own personal footballing arena improved even further - when one day we discovered that there was a gap behind one of the gates that you could just squeeze through if you were a skinny youth. This meant we could now get in to play even when the gates were locked - and naturally we began taking full advantage of this.

All in all, these days were a happy time. My whole world had suddenly become all about football and Forest – indeed, never does your life revolve around the beautiful game more than those first few years when you're first getting properly into it.

All my other childhood passions had been unceremoniously shoved to one side – and my bedroom rapidly became a shrine to Brian Clough and his players. And the posters on my wall were only one sign of my new obsession...

I'd also wear my Forest shirt pretty much every day, until the name of the club's sponsors, Shipstones Fine Ales, started to go a bit crusty and flake off. Today, without seeing a picture of it, I could tell you very little about the current Forest shirt other than the fact that it's red and has the club's tree badge on it – but I can still remember every tiny detail of that 'Shipstones' shirt, from the tessellating parallelograms on the fabric to the detail on the collar.

I'd record Forest stuff off the TV obsessively onto VHS cassette tapes and watch them on repeat. To this day I can still remember bits of TV commentary from that era pretty much word for word.

I'd spend hours poring over my growing collection of Forest matchday programmes. It's not uncommon for football fans to become fervent collectors, and that was very much the case with me. As well as programmes from the games that I'd actually been to, I started accumulating old ones going back to previous decades - finding that car boot sales were a great hunting ground. Naturally, my collection was filed meticulously in date order.

I'd spend hours reading up on Forest's glorious history. A lot of people accuse us Reds fans of being stuck in the past. To be fair though, anyone would be if their team had achieved what Forest did in the late 70s and early 80s.

I'd spend hours mathematically working out what the score was going to be in Forest's upcoming games. For instance, in October 1989, Forest had beaten Crystal Palace 5-0, and then Palace had gone on to beat Luton 4-1 shortly afterwards. It surely stood to reason then that Forest would beat Luton 9-1 when the two sides met a few weeks later? If only it were that simple…

I'd write about Forest pretty much every day at school – something I had the freedom to do, given that primary education was a lot less prescriptive back then than it is nowadays, with teachers more than happy to let you do your own projects about whatever you happened to be interested in.

I also named two pet goldfish Harry and Psycho, in honour of Steve Hodge and Stuart Pearce.

And at one point I even had the Forest tree shaved into the back of my head!

Probably my most disturbing trait of all though around this time was how I developed an almost *Rain Man*-like recall of Forest-related stats. It's funny, but as I've grown older and my brain's become cluttered with more and more information and responsibilities, I find these days that the finer details of what's going on with Forest tend to go in one ear and straight out the other. If you quizzed me now on who scored in the Reds' last home game, I'd probably struggle to tell you. However, ask me what the score was and who scored in any game during Forest's 1989-90 season, and I'd put good money on me being able to give the correct answer.

So there we were then – I'd become a proper Forest nerd.

And as the Christmas of 1989 approached, Dad decided it was time to take our support of the mighty Reds to the next level...

5. Season tickets

"As far as I knew, no-one else at school had a season ticket – so suddenly, I was the biggest Forest fan out of anyone I knew..."

Christmas Day 1989 saw the usual array of presents under the tree at our house – and though it didn't look like the biggest or most exciting of gifts, a small thin package no bigger than my hand proved to be the biggest hit of the day.

Yes, hero that he is, Dad had only gone and splashed out on a 'half season ticket' for the two of us – meaning we'd get to go and see every single home league game during the remainder of the season!

Looking back, buying us a season ticket was probably a decision that Dad had made simply because it made financial sense – as by this point we were going to virtually every Forest home match anyway. So it probably worked out cheaper to have a season ticket than to keep buying tickets for each individual game.

Nevertheless, it was a massive buzz at the time.

As far as I knew, no-one else at school had a season ticket – so suddenly, I was the biggest Forest fan out of anyone I knew.

Our seats were in the now familiar surrounds of the Executive Stand upper tier, and we saw some great matches from up there over the remainder of the 1989-90 season. Our very first game as season ticket holders saw a thrilling 2-2 draw against Liverpool on New Year's Day 1990, where Forest were 2-0 down at half-time after two goals by Ian Rush - but fought back to grab a point with a gritty display in the second half.

It was a brilliant match – and the first game I'd ever been to that was being broadcast live on TV. I remember feeling quite excited at the thought that there would be millions of people across the country who'd be watching – but I was one of the relative few who were actually *there*.

That said, my excitement was somewhat tempered by a sartorial choice imposed on me that day by my Mum.

Now when the winter months began to draw in during that 1989-90 season, Dad had started bringing a flask of soup to the match to warm us up at half-time. This quickly became a ritual we looked forward to on cold afternoons at the City Ground, although there was a bit of an awkward moment at one game when Dad had neglected to screw the top of the flask on properly – so when he gave it the obligatory shake after fishing it out of his bag, he inadvertently covered the entire row in front of us with its contents!

Fortunately, the Liverpool game saw our soup poured without incident. However, Mum had decided that day that a plastic mug of Minestrone wouldn't be sufficient to stop me from freezing to death – and as such, she'd forced me to go to the match wearing a pair of her tights underneath my tracky bottoms!

The fact that Liverpool's John Barnes was also wearing tights didn't make me feel much better.

Luckily for me, the weather conditions weren't as harsh for Forest's next home game against Millwall a couple of weeks later - so I was spared any further enforced covert transvestism. History records that the Reds won 3-1 against the Londoners – although my strongest recollection of that particular game is of the Trent End taunting Millwall's long-haired midfield hardman Terry Hurlock with regular cries of "Gypo!" and "Where's your caravan?" A strange snapshot of the times – these days it's so common for footballers to have extravagant hairstyles that no-one really bats an eyelid.

Meanwhile, other highlights from the various Forest matches that Dad and I went to during that first half-season as season ticket holders included memorable league victories against both the Manchester teams. The 1-0 win against Manchester City was famous for the controversial winning goal, which saw Gary Crosby sneak up behind City goalkeeper Andy Dibble as he was about to launch a drop kick upfield – whereupon the diminutive Reds winger cheekily headed the ball off his outstretched palm and casually rolled it into an empty net.

In the immediate aftermath there was something of a delay in the fans' cheers, as I don't think anyone thought the ref would actually allow the goal to stand

– hilariously though, he did.

Naturally the Manchester City players were furious, spending several minutes remonstrating with the man in black – and what's interesting in hindsight is that one of the most vocal of those protesting City players was a midfielder with frizzy ginger hair by the name of Gary Megson.

Little did any of us know at that time that Megson would wreak revenge on Forest 15 years later - by arriving at the City Ground as the Reds' new manager, and masterminding a terrible voyage to the bottom half of League One.

Personally, I can't help but think this was rather harsh retribution for just one controversial goal!

Meanwhile, the visit of Manchester United during that 1989-90 season saw Forest thrash Alex Ferguson's team 4-0, with all four goals coming inside the first 25 minutes. With three quarters of the match still to go, I remember being giddy with excitement and naïvely thinking Forest may actually end up winning about 16-0.

Of course, football never quite works like that. Still, if you'd told me before kick-off that I'd have to settle for a mere 4-0 win for Forest, I would've been more than happy. What's more, the comprehensive victory was made doubly satisfying by the fact that the United team happened to include former Reds midfielder Neil Webb – the first time he'd been back to the City Ground following his £1.5 million move to Old Trafford in the previous summer.

Webb's decision to leave Forest had appeared to have been mainly motivated by money – and while it's pretty much a given these days that the majority of footballers are a bunch of coin-hungry mercenaries, back then it was still a relatively new concept… and his transfer had gone down like a lead balloon amongst the Reds faithful. He was immediately christened 'Fat Wallet', and roundly booed every time he touched the ball on his return.

Dad and I also showed our disdain for Webb in other ways. When we weren't down at the City Ground cheering on Forest, we used to have hours of fun shooting an air rifle at a target range Dad had set up in the far end of our garage – and a photo of 'Fat Wallet' cut out of the *Nottingham Evening Post* was one of our favourite targets.

All in all then, that first half season as a season ticket holder was a hugely exciting time. That said, I was starting to learn that being a proper football fan is very much a double-edged sword – because much as the victories brought great euphoria, defeats were now something that put a serious dampener on my whole week.

There was one particular midweek game during the 1989-90 season when Forest were humiliated 4-0 away at Everton – a defeat that felt all the more crushing because it was shown live on TV, which meant the whole nation had been able to watch the Reds crumble. It was the infamous night when Brian Clough described his own players as 'pansies' in his post-match interview.

And as if a 4-0 defeat alone wasn't bad enough, that same day Mum and Dad had also taken me into town straight after school to have an eye test - and I'd found out that I needed to start wearing glasses.

Lacking perspective as you do when you're just ten years old, the combination of Forest getting tanked and facing the prospect of life as a 'speccy' honestly felt like the worst day of my life at the time!

And as well as learning to deal with those occasional defeats, I was also discovering that being a football fan involves having to come to terms every now and again with favourite players moving on to pastures new.

Of course, the turnover of players at most football clubs is rapid these days – so much so that you barely get time to develop any attachment to that star striker or tricky winger before they inevitably jump ship.

But back in the late 80s and early 90s, it was completely different. A player coming or going felt like a big deal, and I remember feeling genuinely devastated the first time I experienced a favourite Forest player leaving – namely big striker Lee Chapman, the man who I'd often pretend to be when playing football myself.

I don't know what it was about Chapman that I liked so much, as he was far from the best player in that Forest team. Maybe it was the hint of showbiz glamour he brought to the City Ground, with him being married to a famous actress off the telly? Looking back it's quite funny to think that Chappo stood out at the time for that reason – after all, most footballers these days seem to be shacked up with someone off *Hollyoaks* or *TOWIE*.

Whatever it was though, Chappo was a big favourite of mine – with my devotion even leading to a spot of juvenile forgery during my very early days as a Reds fan. Yes, back in those days when you signed up for Forest's Junior Reds scheme, you got sent a members' pack full of all sorts of goodies – including a photocopied sheet of A4 paper with all the players' autographs. And on receiving mine, I duly spent ages painstakingly practising Chappo's signature, so I could copy it onto a poster of the great man and pretend to my mates at school that it was the real deal.

Sadly I don't think anyone was fooled. Back then at the primary school I attended it was popular to stroke your chin and say "Jeff!" whenever you thought someone was being a bit economical with the truth – and I'm sad to say that my lame attempts at faking Chappo's autograph were 'Jeffed' out of the playground.

But far more distressing than that was the day when Chappo's time at the City Ground came to an abrupt end mid-way through that 1989-90 season, after he fell out with Cloughie and was unceremoniously sold to Leeds. Given Cloughie's well-known antipathy towards the Yorkshire club, you can only assume that packing Chappo off to Elland Road was the worst form of punishment he could think of for whatever indiscretion the big striker had committed!

To say I was gutted that Chappo had gone is an understatement, and I clearly remember sitting in the living room of Mum and Dad's house on the day that the news broke. Dad was listening to a compilation of 60s music – and ridiculous as it sounds now, I can remember genuinely thinking that the kitchen sink melodrama of 'Anyone Who Had a Heart' by Cilla Black encapsulated the pain that I was feeling about the loss of a favourite player.

As it was, it didn't turn out badly for my former hero – within a couple of years Chappo achieved what was almost certainly the high point of his career, when his goals helped fire Leeds to their league title win in 1992.

I don't think I ever forgave him!

Still, life went on, and a young lad by the name of Nigel Jemson took Chappo's place in the Forest team. And given the overall success of Dad's decision to buy us that half season ticket, it was never in doubt really that we'd jump in with both feet and get a season ticket for the whole of the next season.

Looking back though, I was massively guilty of taking this for granted. During my childhood my parents were never exactly swimming in money – so shelling out a couple of hundred quid for season tickets was a fairly hefty outlay for them. In fact, speaking to them about it now, my Mum tells me that the only way Dad could afford it was by doing building jobs at the weekend on top of his full-time day job, in order to pull in the cash needed.

Thanks, Dad.

When it came to making that season-long commitment to the cause of the Reds, Dad decided to move us from the upper tier of the Executive Stand to the lower tier – and he bagged us great seats, six rows back from the front and very close to the halfway line. This brought a new frisson of excitement to the matchday experience as the 1990-91 season got underway – because when watching back the highlights of the game on TV when we got home later, we'd occasionally be able to catch a fleeting glimpse of ourselves in the crowd in the background.

Naturally this was a massive buzz. At that point in my short life, the only time someone I knew had ever been on telly was when Dad and his mate John had bagged the opportunity to be in the studio audience for an episode of *Bullseye* – and we got to see the two of them grinning away in the background for a few seconds when the show eventually made it onto air a few months later.

There were also a couple of other things that were very alluring about the fact that our new seats were so close to the pitch.

First of all, there was a much higher chance of getting to touch the ball if it ever got hoofed into the crowd – something that I managed to do for the very first time at an otherwise forgettable 3-1 defeat at home to Manchester City midway through that first season on the lower tier.

And secondly, if you shouted something at one of the players during a match, there was every possibility that they might actually hear you. At the time I remember feeling quite enamoured by the idea that I could potentially use this proximity to have a tiny amount of influence on the performance of the Forest team - although why any of the players would've paid any attention to the shrill advice of a ten-year-old kid sat in the stands I'm not entirely sure!

Meanwhile, moving down to the lower tier of the Executive Stand wasn't the only significant change when Dad popped down to the City Ground during that summer of 1990 to sort out our season ticket. He'd also upgraded us from having a 'tandem' ticket to a 'tricycle' – as my brother Al had decided that he wanted to start coming along to watch Forest with us.

Now throughout my childhood my parents always tried to treat Al and I fairly – and when Dad started taking me to Forest matches, Al was always asked if he wanted to come along too. Initially though he'd always declined the opportunity, and generally treated any mention of the Reds with a degree of contempt.

Looking back, I think the two of us had a fairly typical brotherly dynamic back in those days, in that we'd often show a healthy disdain for whatever the other was into. And Al's dismissive attitude towards Forest was no different really to the way that I'd sneer at his obsession with the TV show *Red Dwarf*.

But there came a point sometime in 1990 when the lure of the Reds became too great even for Al.

And that moment would prove a significant landmark in my 'career' as a Forest fan – because my esteemed sibling would go on to become my primary matchday companion for most of the next three decades.

In hindsight it was perhaps inevitable that Al would get the bug eventually – as his arrival into the world in 1978 had seen him literally delivered straight into a scene of Forest mania.

Yes, my older sibling was born the same week that the Reds were playing against Liverpool in the League Cup final – and working on the maternity unit at Nottingham's Highbury Hospital where he made his grand entrance was none other than Viv Anderson's mum. As you would expect, she was very excited about the fact her son was turning out at Wembley, and my parents recall that staff even smuggled a portable TV onto the ward so they could keep tabs on the match while they were working.

Of course, Al himself can't remember any of that - but you could hardly blame him for caving in and succumbing to the charms of the mighty Reds some 12 years later. After all, while Brian Clough's team of the early 90s wasn't quite up there with his side of 1978, it was still a great time to be a Forest fan. What's more, football was also undergoing a bit of a surge in popularity in general around this time – something not entirely unconnected with England's brilliant performance in the World Cup during the summer of 1990.

Unsurprisingly, given that I was in the first flush of my love affair with the beautiful game, I was glued to Italia '90 from start to finish. I could vaguely recall Mexico '86 and the sense of outrage at England getting cheated by Maradona and Argentina – but Italia '90 was the first World Cup that I properly followed.

I remember being massively excited in the run-up to the tournament. The fact that footy was going to be on telly pretty much every day for an entire month seemed too good to be true – and while nobody gave them a cat in hell's chance, I was quite excited to see how England would get on.

Later on in my life, in my late 20s, I got into a habit lasting a good three or four years where I'd go and watch England quite regularly – both at home and sometimes even away. In fairness this was partly because Forest were mostly terrible during this period, so it was my only way of actually getting to go and watch some vaguely decent players!

Apart from this little phase though, I've never really been massively passionate about our national team over most of my years as a football fan. Indeed, I think the problem with England for most of us who support a club team is that it's hard to emotionally invest in a side that will usually include at least two or three players who you'd normally be happy to see on the receiving end of a Stuart Pearce two-footed lunge.

Steve McMahon.

Paul Ince.

Gary Neville.

Wayne Rooney.

The list goes on…

However, when it comes to a big tournament, I'm as guilty as anyone of jumping on the England bandwagon - and in the run-up to Italia '90 Dad and I started getting into the spirit of things by collecting a set of commemorative coins that were given out at Esso garages every time you filled your car with petrol. Each coin had a different England or Scotland player's face on them - although looking back, some of the artistic interpretations were about on a par with the attempt by the blind girl to sculpt Lionel Richie's head in the cheesy balladeer's infamous 'Hello' video.

There were a total of 30 coins to collect - 15 England players and 15 Scotland. Of course though, World Cup squads actually had 22 players in them - so I can only assume that someone at Esso must have taken a punt and tried to guess who England and Scotland's first choice elevens and subs would be. They didn't do a particularly good job - there was no Paul Gascoigne among the 15 England players, despite the fact that he ended up being one of the stand-out player at Italia '90.

The coins came in a shrink-wrapped packet which concealed the identity of the player within – so much like my earlier experiences of collecting Panini stickers, it was always with eager anticipation that I'd rip these open for the big reveal. It was always exciting if I got an England player that I hadn't already acquired, although equally it was a bit underwhelming if I opened the packet to find some Scotland player that I'd barely heard of. Murdo MacLeod, anyone?

You could also get a special presentation folder from Esso garages to slot your coins into - and gradually, I reached a point where mine was nearly half full. But there was still a long way to go to complete the set - and even though I was only ten years old, I was painfully aware of the reality that Dad was only ever going to fill his car up so many times during the months either side of the World Cup.

Happily though, salvation was at hand - in the form of an Esso garage that Dad used to go to at the bottom of St Ann's Well Road in Nottingham, and a woman who worked there who took a shine to me for some reason. One day Dad and I had been out in his car when he stopped there to get some petrol, and when we went in to pay my new best friend casually plonked a massive stack of the little shrink-wrapped packets onto the counter - allowing me to just keep opening them until I'd completed the whole set of coins!

As for the actual football in Italia '90, a lot of the games kicked off in the late afternoon – and this being so, I persuaded my parents to let me have my own key so I could leg it home straight from school and let myself in and not miss any of the action. I remember sitting in our living room and watching the opening game between Argentina and Cameroon – and what a game it was.

We all love to see an underdog win, but to see Cameroon pull off a victory against Maradona's lot after what had happened four years previously was extra special. It was also quite satisfying to see them practically kick the south Americans off the park over the 90 minutes – indeed, the challenge that earned big centre half Benjamin Massing a red card when he flattened Claudio Cannigia remains probably my favourite ever foul to this day!

It was certainly a great start to the tournament. It's interesting, but Italia '90 seems to be widely looked back on as a fairly dreary World Cup, marked out by negative football. I had no basis for comparison though, so I certainly didn't see it like that at all at the time. Back in those days there was hardly any foreign talent in English football - so simply acquainting myself with players like Colombia's Carlos Valderama and Italy's Salvadore Schillachi felt very exotic. We actually had an Italian family living next-door-but-one to us at the time – I can still remember them all running out into their back garden screaming when Schillachi bagged a late winner for the hosts in their opening game against Austria.

The tournament was all played out too to an impeccable soundtrack. The official Italia '90 song was of course Luciano Pavarotti's rendition of 'Nessun Dorma' – which still makes the hairs stand up on the back of my neck whenever I hear it.

And then there was 'World in Motion'…

At school we all knew the John Barnes rap word for word. In fact, I still do now! Years later I actually got to meet John Barnes, and I couldn't resist bringing up the subject of his cameo on what is unquestionably the greatest 'official' England song ever recorded. I'd taken along my copy of New Order's 'Best Of' album for him to sign – and brilliantly, he actually wrote "To Rich, you can be slow or fast but you must get to the line! Best wishes, John Barnes."

As for how Barnesy and his England team-mates got on in Italia '90 - well we all know the story. Bobby Robson's team got off to a stuttering start, but slowly started getting better and better with each game – and inspired by some mercurial performances from Gazza in midfield, eventually surpassed all expectations to get to the last four. For us Forest fans it was made all the more special by the fact that two of our own, Stuart Pearce and Des Walker, were mainstays of the England team – although sadly, Psycho is always remembered for the part that he played in England's exit in the heartbreaking penalty shoot-out defeat against Germany.

One thing that Psycho never lacked though was strength of character. He'd have to wait six years to achieve full redemption following his miss from the spot in Turin – however he quickly bounced back as soon as domestic football resumed again in August 1990, by having probably his best ever season in a Forest shirt. As well as offering his usual indomitable presence on the left side of the Reds' back four, he also scored 16 goals – a remarkable total for a left-back.

Of those 16 goals, Psycho's greatest was a winning strike away at Manchester United. With the trip to Old Trafford having come up just a few months into the season, memories of the Italia '90 were still fresh – and early in the game the United fans took great delight in goading Psycho with chants of "Who missed in Italy? Stuart Pearce, Stuart Pearce…"

It didn't take Psycho very long though to shut them up. After just seven minutes, Forest won a free-kick in front of the Stretford End, about 30 yards out. And brilliantly, our hero ran up and absolutely larruped the ball into the top-left corner of the United goal.

It was fantastic strike, and the footage well worth looking up on YouTube. After the ball hits the back of the net the clip briefly cuts to a rammed terrace of travelling Forest fans at the far end of the stadium going absolutely bananas, but Psycho himself remains stony faced - and instead turns, arms aloft, to face the silenced United fans.

As good a 'fuck you' as you could ever wish to see.

Alas, I wasn't there at Old Trafford myself to witness this goal – but by this point in my 'career' as a Forest fan I was very much in the habit of keeping close tabs on the Reds as best I could whenever they were playing away.

Back in those days, the amount of football shown on TV was nothing like the exhaustive coverage we get now. However, ITV would show a live game every Sunday afternoon on *The Match*, hosted by the bumbling Elton Welsby – so I'd occasionally get to watch Forest away games on that. There was also live coverage over on the BBC of selected FA Cup games, often featuring expert punditry from the late Jimmy Hill – a man who quickly became a figure of great ridicule in our household due to both his large chin and tendency to talk absolute rammel.

Most of the time though when Forest were playing away, I'd have to rely on radio and Teletext to keep abreast of how the Reds were getting on. At some point I even bought myself a pocket radio so I could still keep tabs on scores even if I happened to be out and about. I remember one occasion during a family gathering round at my grandparents' house on Boxing Day, when Forest were playing away at Tottenham – and Dad and I were furtively listening to my radio via earphones while sat at the dinner table. Initially, I don't think a lot of our wider family knew what we were up to – although they certainly did when Stuart Pearce smacked in a last-minute winner for the Reds. Dad and me naturally leapt to our feet and shouted in celebration - my elderly Great Uncle Doug spoke many times afterwards about how we nearly gave him a heart attack!

Back in those days, BBC Radio Nottingham's coverage was fairly primitive compared to the full-match live commentaries that Forest fans are able to enjoy today – with the station's Saturday afternoon sports programme only offering occasional updates on how Forest, Notts County and Mansfield were getting on. If any of the three Nottinghamshire teams had scored, the first you'd know about it was the sound of a jingle known as 'the goal chime' - basically a recording of a someone shouting "Goaaaaaaalllllll!" in the style of a South American commentator. This was great, but you always had that agonising few seconds of not knowing whether it was Forest or one of the other two local sides who had burst the onion bag.

And Teletext was a nightmare too - as on a Saturday afternoon when you beamed up page 141, the First Division scores would be split across three scrolling pages… so every time it moved on to the next page from the one that was showing Forest's game, you knew you were about to spend the next few minutes in an agonising black hole of zero information.

Teletext was also the worst way to find out that your team had conceded a goal. With Radio Nottingham, discovering that the opposition had found the back of the Forest net wasn't so bad when the news was broken to you by the soothing tones of Martin Fisher or Andrew James – however, with Teletext you'd simply see a zero turn to a one or a one to a two without any form of warning or fanfare whatsoever.

But for all the frustrations, I do remember some magical times following Forest's progress away from home via radio and Teletext during my early years as a Reds fan – not least an evening League Cup match away at Tottenham in January 1990, when the Reds pulled off a brilliant 3-2 victory that saw me leaping around my bedroom with excitement.

That win against Spurs sent Forest through to the League Cup semi-final, and a tie against Coventry over two legs.

Now in football you sometimes get two teams who don't seem to be able to avoid each other - and around the late 80s and early 90s, Forest always ended up playing Coventry in cup competitions. This resulted in some cracking matches, and also a bit of a rivalry between the two clubs.

And to be fair, Coventry had a decent team around this time, with great players like striker Cyrille Regis and goalkeeper Steve Ogrizovic – the latter who'd been a late starter in professional football, and had actually spent the early part of his adult life working as a copper with the Nottinghamshire Police.

There was a definite sense of anticipation then in early 1990 when the draw for the League Cup semi-final once again saw Forest paired with Coventry – with the first leg at the City Ground. Of course, season tickets don't get you into cup matches - however there was no way we were going to miss out on seeing the Reds and the west midlanders going toe-to-toe – and in the run-up to the first leg, Dad popped down to the Forest ticket office and snapped up our normal seats for the game.

The day of the match was actually the very same day that Nelson Mandela finally walked free after 27 years of imprisonment – an event that's rightly looked back upon as a pivotal moment in modern history. But at the time, this paled in significance for Dad and I compared to the infinitely more important matter of Forest taking on Coventry – and the match an absolute cracker, with the Reds bagging a 2-1 win thanks to possibly my favourite goal I've ever seen.

And once again, it was Stuart Pearce who delivered - as a he so often did back in those days.

Now the fact that the Reds' captain was pretty handy with free-kicks was not exactly news – yet the sheer power with which he hammered this one into the back of the Trent End net off the underside of the crossbar was simply breathtaking.

Take that Cov, and your silly badge with an elephant standing on top of a football!

The game that afternoon was shown live on TV – Dad had set the video to record it, and I remember us replaying Psycho's goal over and over after we got home. I swear the crossbar was shaking for several minutes afterwards.

Over the year there's probably been better goals scored by Forest players – however, mine and Dad's seats were bang in line with the spot from which Psycho hit the ball, so we got pretty much the best view in the ground as it flew into the net. It proved to be a decisive goal too – as with Forest holding onto their slender 2-1 lead by securing a 0-0 draw in the second leg, it ultimately won the semi-final for the Reds.

Which meant that Dad and I were suddenly able to start looking forward to our very first trip to an iconic footballing arena.

As a popular Trent End ditty went at the time – we were on the march with Cloughie's army, and we were all going to Wem-ber-lee!

6. Wembley

"So cruel that it had to be Des – the one man who you could usually rely on to never let us down..."

Dad and I made our first trip to Wembley on a green Nottingham City Transport double decker bus, which departed on the morning of the match from outside the old Ice Stadium.

That day in April 1990 was a glorious sunny one, and with Forest's opponents on the day being Oldham Athletic – who were plying their trade in English football's second tier - the mighty Reds were red hot favourites to finish the afternoon triumphant and lift the League Cup.

Though that's not to say that Oldham were mugs by any means. They had a great team in the early 90s who had caused a fair few upsets in cup competitions, and in the next few years they did eventually make it up the top flight for a few seasons.

However Forest had a great record in the League Cup - indeed they would arrive at Wembley on this occasion as reigning cup holders, having won it the previous season. They'd also got to the final three years on the spin in the late 70s and early 80s, doing a 'Meat Loaf' by ending up as winners two times out of three.

As it turned out, going to watch the Reds play beneath the twin towers for the first time was a brilliant experience. From taking the obligatory walk up Wembley Way, to seeing Stuart Pearce lead a victorious Forest team up the famous 39 steps following a 1-0 victory, it remains one of my happiest memories in all my years as a Reds fan.

One of my most vivid recollections of the day is a moment that occurred just after Psycho had lifted the trophy, when Brian Clough made his way over to the Forest end of the stadium to show his gratitude to the 30,000 or so of us who had travelled down to cheer on the team.

If I close my eyes I can still picture Cloughie in his trademark green sweatshirt getting closer and closer, before suddenly stopping on the running track that surrounded the pitch and saluting the fans.

Sitting as we were quite near the front in the backless seats that they used to have on the lower tier at the old Wembley, Dad and I were just a stone's throw from the great man. We didn't know it then, but that moment in time of him standing with both hands clasped above his head would go on to become an iconic image of Forest's greatest ever manager. In fact, 15 years later I would find myself part of the fundraising drive that led to Nottingham getting its very own statue of Cloughie – with the finished article capturing him in that exact pose.

More of the statue campaign in a later chapter. However, it's worth mentioning at this juncture that my involvement in raising the money for it did lead to a mildly amusing encounter with the very man who scored the only goal of the game back on the day of my first ever visit to Wembley.

Of course, Nigel Jemson was a player who Cloughie would often refer to as having "an even bigger head than mine".

But full of himself or not, the 21-year-old striker - as he was at the time - showed a cool head to tuck home a rebound after Oldham keeper Andy Rhodes had saved his initial shot. For that reason alone, Jemmo is a Forest player I'll always have a massive soft spot for - and on the occasions when I've encountered him during adulthood, I've generally found myself instantly transformed back into the starstruck ten-year-old who was going absolutely nuts behind the goal as the ball rolled into the back of the Oldham net.

Imagine the state I was in then one day in 2005, when I found myself assigned the task of cold calling Jemmo on his mobile!

This mission came about because it had been decided to organise a Q&A event with a panel of former Forest players to raise some cash for the Cloughie statue. With one of the other guys on the fundraising committee having acquired Jemmo's number from a mutual acquaintance, we decided to contact him to ask if he'd be willing to give up an evening to take part - and I was given the job of making the call.

For some reason I'd decided a weekday morning might be a good time to catch Jemmo, and I remember sitting with my phone in my hand for a good five minutes plucking up the courage to make the call – and shaking like a shitting dog when I punched the number in and heard the dialling tone.

Amusingly, when a drowsy-sounding Jemmo eventually answered, it turned out that I'd woken him up!

Oops…

Fair play though to Jemmo, he immediately agreed to come along to the event – and the night helped raise a decent chunk of money towards the statue.

But anyway, back to Wembley…

Having got my first taste of the twin towers in 1990, I was naturally eager for more – and fortunately, the fact that Forest were going through a massive purple patch in cup competitions at the time meant I didn't have to wait for very long. That first trip in 1990 was followed by three further visits – each of which saw my brother Al join Dad and me. Together, the three of us saw a defeat against Tottenham in the 1991 FA Cup final, a defeat against Manchester United in the 1992 League Cup final, and a win against Southampton in the 1992 Zenith Data Systems Cup final. In fact, Mum came with us as well to the Zenith Data Systems Cup final.

Though it ended in defeat, the Wembley trip that I have the most vivid memories of is the 1991 FA Cup final. Looking back, it almost certainly remains the biggest Forest match I've ever been to, and it felt like the entire country was rooting for Brian Clough to win the one trophy that had thus far eluded him during his glorious career as manager. Tickets were like gold dust, and I remember talk at the time that they were being sold on the black market for as much as £1,500 – which was a massive amount of money back then. Still is, to be fair. Indeed, I remember Dad checking his wallet about 20 times on the way down to Wembley, just to check that our tickets were still tucked safe inside.

As well as the sheer sense of occasion, there was also a feeling in the run-up to the game that it had been a hell of an effort by Forest to even get there. To reach the FA Cup final, the Reds had needed no less than five replays – two of them in round three alone, to get past the stubborn test of Crystal Palace.

With those two replays, and also several postponements due to adverse weather, that tie against Palace seemed to go on forever – and it was a relief to finally see the back of the niggly Londoners when Forest finally saw them off at the third attempt.

Inevitably though, who was next up on the fixture list?

Yes, Palace again – in the league this time.

It was like *Groundhog Day* with added elbows.

Both of the next two rounds of the cup saw Forest require replays too – and also dramatic late equalisers to stay in the competition. The fourth round took the Reds up to the north east – and though at the time Newcastle were languishing in the lower reaches of the English football's second tier, they proved a difficult test.

The game certainly made for a tense evening round at my mate Stewart Green's house as we sat and listened to live commentary on the radio. With barely ten minutes gone on the night the Reds were 2-0 down, and were seemingly struggling to deal with the bustling Newcastle number nine Mickey Quinn – who looked more like a darts player than a footballer, yet still seemed to score an absolute shedload of goals every season. The sort of player you sadly don't really see any more, at least not at the top level.

Fortunately though, two late goals by Stuart Pearce and Nigel Clough salvaged a draw – and despite huge support from a large and very vocal away following, many armed with giant inflatable bottles of Newcastle Brown, Forest comfortably beat the Geordies 3-0 in the replay.

It was through to round five then, and another away tie at Southampton. The match was chosen for live TV coverage on a Monday night - and for some reason, Dad, Al and I had gone round to Dad's mate Bob's house to watch it.

It's fair to say that it wasn't a brilliant game. The Reds were 1-0 down with time ticking away – and with the evening getting increasingly foggy on the south coast, you could clearly hear the travelling Forest fans who were at the game singing "Come on you fog!", in the hope that the conditions would become unplayable and force the ref to abandon the tie.

Fortunately, such extreme measures weren't needed – with Steve Hodge snatching a late equaliser for the Reds.

At least I *think* it was Steve Hodge – it was hard to see in the pea-soupy

—

conditions!

Whoever it was though who got the vital goal, there were wild celebrations in Bob's front room - resulting in a stern telling off from Bob's wife, with our commotion having woken their young children who'd been fast asleep upstairs.

As well as being a memorable escape, that night goes down in history as a notable one when it comes to the Forest faithful's vocal repertoire – for I believe I'm right in saying that Steve Hodge's equaliser inspired a very first rendition of a certain Righteous Brothers classic from the travelling Reds' fans. Of course, 'You've Lost That Loving Feeling' is now such an established part of Forest folklore that Bill Medley of the Righteous Brothers would actually end up coming to the City Ground 22 years later, just so he could experience for himself the sound of his song being sung by 20,000 people.

The song quickly gathered momentum over the remainder of the season – much like Forest's FA Cup run itself. For all the nervous moments and narrow escapes in the early rounds, the Reds seemed to get better and better the further they progressed in the competition. A 1-0 win in the quarter finals away at Norwich saw them succeed in getting through a round for the first time without actually needing a replay – and then the semi final saw a comprehensive 4-0 demolition of West Ham, although admittedly this was helped by some highly dubious refereeing.

So that was that, Forest were in the FA Cup final – and it was all very exciting. In the run-up to the big day, it was all anyone was talking about at school – and I remember feeling like a sort of celebrity among my peers, due to the fact that I was actually going to Wembley to watch the game.

Getting our tickets had involved Dad, Al and I standing for hours in a massive queue that snaked its way around the streets surrounding the City Ground. Come the day, Al and I got Mum to paint our faces red and white for the occasion – and once again, we again travelled down to London on a green Nottingham City Transport bus. We were confident of Forest's chances of winning, as after booking their place in the final the Reds had finished the league season in great form – winning five of their final six games, including a 7-0 demolition of Chelsea.

Alas, the big day at Wembley didn't go the way us Forest fans wanted it to. However, the atmosphere was incredible – and as an entertaining spectacle, the game had everything. As we all know, the first half alone saw the Reds go into an early lead thanks to a brilliant Stuart Pearce free-kick, and Mark Crossley saving a Gary Lineker penalty – not to mention Paul Gascoigne charging around like a bull in a china shop and ultimately getting stretchered off.

It was such an absorbing contest that I felt exhausted just from watching it. Not that I was complaining – to be 1-0 up as we reached the half-time interval was a great position to be in.

Sadly of course, the tide started to turn Tottenham's way as the game wore on. It was just heartbreaking though the way the match ended, with Des Walker heading the ball into the back of his own net in extra time to win the cup for Spurs.

So cruel that it had to be Des – the one man who you could usually rely on to never let us down.

We left as soon as the full-time whistle went, not wanting to hang around to see Spurs lift the trophy. I always remember on our way out of the stadium bumping into one of Dad's friends, who was in tears. It was the first time I'd ever seen a grown man crying over Forest.

It wouldn't be the last.

Despite the result though, the players were greeted like homecoming heroes when they arrived back in Nottingham the next day, with thousands of us gathering in Market Square for the team's formal homecoming reception - and Des Walker's name sung loudest of all. For all the disappointment, I think every Forest fan knew that the team had given it everything – the footballing Gods had just chosen not to smile upon us on this occasion.

Decades on, a lot of Forest fans still talk about how the match would've been completely different had the Reds been able to play most of it against ten men – referring to the widely-held belief that Gazza should've had a red card waved at him as he left the pitch on a stretcher.

To be fair, referee Roger Milford equally got some big calls wrong that went in Forest's favour. Stuart Pearce's goal should probably have been disallowed for the way several Reds players interfered with Tottenham's defensive wall; while some refs might also have sent off Mark Crossley after he brought down Gary Lineker to give away the penalty.

But for all the disappointment, the biggest consolation was the unshakeable belief that we'd be back. And we were – with Forest making it to Wembley not once but twice the following season.

If only we'd known though then that those two trips would be the Reds' very

last visits to the hallowed twin towers…

That said, brilliant as it was going to Wembley, the place was never quite the magical footballing Shangri La it was often cracked up to be. With it still being 'the old Wembley' back in those days, my main recollections are of seats miles from the pitch, endless queues to get out of the car-park, and the terrible facilities on the stadium concourse – in particular, trips to the toilet involving having to wade through ankle-deep rivers of urine.

What's more, the 1992 League Cup final was marred by crowd trouble, thanks to hundreds of Manchester United fans having snapped up tickets in the Forest 'end', and also unnecessarily heavy-handed policing. Al and I had both bought flags that day – only to have the sticks confiscated at the turnstiles by a charmless jobsworth in a Met uniform due to them apparently being regarded as offensive weapons. Being only 12 and 14 at the time we were both quite upset – in fact, it put a downer on the day probably more than Brian McClair's goal that won the game for United.

That said, I do hope a trip to Wembley to see Forest is something I get to experience again at some point in my lifetime… especially with the old stadium now obviously replaced with something rather more state-of-the-art.

I have been to the new stadium to see England, a couple of music concerts and a Carl Froch fight – just not a Forest game. As I write this though it's nearly a quarter of a century since the Reds' last visit to Wembley, so I'm not holding my breath...

7. Meeting your heroes

"I can only apologise all these years later to Steve Hodge's aunt if I ever gave her genuine concern that her house was being cased out as a potential burglary target.."

As well as some memorable wins and several trips to Wembley, during those first few years as a Forest fan I also managed to meet a few of my heroes – which is always a ludicrously exciting experience when you're a kid.

Indeed, before I got into football, I don't think I'd ever even met anyone famous.

Certainly not anyone *properly* famous.

Probably the nearest I'd got was during my early childhood, when my family and I lived on Kent Road in the Nottingham suburb of Mapperley. At that time there was a youth called Julian who lived opposite us who did a bit of acting, and actually starred during the mid-80s as the character Mugsy in the ITV children's programme *Murphy's Mob*.

The fact that we had a minor TV star living in our neighbourhood might seem a bit improbable, but it wasn't really – as Nottingham was a hotbed of small screen talent at the time. This was thanks to the launch in 1983 of The Television Workshop, an institution that has kickstarted the careers of numerous well-known names over the years from Shane Meadows to Samantha Morton.

It was through getting involved in The Television Workshop as a kid that Julian had ended up on the telly – and to be fair, he was probably far more famous at the time than any of us ever actually realised.

We never really gave him credit though, simply because we were just used to him being the unassuming lad from the family who lived over the road. During the height of his stardom he would actually supplement whatever he got paid for being in *Murphy's Mob* by occasionally babysitting for my brother Al and me. There was one time when he almost accidentally burnt our house down through a hapless attempt at making some toast – although that's another story!

Sadly when I was six my Mum and Dad played a real life game of Monopoly by trading in Kent Road for another street – and while our new neighbourhood about a mile away was very nice, it was distinctly lacking in minor TV stars.

However, a few years after we'd settled into our new place, and around the time I first started getting into Forest, Mugsy from *Murphy's Mob* was suddenly Top Trumped in quite spectacular style - when I discovered that Steve Hodge's aunt lived just round the corner from us!

Again, this wasn't all that improbable – after all, the tenacious Reds midfielder was a local lad, having grown up only a couple of miles down the road from us in the mining village of Gedling. As such, it was quite likely that he'd have numerous family members dotted around the area.

As it happened, Steve Hodge's aunt was pretty small fry really in the grand scheme of footballing royalty in our neighbourhood. Also living just a few streets away from me during my childhood was Tommy Lawton, who was a resident in a supported housing complex for older people. I'd delivered the legendary former Notts County and England striker's newspaper once whilst helping a friend do his paper round - although I'd never actually seen him.

To be honest though, I don't think Tommy Lawton's status as a true footballing great, and a man who once broke the British transfer record, really registered with me back then. As far as I was concerned he was just an old Notts County player - and Notts were rubbish, weren't they? Frankly, the close proximity of Steve Hodge's aunt was far more exciting - and I started making a point of going past her house all the time on my bike, convinced that it was only a matter of time before I spotted 'Harry' popping in for a cuppa.

Alas, I never once caught a glimpse of the Forest number six - and in the unlikely event that his aunt happens to be reading this, I can only apologise all these years later if I ever gave her genuine concern that her house was being cased out as a potential burglary target!

Despite my lack of success though with Steve Hodge, it wasn't long before I got to meet a Forest player for the first time. In fact, my first experience of rubbing shoulders with members of the Reds' first team actually saw me meet four or five in one go. This occurred after Dad had the brilliant idea of going round to the back of the Main Stand after one of our early trips down to the City Ground to watch Forest, and hanging around by the players' entrance until our heroes emerged – at which point we could go and ask them to sign our copy of the matchday programme.

Finally, after all the hours I'd spent trying to forge it, I was able to get Lee Chapman's *real* autograph!

We actually made this post-match pilgrimage a few times, and usually there'd be a fair few fellow fans gathered by the players' entrance for the exact same reason that we were there. Over time it became apparent that our heroes had clearly devised some sort of 'rota' – as each time, one or two players would emerge first and immediately draw the assembled hordes of autograph hunters like moths to a flame, allowing the others to sneak out relatively unnoticed and make a quicker getaway.

To be fair, this was understandable in some respects. Over the years I've often thought that Forest seem to attract some of life's real waifs and strays - and along with lads and their Dads, you'd regularly find some real oddball characters hanging around by the players' entrance after matches.

In spite of the players' diversionary tactics though, Dad and I did still manage to enjoy fleeting encounters with the freshly-showered likes of Brian Laws, Des Walker, Tommy Gaynor and – finally - Steve Hodge! I'd like to say that I had some deep and philosophical conversations with the various players that we met - but to be honest, I was literally shaking with the excitement at getting to spend a few seconds in the company of my heroes barely an hour after I'd seen them strut their stuff in front of 20,000 people. As such, I largely left all the talking to Dad.

On one of the occasions when we went round to the players' entrance after a match, Dad actually got some photos of me stood with various members of the Forest squad. In this modern age of course, pretty much everyone has a camera on their mobile phone – and as a result, we tend to document every last detail of our lives in photographs. But back in those days, cameras generally only came out on special occasions – so looking back, it was pretty cool that Dad made a point of bringing his along to the match just so he could capture those encounters.

Sadly the photos seem to have disappeared at some point in the years since – although starstruck as I was, I seem to remember that I looked like a rabbit in the headlights in every snap!

All in all, my one abiding recollection of those trips to the players' entrance to get autographs was thinking it was quite bizarre seeing the players wearing normal clothes – and also watching them get into their cars and drive off after they'd finished signing everything that was thrust in front of them. In my innocence, I'd sort of imagined that they all just lived at the ground, and spent their whole lives dressed in full Forest regalia. It was a bit strange when the realisation dawned that, away from football, they actually had regular domestic lives like anyone else.

But despite various illusions being shattered, those early encounters with various Forest players had only made me thirsty for more – and it occurred to me not long after I started going to matches that getting to be a mascot or a ball boy would surely be an absolute guaranteed way of getting to meet pretty much the whole team. Particularly being the mascot – after all, as well as running out onto the pitch with the team and taking a few shots at Steve Sutton, you presumably got to hang out in the dressing room as well?

After I pestered her for ages, Mum eventually rang up the club to find out how you got to become a mascot – only for her to discover that there was a five-year waiting list. This meant I'd have to bide my time until I was 15 – and on that basis, she chose not to put my name down, having felt that I probably wouldn't be up for doing it by the time I was that age. At the time I protested her decision vehemently. In hindsight though she was probably right, as mums invariably are.

As for becoming a ball boy meanwhile, one of my mates from school managed to get in there on that score - but it turned out it wasn't actually the greatest of gigs in reality. Yes you got to watch a match from the edge of the pitch, and also got in for free – in fact, if I remember rightly I think he actually got paid the princely sum of a quid for his 90 minute shift. However, there was no opportunity to mingle with the players – what's more, he also had to spend the whole afternoon wearing a manky old tracksuit that clearly hadn't been washed in about a decade and smelt like a tramp's vest.

But while the possibility of becoming a mascot or a ball boy were both summarily dismissed, I did still manage to acquire numerous further additions for my collection of Forest players' autographs - through a spot of letter writing. This is probably a dying art among the young people of today growing up in the age of electronic communication – however, I was very much a child of the *Jim'll Fix It* generation, and being able to write letters was an essential life skill for any self-respecting youngster.

In fact, there was a period during my childhood when my favourite TV programme was the cult kids' show *Rainbow* – and at one point I decided in my wisdom to write off and ask for a signed photo of its main protagonist, the redoubtable gobshite otherwise known as Zippy. And brilliantly, someone in the offices at Thames Television had humoured me, by scrawling 'Zippy' in biro across a photograph of my hero and sending it back to me!

In stark contrast I never got a reply to the various letters that I sent to 'Jim'll', as I was convinced Jimmy Savile was called back in those days – but then that's probably just as well given what we know now.

Just like my experience though with Zippy, I enjoyed considerable success from writing to members of the Forest team during my early years as a Reds fan. Within a few weeks, I'd usually find that my stamped addressed envelope would arrive back containing a signed photo - particularly if I'd sucked up to the player a bit in my letter and told them that they were my favourite member of the Forest squad!

Some of my heroes would even go to the efforts of writing 'To Rich' before their signature; while it was apparent that others even had a special gold marker pen for the purpose of signing their name.

But getting an autograph by writing to one of the players almost seemed like cheating - the real thrill was when you managed to get a signature in person. And over time I discovered that another good way to get a bit of facetime with some of my Forest heroes was to go to watch the Reds' reserve team at the City Ground – as members of the first team squad would often go along to watch the matches, and sit with the ordinary punters in the Main Stand.

I remember one reserve team game where word spread that Roy Keane was sitting at the back of the stand. Off I shot like a rat up a drainpipe to where he was sitting, and plucked up the courage to ask for his autograph. This was the fresh-faced 19-year-old Roy Keane of 1990 though, who'd not long broken into the Forest first team. Even now as an adult, I don't think I'd dare go and pester the terrifying figure that Roy Keane has become in more recent years!

Meanwhile, my autograph book was filled even further thanks to encounters with Nigel Clough and Steve Chettle – the former at a local DIY store, where he was randomly making a personal appearance, and the latter when he paid a visit to my primary school.

The visit of 'Chet' was all part of Forest's early forays into the Football in the Community movement, which at the time was just starting to get off the ground at clubs around the country. At my primary school, we were lucky enough to have a series of visits from a group of Forest youth coaches as part of the scheme, who basically did our P.E, lessons for a few weeks.

One of the coaches was a guy called Mick Raynor, who was a really nice chap. However, there was another bloke whose name I don't recall, who was a proper sadist, and who seemed to think he was a sergeant major in the army rather than a football coach working with a bunch of nine and ten-year-olds. During one of our sessions a group of us had annoyed him for some reason, and as a punishment he made us stand still for ages in the middle of the Gedling Miners' Welfare playing fields, where we did our P.E., with our arms held out horizontally. Doesn't sound like too much of a big deal – but honestly, try doing it for ten minutes.

Actually, don't – it was bloody agony!

It was all worth it though, as when we completed the Football in the Community coaching sessions we not only got to go on a tour of the City Ground and see everything from the trophy room to the players' dressing room, we also had the 'royal visit' from Chet - who caused enormous excitement as he arrived at our school in his Forest tracksuit to present us with our certificates.

I remember everyone having to queue up in the school hall to meet Chet – and when I eventually got to the front of the line I impressed the great man by producing not just a scrap of paper for him to sign like most of my peers, but my copy of the matchday programme from the 1990 League Cup final, which had taken place a few months earlier. I can't remember exactly what Chet said, but I do recall being surprised by the fact that he was relatively softly spoken in person – as my only previous experience of his voice was the distinctive gruff bark reminiscent of the mating call of an American black bear that you'd occasionally hear booming from the centre of the Reds' back four during matches!

Over subsequent decades I've gone on to meet various Forest heroes past and present, and also a few icons from the wider footballing world – and I'll be sharing tales of some of those encounters in later chapters. By far and away the biggest name I've ever rubbed shoulders with though took place when I was 15, when I got to share a few seconds with the copper-bottomed legend widely regarded as the greatest player in the history of the game. Yes, I refer to Edson Arantes do Nascimento – or Pele, as he is much better known.

Sadly of course, Pele never played for Forest during his distinguished career – although to be fair, during the time he was at his peak in the 60s the Reds had the mercurial Joe Baker banging in the goals, so he would've probably had to settle for a place on the bench.

However my encounter with the Brazilian legend did actually take place at the City Ground, when Forest hosted an international game between Sweden and Japan during the summer of 1995. The match was part of a tournament that was held at various stadiums across the country that summer to ensure facilities were up to scratch in readiness for Euro '96 the following year – and for reasons that were never really made clear, it had been announced in the run-up to the game that Pele would be in attendance as a guest of honour. Around 5,000 of us were present at the City Ground on the day – and while Pele had long since retired from playing and many fans such as myself were too young to have ever seen him in action, he was rightly given a standing ovation when he was brought out onto the pitch just before kick-off to wave to the crowd.

But I managed to go one better than simply catching a glimpse of the great man from a distance…

This all happened around an hour or so earlier, when I'd been wandering along Pavilion Road on my way to the ground – and I suddenly spotted a very cheerful looking Pele making his way through the crowds, flanked by a couple of minders.

Quite why Pele had turned up on foot is unclear – for his sake, I can only hope he hadn't arrived in Nottingham by train and been made to walk all the way to the ground via the less than salubrious environs of the Meadows estate. The world's greatest ever footballer getting 'taxed' by a gang of hoodies certainly wouldn't have been the best bit of PR for the city!

In the heat of the moment though, this mystery wasn't something I really had time to ponder. After all, we're talking about one of the most recognisable people in the world - and it very quickly became apparent that lots of other people had spotted him too.

Naturally he was surrounded within seconds, and as such there was no chance of an autograph - although I did manage to shake him by the hand before he was seemingly swallowed whole by a gaggle of giddy Japanese supporters, all furiously clicking away with their cameras.

Not quite as exhilarating as meeting the great Steve Chettle, obviously – but nevertheless, a pretty exciting moment.

That said, my encounter with Pele had been pre-meditated to some degree. Sure, I hadn't expected to bump into him in the street – but I had turned up at the City Ground that afternoon knowing he was going to be there.

Of course, getting to share a few seconds with the greatest footballer of all time is not something to be sniffed at, whatever the circumstances. If you're going to rub shoulders though with the great and good from the beautiful game, it's always far more memorable when those encounters happen unexpectedly – and particularly if the meeting occurs in a situation that has nothing whatsoever to do with football.

One relatively recent example of a time when I've had a chance meeting along these lines with someone associated with Forest occurred during 2016, when I went to an 'Audience with…' event in Nottingham with Happy Mondays frontman Shaun Ryder – and it suddenly dawned on me during the evening that I was sat just a few feet away from Mark Crossley.

Now by this point during my 'career' as a football fan, I'd long since stopped collecting autographs. After all, there comes a point in your life when it suddenly feels a bit embarrassing asking a grown man to write their name for you on a piece of paper - unless it's some sort of event like a book signing that's been specifically set up for that purpose.

What's more, autographs have become an industry in themselves in the last few decades – and to me, getting a player's signature doesn't quite have the same magic when you know that that exact same scribble could've just as easily been bought over the internet. Honestly, take a look at some of the Forest autographs available on eBay next time you're online– at the time of writing you're just a few clicks from owning the biro scribbles of everyone from your big names like Stuart Pearce (£44.95) to long-forgotten footnotes like Lee Glover (a mere £4.50).

You even get some ex-footballers on the fan convention circuit these days, where they spend a day sat behind a trestle table in some soulless exhibition centre and punters queue up and pay them £15 or £20 for an autograph. I guess it's a pretty lucrative day's work if you can get a couple of hundred punters who are willing to stump up the money – though I can't help but feel that it's only a few steps away from prostitution.

But while autographs don't hold the same allure for me these days, I do like to try and have a quick chat if I ever happen to encounter a Forest player past or present. Happily my social skills have developed significantly since my early days as a Reds fan, when I'd wordlessly proffer a copy of a matchday programme and a pen to my heroes – so upon spotting him at the Shaun Ryder event, I immediately sidled over to Mark Crossley to say hello.

I'm pleased to say that 'Big Norm' was lovely - happily chatting away about his years at Forest, and also what music he was into. Amusingly, I actually spotted him joining the scrum with everyone else later on in the evening to get his photo taken with Shaun Ryder. Just goes to show that no-one is exempt from having heroes – even those who happen to have saved a penalty in a FA Cup final.

Of all the unexpected encounters that I've had though with people associated with Forest, my favourite one was with someone whose connection to the Reds is actually relatively tenuous – namely Sean Dyche, who I randomly bumped into back in 2013 on a Sunday morning on the outskirts of London.

I'd travelled down to the capital the previous day to attend a friend's wedding - and with the marriage celebrations having descended into a mammoth 12-hour drinking session, I was feeling pretty rough the following morning as I checked out of my hotel room ready for the long drive back to Nottingham.

It was the sort of hangover that can only be cured by a McDonalds breakfast – so on my way out of London, I decided just before I hit the M1 to stop at the Maccy Ds in Stanmore. And the first thing I saw as I walked in was Sean

Dyche, who was sat having a coffee with another bloke who I didn't recognise.

It was quite a surreal situation – at first, I actually wondered if I was still drunk and having some sort of hallucination!

Now at the time, Sean Dyche was (and still is, at the time of writing) manager of Burnley - however, it was reasonably well known that he actually began his life in football in the late 80s as an apprentice at Forest.

Goodness knows what he was doing having a coffee in a branch of McDonalds on the outskirts of London on a Sunday morning - naturally though, I couldn't resist going over for a chat.

Given that I was a bit dishevelled and probably still stank of alcohol, you could've forgiven Dyche for avoiding eye contact and being keen to get rid of me as soon as possible. But fair play to the guy known to the Burnley fans as 'the ginger Mourinho', he was an absolute gent.

After saying hello, I explained to Dyche that I was a Forest fan - and that I was pleased to see him doing so well at Burnley, with him technically being 'one of our own'. He seemed genuinely chuffed to hear this, and duly told me a great story in his distinctive raspy tones about how him and some of the other Forest apprentices used to sometimes get summoned to Brian Clough's house to do a spot of gardening – a chore for which the great man would reward them by cooking them lunch and then giving them a crisp tenner each.

After a couple of minutes I decided to let the Burnley supremo get back to his business, so wished him best of luck for the rest of the season before wandering off to order my breakfast. But as I was tucking into my hangover cure a short while later, Dyche got up to leave – and as he walked past me on his way out of the door, he actually gave me a manly cuff on the shoulder accompanied by a cry of "Cheers mate!"

Top man. I'd genuinely love him to come and manage Forest one day on the strength of this incident alone.

That said, I suspect he might be a little bit 'out of our league' these days given the success he's had since our meeting in getting Burnley a firm foothold in the Premier League. And to be fair, it's never ended well in recent decades when Forest have appointed ginger managers!

All in all then, I think it's fair to say that it's still pretty exciting even as an adult when you encounter people from the world of football. However, nothing will ever come close to the buzz that you got from meeting your heroes when you were a kid - and from Steve Chettle to Roy Keane, I think I did pretty well back in those days in terms of how many Forest stars I managed to rub shoulders with.

But one important person indelibly associated with Forest who eluded me throughout that time was the very man for whom Sean Dyche provided an occasional gardening service. Although it wasn't through lack of trying on my part...

8. Cloughie

"Like all Forest fans, I hoped beyond hope that Cloughie could shit one last rainbow.."

Though I'm a bit too young to have experienced the Forest glory days of the late 70s and early 80s under Brian Clough and Peter Taylor, I was fortunate enough to grow up with Cloughie as the Reds' manager.

Of course, when someone's been there for as long as you can remember, it's easy to take them for granted.

But not Brian Howard Clough. I always knew he was special.

It wasn't just the fact that Cloughie was a great manager. His sheer charisma and force of personality were also intoxicating.

As a kid, I acquired a video that told Cloughie's life story, and would watch it repeatedly. I was mesmerised by the man in his pomp - whether old footage from the 70s of him running verbal rings round his old Leeds United adversary Don Revie, or clips of him casually breezing into the City Ground in January 1975 to begin his 18 year reign as Forest manager.

My love of Cloughie was such that I even remember being allowed once to stay up late to watch him make a brief cameo appearance in the TV crime drama *Boon*, which was largely filmed around the Nottingham area. And by the time I'd been following Forest for a couple of years, I didn't think it would be possible for the great man to raise himself any higher in my affections.

But somehow, in the autumn of 1991, he managed it.

Now there have been lots of stories about Cloughie's benevolent side – whether it be paying for old ladies' shopping, or stopping in his car to offer lifts to complete strangers.

—

And on my 12th birthday, I was lucky enough to be on the receiving end of one of his random acts of kindness.

As was customary during my childhood, Mum and Dad had said that I could have a few friends round for tea to mark the milestone of becoming a year older. I duly invited a couple of mates from school – and having always been told 'If you don't ask, you don't get', I also wrote a very polite letter to Cloughie, asking him if he'd like to join us!

Looking back, it's funny to think that I actually thought a busy football manager with a family of his own might turn up to the birthday celebrations of a 12-year-old who he'd never met. Nevertheless, come the day, I found myself running excitedly to the window in our front room every time I heard a car pull up outside – hoping it would be the arrival of the great man.

Needless to say, he never did turn up – and while I still had a great time with my mates, I do remember feeling a tinge of disappointment that my hero hadn't graced us with his presence.

However, this was quickly forgotten a couple of days later when I arrived home from school to find a chunky package had arrived in the post for me.

Now back when you were a kid, getting *anything* in the post was exciting. But when it's a parcel with a Nottingham Forest postmark – well, the levels of anticipation were frankly off the scale. Giddy with wonder, I ripped open the brown paper... and I discovered a letter from none other than Cloughie himself – who thanked me for the invite and apologised for his non-appearance at my birthday celebrations, citing the fact that he'd been away sunning himself in Majorca.

But best of all, accompanying the letter was a football signed by the entire Forest squad.

Naturally the letter and the signed football remain cherished possessions – although little did I know on that day when they arrived in the post that Cloughie would be gone as Forest manager in less than two years.

To this day it still saddens me that the great man's 18-year reign never got the ending it deserved. The speed with which his great team of the late 80s and early 90s disintegrated was alarming – certainly, few could've predicted what lay ahead as his final season in charge got underway.

I always love it when the fixture computer gives Forest a home game on the opening weekend of the season. When the big day finally comes the sun always seems to be shining, and as a fan there's always that buzz of excitement as you return to the City Ground following the summer break, knowing that - in theory - *anything* might happen over the next nine months.

On this particular occasion, in August 1992, Forest were playing Liverpool – and there was also the additional excitement caused by the fact that it was the first ever televised game of the newly-formed Premier League. As it was, the Reds played superbly - and but for an inspired display by David James on his debut in the Liverpool goal, they would've won by much more than 1-0.

A brilliant start then to the new season - but sadly, it was a false dawn.

Immediately after the win against Liverpool, Cloughie agreed to sell Teddy Sheringham – who'd scored the winner against the Scousers, and also been top scorer the previous season – to Tottenham.

Now this wouldn't have been so bad had 'Super Ted' been properly replaced. Sadly though, he wasn't – and with Des Walker having also departed in the summer and Stuart Pearce sidelined with injuries for much of the season, the Forest team was suddenly seriously lacking in leadership and quality.

Consequently, the Reds quickly plummeted down the league table – and Cloughie seemingly fiddled while Rome burned.

To be fair, Cloughie was by no means the only one who didn't seem to really grasp just how grave the situation was. For quite a good chunk of the season, all we heard from the critics was that Forest were too good to go down - and I think the vast majority of us fans believed too that the Reds would manage to claw their way out of danger.

As the season rumbled on, opposition fans visiting the City Ground started taunting the Trent End with chants of "Going down, going down, going down…" – only to be disarmed by an instant response of "So are we, so are we, so are we…" Indeed, the idea of Forest actually getting relegated seemed so absurd that it felt like we could afford to joke about it.

But as we all know, league tables never lie – and months drifted by without the Reds showing any sign of getting themselves out of the mess they were in. And I think all of us knew the game was up in March, when it was announced that Cloughie was signing a striker with proven top flight experience to fire the goals needed to reach safety. Only for that striker to turn out to be Robert Rosario!

The popular joke at the time was that Cloughie had told his assistant Ronnie Fenton to go out and sign the Brazilian international Romario – only for Ronnie to mishear and accidentally sign the lumbering former Norwich and Coventry journeyman instead.

Of course, the Reds manager had been known on numerous previous occasions to turn misfit players into world-beaters. But it was quickly apparent that 'Big Bad Bob' would be a step too far even for Cloughie's celebrated turd-polishing abilities – and upon reaching the business end of the season, Forest went into their final home game against Sheffield United knowing nothing less than a win would do if they were to retain any chance of staying in the Premier League.

With the stakes as high as they were, the fixture in question was already a massive game – and its significance only increased tenfold when the news came a few days beforehand that Cloughie would be bowing out at the end of the season.

That day my brother Al and I had decided to eschew our usual seats in the Executive Stand to go and stand in the Trent End – because the club were intending to demolish it in the summer and build a brand new stand. As it turned out, relegation saw these plans put on hold for a year – at the time though, it looked like it would be our very last chance to experience the unique ambience of the old cowshed.

By this point in my 'career' as a Forest fan I'd stood in the Trent End a few times, usually during cup games – mainly because standing was a bit cheaper than paying for our usual seats. Dad had even acquired a milk crate for me to stand on at those games so I could see over people's heads.

On these forays into the Trent End we'd usually play it safe and stand in one of the outer sections. With the game against Sheffield United being one of such importance though, it felt like there was only one place to be – and so it was that Al and me decided to brave the sardine-like conditions in the centre section, where the Reds' most vociferous fans would congregate.

Unsurprisingly, the game proved to be a highly-charged and emotional occasion at a packed City Ground. Like all Forest fans, I hoped beyond hope that Cloughie could shit one last rainbow, and inspire the team to a win that would enable them to escape relegation by the skin of their teeth. Sadly though, real life is never quite like the movies – and a limp 2-0 defeat saw the Reds condemned to spending the following season in the second tier of English football.

Seeing your team get relegated is normally a sombre affair – yet on this occasion it wasn't. This was probably in part down to the fact that it had been more than 20 years since Forest had last suffered relegation – so an entire generation of fans, myself included, had grown up with no idea how we were supposed to behave in such circumstances.

But more than anything, the fate of the team was genuinely overshadowed that day by the sheer outpouring of love for Cloughie and everything he'd done for Forest over his 18 year reign. Throughout the game the fans sang his name – visiting supporters included - and the atmosphere was one of celebration more than anything.

Come the final whistle, Cloughie was given a standing ovation before disappearing down the tunnel. Slowly, the City Ground began to empty – but those of us who were stood in the centre section of the Trent End all remained where we were. We wanted one last piece of our hero – and we weren't going anywhere until we got it.

Happily, insistent chants of "We want Brian" eventually paid off – for after about 20 minutes, a solitary figure in a familiar green sweatshirt emerged from the tunnel.

Slowly, Cloughie began walking towards the Trent End – at which point those of us who'd remained behind needed no further invitation. Al and me were among the first hundred or so to spill out on the pitch – and thinking about it now, it was probably a bit of a risky move. After all, we all knew that Cloughie took a pretty dim view of those who encroached the hallowed turf.

Any rational thought about what we were doing was lost though in the sheer emotion of the moment, and the police and stewards made little attempt to stop us – knowing it was probably futile. I managed to get within a few feet of Cloughie, although he was soon lost among a sea of fans wanting to grab a final opportunity to show him how much he meant to them.

Looking back, it was astonishing really. Forest fans are as fickle and as quick to reduce heroes to zeroes as any – but the love for Cloughie was unconditional. Yes, he'd messed up badly by allowing the team to slip to relegation. However, after everything he'd done for Forest, we could allow him one monumental balls-up.

The loyalty shown towards Cloughie by the City Ground faithful that day was certainly a stark contrast to the way Arsenal fans have behaved in recent years towards Arsene Wenger – who's had to listen to regular calls for his head from a bunch of ungrateful supporters, who seem to think their team is massively underachieving under his management. This despite the fact that the Gunners have never finished lower than fourth in the Premier League during the Frenchman's 20+ years in charge.

Some people really need to be careful what they wish for…

That said, I do think most Forest fans will look back with the benefit of hindsight and agree that Cloughie should've called time on his glorious career some time before he did. By the time of that fateful 1992-93 season, his judgement had clearly become clouded – need I say more than mention the words 'Robert' and 'Rosario' again?

What's more, even to a kid like myself, it was obvious from Cloughie's blotchy red face and increasingly erratic behaviour that something wasn't quite right with the great man.

For quite some time after he retired, Cloughie's declining health and struggles with alcohol – and also reports of his alleged dodgy financial dealings – cast a long shadow over his entire career.

I got to see first hand what a mess he was two years after retirement, when I acquired tickets to be in the audience for a television programme that was on ITV at the time called *Sport in Question*. Recorded at Nottingham's old Carlton Studios, best known as the place where game shows like *Blockbusters* were filmed, *Sport in Question* was basically like a sporting equivalent of *Question Time* – and on this particular week, Cloughie was one of the panel guests. Sadly though, his shambolic performance was nothing short of embarrassing – and even made national news headlines afterwards, with this having been the very TV appearance where he famously called Alan Sugar a 'spiv'.

In one respect it had been funny to watch from a ringside seat as Cloughie gave the bumptious Spurs Chairman (as he was then) a pasting. But on the whole, it was upsetting to see a man who had once been so razor sharp slurring his words and generally carrying himself with the air of a pub drunk. It wasn't quite George Best on *Wogan* – but it wasn't a million miles off.

In some ways though, Cloughie's vulnerability and frailties made us love him even more.

And above anything else, even the unimaginable success that he and Peter Taylor brought to a previously unremarkable provincial football club, I'll always love Cloughie simply because he cared enough to want to make a 12-year-old lad happy on his birthday.

9. Confessions of a teenage fanzine editor - part one

"A more volatile character than Frank Clark would've probably chinned me - and I would've almost certainly entirely deserved it…"

Aside perhaps from getting sent a birthday present by Cloughie, I guess the tale of my early days as a Forest fan is fairly run-of-the-mill really.

Boy gets into football, starts going to matches with his Dad – it's a rite of passage that's been played out countless times all over the world, and one that will probably be played out countless times more.

There did come a point for me though where things got slightly out of the ordinary – and that was when I decided to launch my own Forest fanzine at the age of just 12.

As you do!

The football fanzine phenomenon of the late 80s and early 90s has of course been widely documented. In the space of a few years, unofficial fan-produced publications were launched up and down the country at pretty much every club in an explosion of Pritt Stick and Letraset.

Sometimes controversial and often funny, fanzines provided an avenue for fans to share their views about what was happening at their club, and also the game in general.

And it was a much-needed avenue. Back in the 80s, football fans were being demonised by everyone from the media to politicians - so fanzines were a way to bite back.

But in addition, fanzines were a form of entertainment. It's almost hard to comprehend in this modern era of 24/7 rolling news, but back in the 80s there wasn't a lot to read about your team. You'd get a bit of coverage in your local paper, bland magazines like *Shoot* and *Match* - whose idea of an in-depth

---

interview with a player was asking them what their favourite food was - and the propaganda of your club's official matchday programme.

But that was about your lot.

Happily though, that all changed when the fanzine boom saw Forest blessed with three excellent publications. *Brian* had been launched in 1988, closely followed by *The Tricky Tree* and *The Trent Times* - and with their mixture of passion and humour, I became an avid reader of all three.

It was *Brian* and *The Tricky Tree* that I discovered first, and I can vividly remember the day those two publications came into my life. It was a sunny afternoon in August 1990, and I was out and about in Nottingham city centre with Mum, Dad and my brother Al. I can't remember what we were doing - possibly a family trip to see a film at the old Odeon cinema. But at some point during the outing we nipped to the newsagent that used to be on St James's Street, just off Market Square - and I remember being stopped in my tracks when I spotted two little A5-sized magazines in the window that were clearly about Forest.

Dad duly did the honours and bought me a copy of each of the two publications – and it's no exaggeration to say that that moment changed my life.

I still have those very same copies of *Brian* and *The Tricky Tree* - and leafing through them now, they're both pretty rough and ready in terms of the way they were put together, as fanzines of the time often were. Highlights in terms of the editorial content include pages of love for Stuart Pearce in *Brian*, following his miss from the penalty spot in England's defeat against Germany in the semi-final of that summer's World Cup; and a hilarious spoof interview in *The Tricky Tree* with John Sillett, who was manager of Coventry City at the time.

I remember finding the spoof Sillett interview particularly entertaining, as the slapheaded Coventry boss was someone who was a great source of intrigue to me at the time. This was largely due to the distinctive home team dugout that Coventry had at their Highfield Road stadium, which actually looked more like some sort of bomb shelter. It had a hole in the roof so the Coventry coaching staff could pop their heads up and get a more elevated view of what was happening on the pitch – and for some reason, I used to find the sight of Sillett's shiny bonce poking out enormously comical. I always thought it looked like he was driving a tank!

In the years since, there's been more than one occasion when I've tried to find photos of John Sillett in his 'tank' on the internet – bizarrely though, there doesn't seem to be a single trace of it anywhere in cyberspace. Which makes me worry whether the whole thing may actually be a figment of my imagination – after all, the mind does work in strange ways sometimes when recalling things from childhood. That said, I have discussed 'Sillett's tank' with various fellow football fans of a similar age, who all swear too that it definitely existed!

But anyway, back to fanzines...

Being just ten years old as I was at the time when I discovered *Brian* and *The Tricky Tree*, I was almost certainly a lot younger than most people who bought the two publications – so I think it's fair to say that some of the content probably went a bit over my head. Nevertheless, I remember absolutely devouring those first copies, and taking them to school and showing my friends. With some of the articles including swear words, it all felt very exciting and slightly illicit.

Looking back, I think it was inevitable that I'd eventually end up starting my own Forest fanzine. I'd always loved writing at school, and I'd also shown a fair bit of business nous for someone of such tender years – not least during my first year at secondary school, when me and my mate Dean Heckford got involved in a bit of a scam with a few other lads where we earned a reasonable amount of extra pocket money by selling watered-down aftershave to our peers!

Inevitably, there came a point where someone ratted on us and we had our entire stock unceremoniously confiscated. You'd have thought the school might have at least acknowledged our precocious entrepreneurial spirit and tried to steer us towards a more legitimate avenue of flexing our business muscles – back in those days though teachers seemed to revel in crushing our spirits, just like the terrifying headmaster portrayed by Pink Floyd in 'The Wall'.

Still, I was unruffled by the experience - although it was actually my brother Al rather than me who was first out of the blocks in putting together something approximating a fanzine when, around the time of Forest's appearance in the FA Cup final in 1991, he cobbled together a magazine called *The Forest Tree*.

The Forest Tree largely consisted of cartoons and jokes – and having persuaded one of our parents to sneakily run off a few copies on their work's photocopier, Al started flogging copies to his mates at school. It went down really well and I quickly got involved, helping produce several further editions - with content including a cartoon called 'Whingin' Gramps', whose central character was entirely based on a moaning old codger who sat behind us at Forest home games.

We even managed to get a rudimentary interview with Mark Crossley, Forest's goalkeeper at the time, by sending him a questionnaire through the post along with a stamped addressed envelope. He was good enough to return it with handwritten answers – and so it was that we were able to share with our readers a series of revelations from 'Big Norm', such as his most disappointing Christmas present being, in his words, "Socks thats too small".

It's amazing really when you look back to think that he actually gave us time of day. It's certainly hard to imagine any of today's top flight players co-operating with a bunch of kids in the same way that Big Norm did.

The Forest Tree ended up lasting for four issues before fizzling out. However, that was enough to make me realise what was possible – and in January 1992, my school friend Sanjay Nijran and I launched *Forest Forever*.

Articles in our first edition ranged from a thought piece on who might one day replace Brian Clough as Forest manager, Archie Gemmill being our suggestion, and a brutal character assassination of Neil Warnock - who at the time was manager of Notts County, and just starting to develop a reputation as one of football's perennial gobshites.

Hard as it is to believe now, both Nottingham teams were actually in the top tier of English football at the time – and it's the only period during all my years following Forest when I can remember Reds fans ignoring Derby, who were languishing a division below, and instead engaging in a proper meaningful rivalry with Notts.

As it turned out though, this only lasted for one season, before Notts began to slide down the leagues again.

In terms of production values, that first edition of *Forest Forever* was fairly basic. The 24 pages were cobbled together using a traditional old-fashioned typewriter and lots of Pritt Stick, with bigger text for things like headlines created by cutting individual letters out of newspapers, ransom note style.

But Sanjay and I were full of unshakable self-belief – and far from being happy to just try and peddle copies to our friends, we actually turned up outside the City Ground before a Forest home game with a bag full of copies of that first issue – again, printed on the sly by a parent on their work's photocopier.

Amazingly, a few dozen people actually handed over 30p to buy a copy… with some even saying nice things about our efforts.

Our confidence buoyed, Sanjay and I immediately got working on issue two – which featured much eulogising about Des Walker's one and only goal for Forest, which he'd scored in a home game against Luton just a few days after we'd completed issue one.

Of course, most of the crowd had gone home by the time Des made a rare burst forward and wellied the ball into the back of the Bridgford End net – as it had been a terrible game that had seemed destined to end in a 1-0 defeat for the Reds. Dad and I had always been firm believers though in staying until the bitter end no matter how badly Forest were playing – and this was one of those rare occasions where we were actually rewarded for our loyalty.

The next few months saw *Forest Forever* slowly start to blossom, with Sanjay and I publishing a new issue every five or six weeks. It was hard work - but we discovered that hard work doesn't actually feel like hard work when you love what you're doing. And Forest being Forest, there was never any shortage of topics to write about – indeed, that 1991-92 season when we launched the fanzine saw the Reds get to not one but two Wembley cup finals.

At this juncture it's only fair to give recognition to my family for the enormous contribution that they made to *Forest Forever*. They helped in all sorts of ways – and I'm not just talking about my parents' illicit commandeering of work photocopiers for those early editions!

We also utilised Al's artistic talents for cartoons, while he and Mum and Dad all became part of the sales team outside the City Ground on Forest matchdays. Mum's regular 'pitch' come rain or shine was outside the entrance to the Main Stand car-park, where she was regularly brought cups of tea by the club's car-park attendant at the time, a chap called Terry Farndale. In later years, Terry went on to achieve minor cult status with Forest fans when he became the club's kitman.

Meanwhile Dad did a sterling job flogging copies of the fanzine to his friends at work, and also members of our wider family. My Uncle Mick in particular became probably our most loyal and enthusiastic reader.

Over those early months of *Forest Forever*, Sanjay and I got to know the guys behind the other Forest fanzines. You'd have thought there might have been a bit of a rivalry between us, but it was nothing like that. In fact, at home matches before kick-off, we'd all stand in a line selling our wares on what became known as 'Fanzine Corner', next to what was at the time the Wurlitzers bar – myself and Sanjay with our *Forest Forevers*, Bob Stevens with his *Brians*, Andy Lowe with his *Tricky Trees* and Sheldon Miller with his *Trent Times*es.

I was actually a bit starstruck when we first got to know the likes of Bob, Andy and Sheldon. After all, I'd been an avid reader of the other Forest fanzines for a good year, so I was accustomed to seeing their articles in print.

One key player in the world who I never really got to know though was the mysterious JS Pritchard - editor of *Brian,* and one of football's very few female fanzine editors. She always seemed to keep a fairly low profile – however, she did send me a lovely handwritten letter not long after Sanjay and I started *Forest Forever*, offering us stacks of useful advice.

Indeed, all of the folk involved in the other fanzines were incredibly encouraging of what Sanjay and I were doing. When we launched issue two of *Forest Forever* at a home game against Norwich, Bob Stevens was also out selling copies of *Brian* – and with *Brian* priced at 70p and *Forest Forever* 30p, he jovially bullied all of his customers into buying both for a quid. This was a massive help to us in building our readership.

Over time we discovered that there was also a brilliant sense of community within the wider fanzine underworld. Around the time Sanjay and I started *Forest Forever* a Nottinghamshire fanzine five-a-side tournament was being held every year, where teams representing all of Forest's, Notts County's and Mansfield Town's publications would go head-to-head. It was a bit like a fan version of the long-forgotten County Cup, that annual competition that used to be contested by the three Nottinghamshire clubs every season – which was eventually consigned to the dustbin of local footballing history sometime around the mid-90s, presumably because Notts and Mansfield found it a bit demoralising getting thrashed most years by Forest's reserves.

We entered a *Forest Forever* team into the Nottinghamshire fanzine five-a-side tournament a couple of times, and our first attempt saw us win the wooden spoon by some distance – though with the average age of our squad being only about 14, it was literally men against boys. Indeed, rumour has it that Alan Hansen's famous "You can't win anything with kids" comment a few years later when talking about Manchester United was largely based on our hapless efforts that day!

Those tournaments were brilliant occasions though. The camaraderie between the competing teams was fantastic, and it was always great to meet some of the movers and shakers from the other Notts clubs' fanzines – such as Steve Hartshorn of Mansfield's *Follow The Yellow Brick Road* and Jim Cooke of Notts' *The Pie*. The *Forest Forever* team also improved considerably following our first doomed tilt at glory, after a canny managerial decision to start recruiting some of my Dad's mates who played Sunday league football to give us a bit of steel and experience.

Over time Sanjay and I also got to know quite a few people from fanzines beyond Nottinghamshire. At the time, the national football magazine *When Saturday Comes* used to publish a two-page directory in every issue with contact details for all the publications up and down the country, so we'd often hear from editors of other titles. It was all very mutually supportive – and a far cry from the negative way in which football fans were often portrayed in the media at the time.

Sanjay and I certainly gained a lot of ideas for *Forest Forever* by reading fanzines from other clubs. Favourites of mine included Everton's *When Skies are Grey* and Manchester City's *King of the Kippax*. There was also a QPR publication around at the time called *All Quiet on the Western Avenue* – whose editor, a certain Peter Doherty, went on to achieve tabloid infamy a decade or so later as frontman with indie rockers The Libertines.

After a few issues *Forest Forever*'s circulation steadily rose up to the dizzy heights of 500 copies per edition – with the majority of them sold on matchdays. It was custom in those days for fanzine sellers outside football grounds to draw attention to themselves by shouting the name of their publication in the manner of a market trader – and Sanjay in particular threw himself into this task with such ear-splitting gusto on our pitch on Fanzine Corner that most people within a radius of about ten miles probably had a fair idea of what our game was!

Over time we started to get to know quite a few of our regular readers, who would often stop and say hello – although our first customer of every matchday would invariably pay with a tenner and clean us out of all of our change! I also remember one occasion before a game against Aston Villa when the violinist Nigel Kennedy – well-known for being a Villa fan - casually wandered past us, wearing a battered, ankle-length leather jacket. Alas though he didn't stop and buy a copy of *Forest Forever* or any of the other fanzines, the miserable bogger.

From issue four of *Forest Forever* we were able to take the plunge and start getting the fanzine printed professionally. It was a stretch at first though to pay for this, so for a few editions we saved a few quid by doing the folding and stapling ourselves. This was a mammoth task that invariably saw my Mum and Dad's living room floor turned into a production line, and numerous family members pitching in to get the job done – all of us ending up with black inky hands by the time we'd finished.

By this point Sanjay and I had begun to improve the layout of *Forest Forever* by using Letraset to create our headlines, and we also started to get copies of the fanzine on sale in various shops. These outlets were mainly in Nottingham, but we also managed to get a few places further afield to stock our wares – such as Sportspages, a specialist sports bookshop on Charing Cross Road in London. Generally, most places would take an agreed amount of copies of each issue on a sale or return basis, and take a 20% cut of the cover price for each one that they managed to sell.

Places in Nottingham where *Forest Forever* could be found on sale included a couple of retailers that sadly no longer exist - the legendary and much missed record emporium Selectadisc in the city centre; and a wonderfully chaotic store round the corner from the City Ground called Sport in Print, which always reminded me a bit of the book shop in the cult 80s film *Never Ending Story*.

We also got *Forest Forever* on sale in a small chain of newsagents scattered across Nottinghamshire. These shops were run by a brilliant fella called Mick Garton, and it was great for us because it meant we could deal with one person but have the fanzine on sale in numerous different locations. Nottingham being the small world that it is, the arrangement came about because Mick's Dad happened to be a neighbour of my grandparents. I'm happy to say that Mick's business has flourished since those days, and his MSR Newsgroup empire has spread beyond Nottinghamshire into Derbyshire and Lincolnshire.

It was also around the time of issue four of *Forest Forever* when some of our readers started sending in articles to be published. This was great for Sanjay and I, as it meant less pressure on the two of us to write all the content ourselves. It also made the fanzine a better read – slowly but surely, it started to become diverse mix of different views and opinions, rather than just mine and Sanjay's. As was the fashion with fanzines in those days, a lot of our writers wrote under pseudonyms – and we regularly published articles by the likes of 'the Hollywood Red' and 'Robert Rosario's Biggest Fan'.

One particular article by the Hollywood Red covered Forest's glory days of the late 70s and early 80s. As part of his piece, he had a bit of a dig at the Nottingham one-hit wonders Paper Lace, who'd recorded a single with the Reds' league title-winning squad called 'We've Got The Whole World In Our Hands' – a song which actually made it to number 24 in the charts. Amusingly, the Hollywood Red's snide comments about the band inspired an angry letter from the son of Paper Lace bassist Cliff Fish, which we published in the next issue!

In terms of *Forest Forever*'s editorial content, Sanjay and I also began to dip our toes into the world of proper journalism, by doing interviews with Forest players past and present. What's more, these were actual face-to-face interviews too, rather than simply sending a questionnaire through the post as Al and I had done with Mark Crossley.

Our first proper interviewee was John Winfield, who had made over 400 appearances for Forest in the 60s and 70s, and played at left-back in the great Reds' team that came close to doing a league and FA Cup double in the 1966-67 season.

After finishing his playing career in the mid-70s, John had had to go and get a 'proper job', as all retired footballers did back those days – and nearly 20 years on, it was common knowledge in Nottingham that he ran a newspaper kiosk in the city's Victoria shopping centre. One day then, Sanjay and I decided to go along and ask him if he'd been willing to spare half an hour to chat to us –

and amiable fella that he was, he immediately said yes and suggested we pop down the following Saturday.

Sanjay and I duly scurried away and came up with a set of questions - although there was the small matter of us not actually having possession of a proper tape recorder. However, the two of us were never anything less than resourceful... and we decided we'd record our chat with John using my ghetto blaster.

Come the day of the interview then, the two of us probably looked like the world's least convincing breakdancing crew as we lugged my bulky boombox through the Vic Centre. Happily John was very generous with his time – indeed, we bade farewell to him having exhausted our list of questions, only to then realise that we'd been a pair of prize tools and neglected to actually press 'record'!

Sheepishly, we headed back – and fortunately John was happy to do the whole interview again...

Over the course of our two chats with John he gave a fascinating insight into what life was like as a professional footballer in the 60s and 70s. That said, something that made Sanjay and I feel a bit sad was when we asked him if he still kept tabs on Forest – and he responded by telling us he didn't really follow football any more, saying that he felt the sport had been ruined by money.

If he felt like that then, back in 1992, goodness knows what he must make of the game now.

Having broken the interview duck with John Winfield - and also acquired a proper dictaphone - I started to get a bit more confident, and began to acquire interviews with members of the current Forest team. This was something I achieved by simply going down to the City Ground on a weekday, and hanging around and seeing who I could collar after the team had completed their morning training session - sometimes skipping school in order to do so. I always got away with bunking off, though to be fair I was always very low-key about my non-attendance, whereas my peers who did get caught skiving would usually get busted because they'd spend the time they should've been in school standing outside the local shops smoking and trying to look hard - and inevitably get spotted by a teacher.

Looking back, it's funny to think that those members of the Reds squad who I pestered for interviews for *Forest Forever* were some of the very same players who had rendered me speechless with awe only a few years earlier on autograph-hunting trips with my Dad. In some ways, having a journalistic mission did actually make it easier to go over and talk to them - although at times I'd still feel a bit starstruck inwardly beneath my attempts to try and play it cool and look vaguely professional.

Getting interviews was often a bit of a waiting game – sometimes I'd spent hours loitering around by the players' entrance at the back of the Main Stand. Sometimes I'd end up chatting with Martin Fisher -no relation - who was the Forest correspondent for BBC Radio Nottingham at the time, and as such would often be down at the City Ground for pretty much the same reason that I was. For someone who always seemed so passionate about the Reds when he was doing live commentary on matches, I was horrified on one occasion as we were chatting when he let slip that he was actually a Derby fan! He was a nice bloke though who always had some friendly words of encouragement for me, and over the years I've been pleased to see his career in broadcasting go from strength to strength. At the time of writing he regularly commentates on big games for *Match of the Day*.

And all the waiting around by the players' entrance definitely proved worth it - as over the years, I managed to grab chats with numerous players. Stan Collymore agreed to give me an interview midway through his first season at Forest, which felt like a massive coup – because at that time he was banging in stacks of goals and grabbing a lot of headlines. I still maintain to this day that he's the most exciting footballer I've ever seen in a Forest shirt.

That said, Collymore was also starting to develop a reputation that would stick with him for the remainder of his career for being a somewhat wayward figure – with regular rumours of everything from missed training sessions to bust-ups with team-mates. The day I interviewed him was just weeks before a game that probably summed up his time at Forest – a home match against Bolton in March 1994, when Collymore made a glorious return from injury by coming off the bench and scoring a brilliant goal with his first touch… only to then get sent off a few minutes later for lamping Bolton's Phil Brown. Of course, the very same Phil Brown went on in subsequent years to become one of the most ridiculed people in the game, after he hung up his boots and embarked on a largely hapless managerial career at various clubs including Hull and Derby.

For all the tittle tattle though, I found Stan the Man to be a lovely bloke. With it having been a cold day he invited me inside to do the interview - sitting and answering my questions inside what was then known as the Jubilee Club. Amongst other things he told me how he regretted missing out on the opportunity to work with Brian Clough, with his move to the City Ground having initially been lined up during Cloughie's final few months as manager - only for the deal to fall through because Southend suddenly wanted more money and Forest refused to stump up.

Meanwhile, a player who would later create a lethal strike partnership with Collymore also agreed to give me an interview a few months after his arrival at the City Ground in the summer of 1994. Amongst other things, Dutch international Bryan Roy offered an amusing insight into the musical education he was getting at Forest, saying that he'd developed a big love for the band Madness through Stuart Pearce's habit of always putting their tunes on in the dressing room before matches.

As well as players, I also managed in the summer of 1993 to bag an interview with Frank Clark, who had just arrived at the City Ground to begin the unenviable task of replacing Brian Clough as Forest's manager. We actually sat and did the interview in Frank's office, which felt quite strange knowing it had been Cloughie's office only a matter of months earlier. If walls could talk...

Being only 13 as I was at the time, I was still very much developing my interview skills. Frank had been appointed by Forest after a long spell at Leyton Orient, where he'd initially been the manager but then gone on to become the club's managing director. And having presumably decided to model myself on Jeremy Paxman, one of my questions was basically "So then Mr Clark, I've heard from a Leyton Orient fan that you did a good job as managing director but were pretty useless as a manager – what do have to say about this?"

I cringe when I look back at my utter lack of tact. A more volatile character than Frank Clark would've probably chinned me - and I would've almost certainly entirely deserved it!

But nice bloke that he is, Frank was unruffled and answered the question. Unsurprisingly he felt the 'useless' verdict was an "unfair assessment" of his managerial abilities – and fair play to him, he would go on over the next three seasons to prove that he was right.

Probably my favourite *Forest Forever* interviewee though was one of the Reds' lesser known players, Paul McGregor - who is best remembered by Forest fans for juggling his life as a professional footballer with singing in an indie rock band. And he looked the part too, with proper rock star hair and everything – although there's a fine line between cool and ridiculous, and there was a point when his barnet started to look less like Brian Jones from the Rolling Stones and more like Jareth the Goblin King from *The Labyrinth*.

McGregor's band were called Merc – and being at a stage in my life when I was starting to get into music, there were a couple of times when I went to see them play in Nottingham. There was one particular gig where pretty much half the Forest first team squad were there – at one point while the band were playing I remember looking to my left and suddenly realising that I was stood next to Mark Crossley, who had a bottle of beer in each hand!

Of course, late nights playing smoky venues is the sort of thing you can imagine a lot of managers taking a pretty dim view of. However, with Frank Clark well known for playing a bit of guitar himself, he was probably more likely to have been down the front at one of one Merc's gigs! And to be fair, Merc were actually pretty good. Both times I saw them they played an entire set of original material - before finishing, bizarrely, with a cover version of David Essex's 'Rock On'.

At one of the Merc gigs that I went to, the support act had been advertised on flyers as Blood Clart Rasta of the Wicked Bitches – which, as it turned out, was the DJ-ing alterego of none other than McGregor's Forest team-mate Scot Gemmill. But as it turned out, Gemmill ended up having to miss the gig after he was called up for international duty by Scotland – so we'll never know if he was any cop on the wheels of steel.

Sadly Merc existed in a pre-YouTube age, so I don't think there are any recordings of the band in existence - at least not in the public domain - although it wasn't for lack of trying on my part. Taking inspiration from *Brian*, which back in 1992 had given away a flexidisc by the Sultans of Ping - featuring a live recording of a song the cult indie rockers had written about Nigel Clough - I actually offered McGregor the opportunity to release some of Merc's music through *Forest Forever*. Alas though, this never came to anything.

Ultimately McGregor's footballing career never really lived up to his early promise at the City Ground, and he ended up drifting down to the lower leagues before retiring from football altogether. Lovely bloke though. The interview that I did with him for *Forest Forever* covered all sorts of ground - everything from his fear of spiders, to some amusing dressing room shenanigans in which he had a prized pair of Dunlop green flash trainers mysteriously vanish and then returned to him through the post, but with each trainer chopped up into lots of pieces. His belief was that a certain S Pearce was behind the prank!

Perhaps inevitably, the fact that I was producing a fanzine at such a young age grabbed a lot of people's attention. In 1993 I won the *Nottingham Evening Post*'s 'Young Achiever of the Year' award - and unless anyone can tell me differently, I think I was definitely the youngest person in the country to be editing a football fanzine during this period.

Of course, when you're a kid you tend to just crack on with whatever you're doing without reflecting on it too much - so it never really occurred to me that what I was doing was anything special. But in hindsight I guess it was pretty extraordinary, launching what proved to be a successful magazine at the age of just 12. Around this time a lot of people used to talk me up as the next Richard Branson, which was a plausible parallel I suppose given that he'd also started out in business at a young age by launching a magazine – in his case a publication called *Student*. Not to mention the fact that he and I were both scruffbags called Richard!

Being quite a shy kid though as I was, I was never entirely comfortable with a lot of the attention I used to get through my exploits in putting together *Forest Forever* – or indeed the comparisons with Branson. And several decades on, I think it's fair to say that my career has never shown the remotest hint of being as spectacular as that of the Virgin founder.

In fairness though, I don't think I've ever had either the drive or ambition to build on my success with *Forest Forever* to become some sort of globe-straddling media tycoon. What's more, if I'd ever had such lofty entrepreneurial aspirations, there would've probably come a point where I would've had to move to London – and much as I love visiting our wonderful capital city, the amount of people I've known over the years who have relocated down there and quickly disappeared up their own backsides has always put me off from ever wanting to go and live there myself.

Besides, I've developed a strong belief over the years that success in life is not something you really measure by how high you manage to climb up the career ladder.

My status as the youngest fanzine editor in the country did lead to me being interviewed though on national TV, when I was featured on a TV show called *Standing Room Only* – which was presented by a certain Shelley Webb, who was married to former Forest and England midfielder Neil Webb. Perhaps wisely, I chose not to mention the fact that a photo of her husband had been a favourite target during sessions in our garage firing Dad's air rifle earlier in my childhood, after his controversial move from the Reds of Nottingham to the Reds of Manchester!

Talking to the media was something I ended up doing quite regularly during the years when I was publishing *Forest Forever*. Journalists from both the local and national media would often get in touch if they wanted a fan's perspective on anything Forest-related; while in 1997 there was also a further TV appearance, on Sky Sports' Saturday morning show *Soccer AM*.

As those of you familiar with *Soccer AM* will know, each week the programme has a group of fans in the studio from a different team – known as the 'Fans of the Week'. One of my regular *Forest Forever* readers, a lovely bloke called Dave Fitzmaurice, had decided it was time they had some Reds fans on, so wrote off to the show to ask if he could assemble a suitable group of reprobates.

Happily, the answer was Yes – and going down to London to appear on *Soccer AM* proved to be brilliant experience. As well as fulfilling our role of creating bit of background terrace atmosphere throughout the programme and generally being quite noisy, we got to meet all the celebrities who appeared as guests on the show - including a 17-year-old Rio Ferdinand. Who was lovely.

That said, we did also get ourselves into a spot of trouble that day...

When the 'Fans of the Week' are first introduced at the start of each episode of *Soccer AM*, they make their arrival on the show known by launching into one of their team's terrace songs. Our choice of song had been the subject of some discussion on the way down to London – and in the end we'd decided to take the opportunity to have a dig at Forest's main rivals and go with "We hate Derby and we hate Derby…"

Forgetting though that we were on live TV, we went the whole way with the song – "Sheep, sheep sheep shaggers" and all. As was perhaps to be expected, this went down like a lead balloon with the show's production crew, causing lots of panicked faces and frantic waving of arms - and as soon as the show went to its next ad break, a stern-faced bloke with a clipboard came over and gave us a massive telling off.

We felt a bit like the Sex Pistols after their infamous appearance on *The Bill Grundy Show* in 1976!

Probably the funniest thing that happened though during that trip to appear on *Soccer AM* actually took place after the show finished, when we were making our way to the exit of the Sky studios and spotted Harry Redknapp arriving – presumably to do a TV interview. 'Arry was manager of West Ham at the time - and with him being one of football's renowned wheeler dealers, I decided to stop him and make a cheeky attempt to try and get him interested in buying a Forest player who was massively under-performing at the time.

"Alright 'Arry," I said, "I'm a Forest fan – can you do us a favour and sign Kevin Campbell off us?"

Bless him, Redknapp was quick as a flash with his response: "Yeah, go on then – I'll swap him for Ian Dowie!"

Needless to say, all of this made for a great feature in the next issue of *Forest Forever* - and with each new edition, the fanzine continued to improve. Along with match reports, readers' letters, and interviews with players past and present, one regular feature that was always popular was called 'Gossip, rumour, malicious lies' – basically a round-up of the latest scurrilous whispers relating to the mighty Reds, with much of the material sent in by readers. A quick flick through some old copies of *Forest Forever* reveals an absolute wealth of tittle tattle – everything from Stan Collymore losing the key to the crook lock for his car and having to call the AA, to Mark Crossley being spotted in a supermarket doing his food shop but not exactly showing much evidence of a professional athlete's dedication to nutrition, with his trolley containing nothing but a load of beer and a packet of cream crackers!

On a more serious note, *Forest Forever* also provided support over the years to a number of very worthwhile national movements. Some of the more savvy campaigning organisations operating in the UK at the time began to realise that fanzines were a very effective way to get messages to the sorts of football fans who were engaged with social issues – and I was always very happy to give a few column inches to groups such as Football Fans Against the Criminal Justice Act and, in particular, Let's Kick Racism Out Of Football.

During the time I was publishing *Forest Forever* it was only a few years since the famous photo had been taken of the Liverpool footballer John Barnes backheeling a banana off the pitch after having it thrown at him from the stands – and growing up as I did in the 80s and 90s, it was pretty common to hear people use derogatory language when talking about people from minority ethnic backgrounds. At best these behaviours would be borne of ignorance and intended as no more than 'banter'; but at worst it could be downright nasty.

I grew up in what was at the time a predominantly white part of Nottingham, and I have very clear memories of when a new Asian boy started at the infant school that I attended. On his first day everyone surrounded the poor lad on the playground and gawped at him like he was some sort of circus freak – and you can probably guess the sort of names he got called.

Naively, it didn't really register with me at the time that there was anything wrong with those names. In fact, I remember going home that day and cheerily telling my Mum that we'd had a new brown boy start at school - and that everyone called him 'Paki'.

Fair play to her, Mum immediately gave me possibly the biggest telling off I can ever recall her subjecting me to during my entire childhood – even though I hadn't actually been an active participant in the events on the playground that day.

As it happens, I actually went on to become quite good mates with that brown boy. And of course, it was an enduring friendship with another brown boy, Sanjay, that ended up leading to the birth of *Forest Forever.*

Over those years I must have spent hundreds of hours round at Sanjay's house – some of them working on the fanzine, but a lot of the time simply hanging out. His family were always great to me – his mum and dad had their roots in the Philippines and India respectively - and through their hospitality I was offered me a window into their heritage and culture: from the music they listened to, to the food that they ate. In terms of the latter, Sanjay's mum would sometimes whip up a wonderful fusion of eastern and western cuisine

– chapatis with freshly-fried chips, accompanied by the sphincter-punishing joys of Tabasco sauce.

Looking back, my friendship with Sanjay played a huge part in shaping my worldview, and helped me learn from an early age to have an open mind about different cultures. I'm incredibly grateful for that.

Sadly there's still work to be done in the world of football, and indeed British society in general, to stamp out racism. Maybe there always will be.

I do think though that significant progress has been made in the last few decades. And through supporting the Let's Kick Racism Out of Football campaign, I'm proud of the fact that *Forest Forever* played a small part in spreading the message that there was no place in the beautiful game for atrocious behaviours such as monkey chants and throwing bananas.

We were spreading the message to quite a few people too. Over the first couple of years of its existence, *Forest Forever's* circulation rose steadily – and by around issue ten our print run for each issue was up to 1,000 copies.

I also discovered over time that the fanzine regularly made it into the players' dressing room at the City Ground – which was great for my ego! That said, some of the content might not have made comfortable reading for some members of the Reds squad – as myself and the other writers generally pulled no punches when they weren't performing. As far as I could gather though, most of the players took the fanzine in the spirit with which it was intended.

Those who probably weren't so amused by *Forest Forever* however were the members of the Forest board. The Chairman at the time was a former policeman and publican called Fred Reacher, and he in particular came in for some scathing criticism within our pages – most notably when alleged dodgy dealings in the club's ticket office were featured on the national TV programme *World In Action*. Reacher had agreed to give an interview as part of the programme, but didn't exactly present Forest in the greatest light when all he could say in response to the allegations was "Prove it."

Naturally the Reds' Chairman was hammered for this in the pages of *Forest Forever*. During this particular era you'd sometimes hear about football clubs banning fanzines or taking taking legal action to try and get them shut down. We never had any of that sort of treatment from Forest – although looking back, some of the criticism of Reacher in particular was quite close to the knuckle.

All in all, I think the best way to describe the feelings of the powers-that-be at the club towards *Forest Forever* – and indeed the other Reds fanzines – was that they tolerated us.

I guess they had little choice – we certainly weren't going away...

10. Away games

"I was slowly starting to understand that away trips were just as much about the adventure itself as the actual game..."

When you start supporting a football team, you'll invariably begin by going along to a few home games. You might even take the plunge and get a season ticket.

But it's not until you start going to watch your team away from home regularly that you know things are getting *really* serious.

My first ever Forest away trip was in my first season of going to matches – the 1989-90 season - and just like my first home game, the opponents were Arsenal.

The trip came about because my Dad had a mate at work who was an exiled Arsenal fan. He regularly drove down from Nottingham to watch the Gunners, and he kindly got tickets for Dad and I so we could join him for the Reds' visit to Highbury.

Initially the match was scheduled for a Saturday afternoon – but Forest's continuing involvement in the League Cup that season meant the game ended up being postponed and rescheduled for a midweek date. This meant we'd be setting off in the early afternoon to get down to London in time – so excitingly, I got to skive off half a day of school.

The thing I remember most about that trip down to Highbury is actually the music that was played when the players came out of the tunnel. Like most boys who'd grown up in the 80s I was a big fan of *The A-Team* - so I was massively impressed when the Arsenal team emerged to the strains of the show's theme music. It certainly seemed a better way of getting the crowd going than the slightly embarrassing Robin Hood theme that Forest were running out to at the City Ground back in those days.

As well as being my first away game, the trip to Arsenal was also my first experience of attending a match incognito – as Dad's mate had got us tickets to sit with him in one of the home sections. As it was though, there wasn't really all that much to cheer about from a Forest point of view; the Reds took a 3-0 hiding on the night, with Nigel Clough also missing a penalty to add insult to injury.

Maybe *we* should've hired the A-Team?

But nevertheless, I'd broken my away duck, and Dad would take me to further away games over the next few seasons – most memorably a number of trips on Forest's run to the 1991 FA Cup final, where we went to Norwich in the quarter final and then Villa Park for the semi-final against West Ham.

For the trip to Norwich, Dad had surprised me by getting us tickets but not actually telling me until the day. Being an FA Cup quarter final, the game was obviously a big deal – and my plan for the day had been to watch *Saint and Greavsie* on the telly before spending the afternoon listening to the match on the radio. However, at about 10am Dad casually said "Come on Rich, get your coat and your scarf, we're off to Norwich!"

We'd got a lift to Norwich that day with another of Dad's mates from work - and a pea-roller of a shot from Roy Keane and some frantic, backs-to-the-wall defending saw the Reds triumph and go through to the semi-finals. That said, we nearly never made it to Carrow Road, with Dad's friend's car suffering a flat battery en route – creating an unexpected delay that saw us only just make it in time for kick-off.

This was just my first taste of the occasional pitfalls of away travel – those times when things go a bit pear-shaped for reasons beyond anyone's control. That said, the *Challenge Anneka*-style race against the clock after Dad's mate finally managed to get his car going again was strangely exhilarating – and I was slowly starting to understand that away trips were just as much about the adventure itself as the actual game.

Before long of course, there would plenty of new adventures to be had for us Forest fans – with the Reds' relegation from the Premier League at the end of the 1992-93 season meaning the Manchester Uniteds and Liverpools were unceremoniously replaced on the fixture list with mysterious places like Grimsby and Southend.

Sadly, the Blundell Parks and Roots Halls of this world have become all too familiar to us Reds fans over the last couple of decades. Back in the summer of 1993 though, as we prepared for the brave new world of the Frank Clark era, they held a genuine sense of intrigue – and I think we all felt a bit like Marco Polo as we counted down the days until the new season and prepared to conquer uncharted lands.

And conquer those lands we did. By the start of that 1993-94 season, my brother Al and I had reached the ages of 15 and 13 respectively – and brilliantly, Mum and Dad had decided that we could be trusted to start going to away games without adult supervision.

Obviously Al and me were too young to drive at this point in our lives. We'd discovered though that the Gedling branch of the official Forest Supporters Club ran a coach to away matches - which departed from the Chesterfield Arms pub in Gedling, just a couple of miles down the road from where we lived. Stumping up our hard-earned paper round money, we duly took the plunge and booked places on board for a trip to Luton – the Reds' first Saturday away game of the season.

I recall being slightly nervous as Al and I arrived at the 'Cheggo' ready for our first trip on the bus, armed with a carrier bag containing an epic 'pack-up' lovingly prepared for us by Mum to save us from having to rely on football ground dog burgers for sustenance. But happily we had a brilliant day - with a 2-1 win for the Reds getting our 'career' as proper home-and-away fans off to a flying start.

Further trips followed over the next few months to all sorts of places from Wolverhampton to Leicester – and while football grounds are getting increasingly bland these days as more and more clubs move to new-build stadiums, back then it was fascinating to see the many quirks of all the different arenas up and down the country. At Luton, we'd discovered that entry to the away end was via some turnstiles built into the middle of a row of terraced houses – and that after clicking your way through, you had to walk down a passage running between people's back gardens to get to the stadium concourse. At Watford meanwhile, you had to trudge past a load of allotments along a meandering footpath – or a twitchell, if we're to use proper Nottingham parlance - to get to the away fans' entrance.

In those early days of travelling to away games on the Gedling bus, one trip that particularly sticks out was a journey to see Forest away at Wrexham in a midweek League Cup game. With the bus leaving from the 'Cheggo' at 4pm, it meant a mad dash for Al and I to get there straight from school. Bless him, I seem to remember Dad sneaking out of work in order to come and pick us up as soon as our lessons had finished and then ferry us down to the pub, where we made the departure in the nick of time. It felt like a proper adventure to be heading to a different country on a school night in order to watch a football match – and it was an evening that would in hindsight prove not insignificant in modern-day Forest history, with Stan Collymore breaking his Forest scoring duck by bagging a hat-trick. Stan the Man of course went on to score an absolute hatful of goals for the Reds over the next couple of years.

As well as stadiums and motorway service stations up and down the country, our adventures on the Gedling bus also saw Al and I quickly became familiar with all of the many weird and wonderful rituals of awayday coach travel - from the first goal sweepstake to the rank horrors of the on-board chemical toilet. We also became acquainted with the many characters of the Gedling bus – some known only by nicknames such as Mad Mick, Moustachio, Fuckin' 'Ell Fred, Speechless and Programme Dave.

The greatest Gedling bus character of all though was the lady who ran it – a brilliant and selfless woman called Joan Bakewell, who was secretary of the Gedling branch of the Supporters Club. As part of this role Joan not only ran the coach and sorted out our tickets for the various away matches, she also organised regular social events for all the Gedling branch members.

Joan was a lovely woman who always looked out for Al and me, with us being among the younger clientele on the Gedling bus. I'm sure there are hundreds of Forest fans who have been part of the Gedling branch of the Supporters Club over the years who have been grateful to Joan and all her efforts - in fact, at the time of writing, over 20 years on from those heady days of the mid-90s, I believe she's still branch secretary and still running the Gedling bus. A proper legend.

As well as the stalwarts of the Gedling bus, all the trips around the country saw Al and I get to know many of the other 'characters' from the wider community of regular Forest away travellers. Everywhere we went we'd always see loads of the same friendly faces - and while half the time we never got as far as actually knowing names, we'd invariably end up on nodding terms.

As humans, we all have an instinctive need to feel a sense of belonging within a community – and through travelling to watch Forest away, I really felt as though I'd found my people. I already knew plenty of Reds fans – but now I was among the elite band of nutters who thought nothing of spending hours sat on a bus to go and watch a 0-0 draw away at Grimsby.

Some of my favourite characters from the wider Forest awayday community included an old bloke who always wore a bright pink raincoat, presumably to increase his chances of being spotted on TV; and two brothers referred to affectionately by many as Smashie and Nicey, due to their resemblance to the Harry Enfield and Paul Whitehouse TV characters. We'd also sometimes bump into my Uncle Stephen - who always seemed proud that Al and I were following in his footsteps by taking our passion for Forest beyond the mere confines of the City Ground. My illusions were slightly shattered though when I finally clocked the face of the bloke with a gruff Joe Cocker-like voice who seemingly started all the songs at the time – and he turned out to be a spotty oik rather than the towering man mountain of my imagination.

Meanwhile, our escapades around the country following Forest also gave Al and I an initiation into something that - rightly or wrongly - has long been regarded by many football fans as an essential part of the matchday experience.

Yes, those trips on the Gedling bus were pretty much an apprenticeship in the art of drinking...

Of course, no alcohol was allowed on the bus by law - and everyone respected Joan too much to even consider getting her into trouble by smuggling any on board. However, most away trips would involve a pub stop on the way to the game – and for many of the Gedling bus regulars, the primary focus during these relatively short windows of drinking time would be on trying to cram in as much booze as possible!

Inevitably, the combination of stomachs full of booze and coach travel would sometimes have messy consequences. There was one memorable occasion on a trip to Norwich when one of the lads had a bit too much to drink – and upon getting back on the bus, proceeded to splatter one of the seats with a spectacular rainbow of vomit.

What made this episode even more amusing than it would've been anyway was the fact that the lad in question was betraying his position as a serious figure of authority within the world of Forest – because away from the

Gedling bus, he actually spent matchdays working as a steward when the Reds were playing at the City Ground!

The fact that 'steward 41' had eaten a prawn sandwich earlier made his decorating job particularly special – although the funniest thing was that the very same bus was being used the next day by the Barnet FC first team for an away trip to Gillingham.

The following evening I made a point of checking to see how Barnet had got on. Unsurprisingly, they lost!

Now those trips on the Gedling bus were by no means the first time I'd been exposed to alcohol. Growing up as I did in a pretty working class family in 1980s England, drinking and smoking were both common pastimes among my elders. My Dad even made his own home brew for many years; while every now and then during my childhood, there would also be trips to the pub with my parents.

Of course, kids such as myself were never actually allowed inside pubs back in those days – so our visits were restricted to warm summer afternoons when we could all sit outside. I'd only ever get to see what lay within when the doors opened as folk came in or out – and those fleeting glimpses would invariably reveal a gloomy scene featuring lots of men and omnipresent clouds of smoke. It always felt like a brief window into a deeply mysterious grown-up world - and pubs became places of enormous intrigue.

All in all, I regarded both booze and fags as being pretty much a staple part of everyday adult life – a belief that was probably only enforced by the relative lack of the cautionary warnings that we see plastered left, right and centre in the modern age. In fact, I'd go as far as to say that kids of my age almost received gentle encouragement to follow in the path of our elders. It seems scarcely believable in the politically correct times that we now live in, but at Christmas during my childhood I'd often get something called a 'Little Smoker's Kit' as a stocking filler – basically a little box containing a pipe, cigars and fags made out of chocolate.

For all the dubious influence though that surrounded me as a kid, my experience of alcohol up until the point when I started travelling on the Gedling bus didn't really stretch much beyond having a few sips of Dad's beer. And while he was a couple of years older than me, I don't think Al's drinking career had progressed much further either. However, with copious amounts of boozing going on around us as we travelled up and down the country following Forest, it was probably inevitable that the two of us would end up becoming active participants.

Back in those days it was pretty much the rule in the male universe that if you were young you drank lager and if you were of more senior years you drank bitter. Having discovered though that I actually hated the taste of both, I usually opted for a pint of Strongbow – something that a lot of the lads on the bus would hammer me for. It's hard to believe now given how popular it is today, but back in the 90s cider was regarded as deeply uncool and a bit of a 'girl's drink'.

But while my choice of beverage was widely derided, a few pints on Forest away trips became the norm for me from around the age of 14 – and despite being a good few years underage, I never had any trouble getting served. Pubs weren't anywhere near as strict as they are nowadays when it came to challenging possible underage drinkers - although to be fair, Al and I were both tall lads, and usually part of a group of people who were generally a good few years older. As such, bar staff probably just assumed we must be over 18.

Matchday drinking never really became a part of my routine before home games though – mainly because I'd be too busy on 'Fanzine Corner' flogging copies of *Forest Forever* until five minutes before kick-off. Nevertheless, the fact that I was enjoying a few pints on away trips gave me significant bragging rights with my mates at school on a Monday morning, with us all being at that age where alcohol was regarded as some sort of holy grail. For most of my peers at that time, consumption of booze was largely restricted to hanging out down at the park and necking bottles of cheap cider, or a grim fortified wine that was popular back then called 20:20. I was never one of the cool kids during my school years – but the fact that I was actually getting served in pubs did earn me a certain grudging respect.

Looking back, I'm not particularly proud of any of my underage alcohol consumption. What's more, all those pints of cider on Forest away trips were the beginning of a heavy drinking habit that I would maintain for well over a decade - and while I don't think my boozing ever reached levels where it was in danger of becoming a serious problem, it did get me into numerous scrapes over the years.

And I still cringe when I recall the day when my GCSE grades were published in August 1996…

The night before Forest had played Sunderland at home and unexpectedly got thumped 4-1 - and after the game, I'd decided to go to the pub to drown my sorrows. I ended up getting so wrecked that I have no idea how I got home, and I was found the next morning lying comatose on the kitchen floor. When I eventually regained consciousness I felt so rough that I actually had to send my Mum down to the school to go and collect my envelope with my results!

Not my finest hour.

That said, it does make me smile when I think back to some of the ridiculous lengths that were gone to back in those days in order to acquire alcohol. I'm not sure if booze still has the same allure for teenagers today – as far as I can see, they're all far too engrossed in their smartphones and Playstations to be bothered about getting wrecked. And in many ways, that's probably not a bad thing. During my own teenage years though, popular schemes that were employed to access alcohol included sending off for fake ID, half-inching small amounts from your parents' booze cupboard in the hope that they wouldn't notice, or persuading somebody's older sibling to go into the shop to buy you whatever your chosen poison was. Around the age of 15 I also discovered the existence of a dodgy off-licence in a particularly shady area of Nottingham - and would happily walk miles to go there just because I knew they'd gladly serve me.

I had a phase as well during my final year at secondary school when I'd 'borrow' a tie from my Dad's wardrobe – and then put it on at lunchtime in place of my school tie, and slope off into Arnold town centre for a quick pint in one of the pubs.

At the time when I was doing this I thought my ruse was absolute genius – that I was a master of disguise on a par with Hannibal from *The A Team*, and that everyone would think I was a young office worker on his lunch break. In reality, it was probably more a case that the pubs didn't really give a monkey's and were just happy to take my money!

All in all, away games were something I quickly found myself looking forward to far more than home games. As well as the illicit joys of a few pints, I relished the adventure of visiting new places every other weekend and all the laughs that were had along the way. What's more, far from the relatively sedate atmosphere that I was used to at home games in the lower tier of the Executive Stand, I loved the fact that away trips would usually involve

---

spending the whole game on our feet singing ourselves hoarse, and generally trying to be the Reds' '12th man'. It was incredibly exhilarating – and on those occasions when Forest were triumphant in bagging three points on the road, you genuinely felt like you'd won it with them.

Over time I gradually became confident enough, probably through the Dutch courage of those pre-match pints of cider, to start off the odd song myself. Puberty had kicked in sufficiently by this point for me to be able to make myself heard, and it was always a massive buzz when you started belting out "THROUGH THE SEASONS BEFORE US…" or whatever at the top of your voice - and immediately found yourself accompanied by a choir of hundreds of fellow fans.

That said, it could go either way if you tried to seize the initiative and get a song going. If for whatever reason no-one joined in, you'd invariably look a bit of a tool - and end up getting serenaded yourself by those sitting around you with a rendition of "Solo! Solo!"

But more than anything, the biggest reason why those adventures on the Gedling bus were such a joy was Forest themselves.

The Reds had got off to a slow start at the beginning of the 1993-94 season, as they adjusted to life in English football's second tier following relegation from the Premier League. However, around the November Frank Clark's team slowly started to get its act together, and prove that there *was* life after Brian Clough. Stan Collymore had begun scoring for fun – and from Sunderland to Bristol City to Tranmere to Stoke, it seemed everywhere we went on the Gedling bus, we'd end up rolling back into Nottingham triumphant knowing that Forest had another three points in the bag.

That said, there were odd times when Al and I used alternatives means of transport to get to games rather than the Gedling bus. For a trip to Charlton towards the end of the 1993-94 season, we decided to accept the offer of a lift from one of my regular *Forest Forever* writers – a brilliant fella called Charlie Vaughan, who wrote under the pseudonym of the Mad Irishman.

But what we didn't realise until Charlie came and picked us up was that we'd be making the trip down to London in the back of his knackered old Metro van – a vehicle whose back doors had a habit of flying open without warning!

Happily, three points for Forest thanks to a goal from big striker Jason Lee made the white knuckle trip worthwhile. It was back to the creature comforts of the Gedling bus though for our next away trip a few weeks later - a midweek trip to Derby, where a glorious 2-0 win put the Reds within touching distance of a return to the top flight.

Now for us Forest fans, beating Derby is always satisfying no matter how the victory is achieved. But on this occasion, it was one of those games where you couldn't have written a better script - with the three points all but secured for Forest thanks to a hilarious and utterly unnecessary own goal by a much-maligned former Reds player, who badly mishit a backpass into the back of his own net!

Of course, the history books credit the goal in question to Reds midfielder Steve Stone, who the ball took a slight deflection off on its way in. To any Forest fans who were there that night though, crammed into the awful away terrace at the old Baseball Ground, it will always be Gary Charles' goal.

As the song went on the night: Nice one Gary, nice one son, nice one Gary – let's have another one…

All these years later, I'd be really interested to know what Gary Charles' feelings are on that goal – and more than anything, what on earth he was *thinking*. Sadly, a number of attempts to make contact with the beleaguered former full-back in the process of researching this book went unanswered.

Still, the win that night at Derby set up a huge game just three days later, with a trip to Peterborough and the knowledge that a win would guarantee promotion for Forest back to the Premier League. Around 10,000 Reds fans made the trip to London Road on a sunny Saturday afternoon – with many of the Gedling bus regulars in fancy dress.

Unfortunately though Forest seemed to freeze on the big occasion, and quickly found themselves 2-0 down to a Peterborough side who had already been relegated.

Myself and Al were stood on the terrace behind the goal - and there was a bloke just in front of us who'd clearly had too much to drink before the game, and was fast asleep by our feet on the concrete steps. About 20 minutes into the game however, the chap in question suddenly regained consciousness, and naturally enquired what the score was. The incredulous look on his face when someone told him that Forest were 2-0 down is one I

—

will never forget – and you can probably imagine the string of expletives that came tumbling from his mouth!

But in hindsight, going two goals behind was all part of what made that afternoon at Peterborough so magical. It provided the set-up for what was probably the most memorable Forest fightback I've ever seen, with the Reds pulling a goal back just before half-time and then coming out in the second half and scoring two more to win 3-2.

When Forest fans reminisce about that game at London Road they invariably go all misty-eyed about Stan Collymore's winning goal. Brilliant a strike though as that was, the moment that always sticks out the most for me was Stuart Pearce's goal that levelled the score at 2-2.

Psycho had of course surprised a lot of fans the previous summer when he chose to stay at Forest despite the club's relegation from the Premier League. And that afternoon at Peterborough, he typified his commitment to the club, by braving a crowd of boots to dive headlong into the six-yard box and head the Reds level. It was right in front of where Al and I were standing – and with news filtering through that Forest now only needed a draw to seal promotion due to the way results were going elsewhere, 10,000 Forest fans went absolutely barmy, with a number spilling out onto the pitch in celebration. But there was still a fair bit of football to be played at this point in the game, and I remember a stern-faced Psycho running over to tell everyone to get off the pitch – "Use yer fackin' heads" being the wise words he chose.

As soon as the pitch cleared the two teams were able to get going again. Collymore's goal a few minutes from full-time sealed the deal in terms of securing Forest's return to the top flight – and at the final whistle, Al and I joined the thousands of travelling fans who swarmed onto the pitch in celebration.

A fantastic day – and happily, Forest continued the momentum the following season, getting the 1994-95 campaign off to a great start with a 1-0 victory at Ipswich in their opening game. The winning goal was a superb debut strike by the club's big summer signing Bryan Roy – and brilliantly, we were able to go straight on the lash to celebrate, with Joan Bakewell having decided to push the boat out for us Gedling bus regulars and organise not just a trip to the game but a whole weekend in nearby Great Yarmouth!

For me, that victory at Ipswich was the start of a run of two whole seasons without missing a single competitive Forest game home or away. What's more, though I'd been a regular away traveller for a year by this point, that year had been one where Forest were playing in English football's second tier. As such, the 1994-95 season was my first experience of visiting many of the country's biggest stadiums – with trips to places like Anfield, Maine Road and Stamford Bridge.

That said, it was a bit of a mission to get tickets for some of these games – as many Premier League clubs, Forest included, were carrying out major redevelopments of their grounds in order to comply with the new requirements in the wake of the Hillsborough disaster for top-flight clubs to have all-seater stadiums. For much of the 1994-95 season then, many clubs were having to operate with lower ground capacities – and inevitably, most dealt with this by reducing the number of tickets allocated to away fans

Our first experience of this came a month or so into the season, when it was announced that there'd only be 300 tickets available to Forest fans for the Reds' trip to Tottenham. Given that Forest's typical away following was around 3,000 at the time, it was never going to be enough to go round. In fact, there weren't even enough for those of us who had stamps on our away ticket loyalty cards to show that we'd been to every Forest away game during the season so far.

There was only one thing for it then. With the tickets going on sale at 9am on a Saturday morning a fortnight before the game, myself and Al and a few other brave souls from the Gedling bus decided the only option was to do exactly what hardcore Cliff Richard fans do when their hero announces a new tour.

Yes, armed with deckchairs and sleeping bags, we headed down to the City Ground on the Friday afternoon in order to queue overnight!

Of course, most fans will have gone to ridiculous lengths at some point in the name of supporting their team – and for me, above even far flung away trips to watch meaningless pre-season friendly matches, spending 17 hours in a queue was by far and away the furthest I'd ever gone.

That said, the long night spent camped out outside the Forest ticket office was actually quite entertaining – though this was largely due to the effects of all the alcohol we necked in our desperate attempts to make the evening as bearable as possible.

Happily, we were successful in getting our hands on the golden tickets when the ticket office finally opened in the morning – and the trip to White Hart Lane a couple of weeks later resulted in a glorious 4-1 win for Forest.

It was a brilliant performance from the Reds that afternoon. Every player played their part - from Mark Crossley saving a penalty by former Forest man Teddy Sheringham, to Norwegian midfielder Lars Bohinen executing a sublime 25-yard lob for the fourth goal.

All these years later, the game that afternoon remains one of my favourite matches I've ever been to. And it wasn't just the fact that it was such a great performance and result – there was also who it happened to be against. Though they ended up underachieving and finishing in mid-table that season, Tottenham had just signed Jurgen Klinsmann, and were being tipped for big things. Furthermore, Forest fans generally had very little love for Spurs at the time - as for some years they'd generally been quite a nasty, horrible team, and memories of the 1991 FA Cup final were still relatively fresh. So seeing the Reds give them a good pasting on their own turf was a sweet feeling.

It was strangely satisfying too knowing that Spurs' Chairman at the time, Alan Sugar, had been there to his team getting dismantled – as having been for a bit of a wander around the outside of the stadium following our arrival at White Hart Lane, we'd seen the diminutive tycoon arriving in a Rolls Royce.

But more than anything else, the victory felt special simply because we were among the few Forest fans who were there to actually see it.

Having said that, the 300 of us who were at White Hart Lane that afternoon 'officially' weren't quite alone – as there were numerous instances of other Reds fans who'd clearly gone to great lengths to blag their way into the stadium. In particular, we were amused to see a paramedic on duty who was wearing a Forest shirt underneath his uniform – presumably having pulled a few strings at work to ensure he'd been on duty for the game.

There was a point during the 90 minutes too when myself and the other 299 Forest fans in the tiny away section were politely reminding the silent and solemn-looking Tottenham fans sat in the stand to our right what the score was - at which point a bloke on the front row surrounded by glum Spurs faces got a massive cheer when he discretely unzipped his tracksuit top to reveal a Forest shirt underneath!

Beyond the actual game, there were also a couple of things about that trip to White Hart Lane that will live long in the memory.

As usual, Al and I had travelled to the game on the Gedling bus – and having applauded the Forest players off the pitch after the full-time whistle, we were in high spirits as we left the stadium and made our way back to our Dunn-Line charabanc ready for the return journey back to Nottingham. Unfortunately though, we arrived back at the bus to find a very sheepish Driver, who'd been out for a leg-stretch and a bite to eat while we were all at the game – and managed to lose the keys!

We were basically stranded then in London – and while one of the dodgier characters of the Gedling bus kindly offered to break into our vehicle and hotwire it for us so we could get going, it was decided that the best approach would be to arrange for someone from the bus company to drive down from Nottingham with a spare set of keys.

Naturally, this meant we were in for a fair old wait – and worried about the implications of a group of about 40 Forest fans wandering the streets around White Hart Lane just after the Reds had tanked Spurs 4-1, the local police perhaps sensibly made arrangements for us to be quarantined in the back room of a nearby pub called the Bell and Hare. This was great, as it meant we could all have a few drinks to celebrate the result – something we didn't normally get a chance to do after an away victory, with it usually being a case of getting straight back on the bus for the journey home. And the landlord certainly wasn't complaining given how much money we were putting in his till!

Finally the spare keys for the bus arrived and we were able to get on our way. We eventually arrived home much later than we'd expected, but very happy.

A brilliant day then – and to cap it all off, a photograph of Al and me at the game actually appeared in a national newspaper a few days later!

Whilst enjoying the match, we had noticed one of the photographers by the side of the pitch pointing his lens in our direction – but at the time, we hadn't really thought much of it. It was only when I went into the newsagents at the end of our road on the Monday morning, and the bloke who worked there waved a copy of *The Daily Star* in my face, that we realized exactly *why* the guy had been taking photos of us. Yes, it turned out Al and me were featured in the 'Face in the crowd' slot in the paper – with Al the lucky one who'd been chosen to win a case of Harp lager.

Unsurprisingly this caused a great deal of hilarity among our friends and family – with possibly the funniest thing being the fact that Al was only 16, and thus still a couple of years away from legal drinking age. He wasn't going to tell *The Daily Star* that though - and he wrote off to them and successfully claimed his prize.

Needless to say, Harp probably wouldn't have been Al's lager of choice – but as an underage drinker you tend to be no more discerning than the average tramp when there's free alcohol available, so it was received gratefully!

All in all, that trip to Tottenham was one of those rare occasions when you're actually rewarded for going to silly lengths to support your team – and Al and I went on to queue overnight to get tickets for away games on two further occasions during the 1994-95 season.

The first of these was Forest's trip to Liverpool in November. Once again, tickets had gone on sale at 9am on a Saturday morning - and after succeeding in our mission to get our hands on some, Al and I actually got straight on the Gedling bus to go and see Forest away at Aston Villa.

Hardcore!

By this point in time, queuing for a ridiculous amount of time for tickets was something that earned you a strange sort of bragging right within the community of regular Forest away travelers. To get tickets then for the Liverpool game, Al and I had decided to go to even greater lengths than we had for the Tottenham game – and having both bunked off school, we got ourselves down to the City Ground at 9am on the Friday morning, a full 24 hours before the tickets went on sale.

Unbelievably, we actually arrived at the City Ground that day to find that there were already a few people who'd arrived even earlier than us. And these folk had come prepared – they'd even managed to get a portable TV and video set up as part of their little camp at the front of the queue!

It was actually quite interesting watching the comings and goings at the City

Ground on a typical weekday. We got to see the players arrive for training –
with Stuart Pearce turning up in a filthy Volvo blaring out loud punk music,
and Stan Collymore rolling up late and being made to carry all the gear as
punishment.

After completing their training session, the players all got on the team bus in
order to travel to Birmingham ready for their game at Villa the following
afternoon. And to be honest it was a bit of a kick in the balls knowing that
they were off to stay in a fancy hotel, while we'd be spending the night sat in
the cold outside the Forest ticket office.

That said, we weren't stood in the queue for the whole time. On this occasion
there was quite a large group of us all queuing together – mainly regulars from
the Gedling bus. This meant we were able to take it in turns to go off in small
groups to stretch our legs, while the others held our places.

At some point during the evening, we'd discovered that the programme hut
by the gates of the Main Stand car-park had been left unlocked. This became
a welcome refuge throughout the night – and a few of the group couldn't
resist the opportunity to add a few bits of Forest-related graffiti to the walls
inside.

Their doodlings are probably still there!

Once again we were successful in getting tickets – although by far the
toughest overnight queue came a few months later, when the time came for
us to try and acquire our means of admission for Forest's trip to Newcastle.
With the game taking place in early February, the tickets went on sale in late
January. And naturally, it was absolutely bloody freezing!

Once again we got ourselves down to the City Ground a full 24 hours before
the tickets were due to go on sale – and as we braced ourselves for a long
night, Fred Reacher came along to chat to those of us who were in the queue.

"We're doing as much as we can at the club to try and make sure you're as
comfortable as possible," he told us.

"What, are you resigning?", came an immediate reply from the queue!

To be fair though to the much-maligned Forest Chairman, he not only
presented the group at the front of the queue with a bottle of whisky, he also

arranged for a gate to be left unlocked overnight by the side of the Main Stand, allowing us access to the ground so we could use the toilet facilities. What's more, another of the club's directors, Chris Wootton, arranged for some contractors who were building Forest's new Trent End stand at the time to bring over some metal fencing and blue plastic sheeting and build us a shelter!

Of course though, having access to the City Ground for an entire night, we did far more than just use the toilets.

Yes, the opportunity to go and have a snoop round was too good to resist – and with seemingly no security on duty, we ended up checking out all sorts of places from the managers' dugouts to the TV camera gantry. One intrepid soul even decided to have a crack at climbing up the floodlight in the Main Stand-Trent End corner - although after getting about halfway up he lost his nerve and slowly began inching his way down again.

At one point there was even a serious discussion about sending someone home to get a football so we could have a kickabout on the pitch - but in the end we decided this would've simply been sacrilege.

All in all, the best thing about our nocturnal explorations was when we climbed into the directors' box in the Main Stand and found that the heated pipes under the seats were still switched on. Given the sub-zero conditions it was a welcome discovery – it was so warm and toasty that myself and a couple of others actually took the opportunity to grab a cheeky hour's kip in there to warm ourselves up!

Once again we were successful in getting tickets. However, whereas our efforts were rewarded handsomely when we queued overnight for Tottenham tickets, this was far from the case with the Liverpool and Newcastle matches – with Forest losing both games.

The defeat at Newcastle was particularly forgettable. Due to bad traffic on the way up we actually missed the first 20 minutes of the game - and to add insult to injury the Geordies' winning goal was a header by Ruel Fox, a player who was by far and away the shortest man on the pitch.

As it was though, those defeats at Anfield and St James Park were two of only six losses on the road for Forest during the 1994-95 season. It was a happy time to be a travelling Red – with Forest enjoying memorable wins away at

Manchester United (2-1) and Sheffield Wednesday (7-1) on their way to a third-place finish in the Premier League.

The Reds finishing third in their first season back in the top flight was certainly a far better league placing than anyone had dared hope for at the beginning of the season. And 12 months on from those scenes of celebration at Peterborough, it was perhaps inevitable that there'd be a pitch invasion once again when the final whistle blew at the end of the Reds' last game of the season - a 2-2 draw away at Wimbledon.

In fact, the travelling Reds fans who'd made the trip to Selhurst Park that day were so eager to get the party started at that they started making their way down to the pitch before the match had even finished. There was one point where the swell of fans had to be pushed back from the touchline so Forest right-back Des Lyttle could actually get off the pitch to take a throw-in!

It was a party atmosphere all-round that day – as Wimbledon were also celebrating yet another season of punching massively above their weight and finishing in the top half of the table. They'd decided to celebrate this in typical 'Crazy Gang' fashion – by arranging for the players to be led out onto the pitch by an elephant! Still one of the strangest things I've ever seen at a football match.

Happy times then – although there were also some low points too during all those years that I spent travelling to watch Forest away from home. For one, the fact that I've endured just about every Chubby Brown video in existence numerous times is entirely down to all those trips on the Gedling bus!

Perhaps inevitably, we also had one or two hairy moments with opposition fans on our travels - and while football hooliganism wasn't as bad in the mid-90s as it had been during the previous couple of decades, there were definitely some away grounds that felt like hostile places to go. As a Forest fan I never felt massively welcome anywhere in Yorkshire, with most trips to that county usually involving spending the entire 90 minutes being called 'scabs' by the natives – a reference of course to the miners' strikes of the mid-80s. The fact that I was only about five during the dispute didn't make a blind bit of difference – I was from Nottingham, and therefore I was as guilty as anyone of letting the miners down.

Leeds in particular always felt like a nasty place to go. When you travel away regularly to watch your team you get used to home fans serenading you with charming songs like "You're gonna get your fucking heads kicked in", and generally laugh it off. And to be fair, the Trent End would sing the exact same songs to the away fans at Forest home games. At Leeds though, it always felt like more than just an empty threat!

I'm not sure if it's still the same now at Elland Road, but back in the 90s after the game had finished you had to walk through a dingy concrete underpass to get to the place where away fans' coaches were parked - and there was always the fear that the infamous Leeds United Service Crew might be waiting in the shadows ready to give you a good hiding. All in all, it was definitely a place where you kept your head down and your colours hidden.

That said, I did always find it strangely exciting at away grounds when you felt that tension in the air – and while we never went looking for trouble, there were one or two occasions when trouble came looking for us. Al and me had a mate called Sam who often used to join us on the Gedling bus, and he got lamped by a Manchester City fan once during a trip to Maine Road as we made our way out of the stadium at full-time. The Stone Island-clad knuckledragger who'd attacked him was presumably furious at the fact that Forest had just nicked a draw, thanks to a jammy last-minute equaliser from Ian Woan.

Meanwhile, other low points during those years of away trips came in the shape of the football itself. While Forest had been brilliant in the 1993-94 and 1994-95 seasons and given us fans a lot to cheer about on our travels, they sadly weren't able to sustain that success – and slipped into a steady decline following the departure of the talismanic Stan Collymore in the summer of 1995.

Collymore had been such a good player that it was always going to be a huge challenge for Forest to fill his shoes - and over the summer months, the Reds were linked with all sorts of strikers by the media. At one point the *Nottingham Evening Post* even reported that Italian superstar Roberto Baggio might be on his way to the City Ground, with a memorably hyperbolic headline of 'IT'S BAGGIO!' plastered across the paper's back page.

As it turned out, Forest actually ended up signing two players to replace Stan the Man - Kevin Campbell and Andrea Silenzi. Sadly though, neither of them were much cop.

Silenzi's arrival had actually seen him become the first ever Italian international to play in England - and while he had a girl's name, his record in Serie A had suggested he was worth a punt at £1.8 million. In fact, during the early part of his career he'd played for Napoli and had actually lined up in a three-pronged attack on a number of occasions alongside Maradona and Careca.

But as it turned out, the gangly and mulleted Silenzi that appeared in a Forest shirt was about as menacing as a Care Bear – and after only two goals in two seasons, he eventually skulked back to Italy in 1997 and faded into obscurity.

Despite being hampered though with lumbering buffoons like Silenzi, Forest actually made a decent fist of soldiering on at the beginning of the 1995-96 season – starting the campaign unbeaten with six wins and six draws in their opening 12 games. Having also not lost during the final 13 games of the previous season, this all added up to a run of 25 Premier League games without defeat – a record at the time, and one which stood for a few years before eventually being broken by Arsenal's 'Invincibles'.

But Forest's next game was a trip up north to play Blackburn, who were reigning Premier League champions at the time. And while undoubtedly a tough fixture, we were all confident that the Reds could bag at least a point – after all, they hadn't lost in the league since February.

Of course, we all know what happened next on that fateful afternoon…

I think those of us who'd made the journey to Ewood Park to cheer on Forest that day actually took the 7-0 thrashing pretty well. Travelling a long way to see your team take a battering can be quite a dispiriting experience – in this instance though, it was such a comprehensive tanking that all you could do really was just shrug your shoulders and laugh about it. At one point during the second half there was even an ironic conga around the away end.

And to be fair, if you're going to end a record-breaking unbeaten run, you may as well do it in style!

Joking aside though, in hindsight that hammering at Ewood Park was almost certainly a watershed moment for Forest. The Reds only managed another two league wins away from the City Ground during the entire remainder of the season - and suddenly, those away trips on the Gedling bus didn't feel quite so much fun any more. Most disappointing of all was Forest's final away match of that 1995-96 season - a trip to Manchester United.

Memories of beating United at Old Trafford the previous year were still relatively fresh in everyone's memories, but on this occasion the Reds were thrashed 5-0 – with a certain 20-year-old by the name of David Beckham, who'd not long broken into the United team, getting a couple of the goals.

Looking back, it's actually quite strange to think of Beckham and Stuart Pearce being on the same pitch that day – as you tend to think of them as being synonymous with two completely different footballing eras. That said, the age of Psycho in his pomp in a red shirt was very much coming towards its conclusion. We didn't know it at the time of that heavy defeat at Old Trafford, but the following season would prove to be his final year at the City Ground.

And disappointingly, the 1996-97 campaign was anything but a happy ending for Forest's inspirational captain after 12 years and over 500 appearances – as the frailties first exposed the previous season on that fateful afternoon at Blackburn started to become and more apparent. By Christmas the Reds were rooted at the bottom of the Premier League table – with Frank Clark relieved of his managerial duties as a result.

Initially Psycho actually took over as caretaker player-manager - and for a few weeks, results did pick up. January 1997 began with five successive wins, including a memorable victory away at Newcastle in the FA Cup, which most Forest fans remember for a spectacular winning goal by Ian Woan.

By the end of the January Psycho was rightly presented with the Premier League Manager of the Month award. Unfortunately though, the oft-talked about 'curse of the Manager of the Month award' struck at this point – for after that run of five wins, Forest only won one more game for the entire rest of the season. With the Reds sliding back towards the bottom of the table, the club brought in Dave Bassett as manager and asked Psycho to go back to being just a player. However, despite breaking the club's transfer record to bring in striker Pierre van Hooijdonk, Bassett wasn't able to stop the rot – and the season ended with relegation from the Premier League.

A pretty dismal period then for us Forest fans. And it was particularly depressing for those of us who were travelling to watch the team away – with the Reds winning only three league games on the road all season.

I guess it's not entirely coincidental that it was during the back of the 1996-97 campaign that I stopped going to away matches on the Gedling bus.

Nevertheless, I look back with enormous affection on those four years that I spent as a 'regular' on board - and several decades on, it makes me feel all warm inside to know that the bus is actually still running. As far as I'm aware it still departs from the 'Cheggo' too, although it's a sign of the times that the place is a fancy gastropub these days – a far cry from the slightly grotty boozer we knew and loved back in the day, where my Dad once nearly got lynched by some of the regular clientele after he had the audacity to win the Sunday meat raffle.

As well as the various adventures themselves, probably my favourite thing about all those years spent travelling on the Gedling bus is the various friends I made. Of all the guys who travelled regularly on the bus, Al and I became particularly pally with a couple of lads called Darren and Dave – or 'Dodgy Darren' and 'Shifty Dave', as we affectionately referred to them.

Darren and Dave were both a few years older than us - and given the strange hierarchy you have as a teenagers where it's deeply uncool to associate with kids who are younger than you, they could've been forgiven for completely ignoring Al and I, or merely tolerating us at best. Fair play to them though, they were great friends to my brother and I, and we had some right laughs with them over the years whilst travelling up and down the motorways of England following Forest. I used to particularly enjoy their company on London away trips, as if we arrived early enough we'd often eschew the option of going for a few drinks near Stamford Bridge or Loftus Road or wherever, in favour of finding the nearest Tube station and heading off into central London. As a kid, it felt like a great adventure getting to see some of the places I'd only ever seen previously on the Monopoly board.

And while nothing to do with the mighty Reds, Darren and Dave also played a huge part in shaping another big passion of mine. Around the age of 12 I'd started getting into music in a big way – although as a kid growing up at a time when MTV's *Beavis and Butthead* were fairly ubiquitous, my tastes were initially restricted to a very narrow spectrum of heavy rock. However, Darren and Dave would often turn up for away trips armed with tapes of whatever stuff they happened to be listening to at the time - and it was largely through that that I was exposed to all sorts of bands from Oasis to the Specials.

All in all, my world back in those days pretty much revolved around Forest, music and alcohol. Before long, the latter two preoccupations would gradually start to elbow the mighty Reds out of the way for a good couple of years. For a good chunk of the mid-90s though, the three things happily co-existed in

109

complete harmony – and it felt like a glorious time to be alive.

Several decades on I haven't seen either Dodgy Darren or Shifty Dave for years, but we do occasionally chat on Facebook and invariably end up reminiscing about the good old days of the Gedling bus – with one particular story about a brown and orange sleeping bag usually getting brought up. Pretty much all of the funny stories from our numerous trips up and down the country fall firmly though into the 'You had to be there' category, so none of them are really worth repeating here.

There also came a point where Darren became a companion for not just away games but also home games. By the summer of 1995 I was approaching my 16th birthday and at that stage in my life when I was desperately craving more and more independence – so after six seasons of sitting with Dad in the Executive Stand, I decided it was time to cut the apron strings and to get a season ticket in the Trent End with Darren. Suddenly, Forest was now officially something I did with my mates rather than my Dad.

Looking back, I feel quite bad really about how I unceremoniously jettisoned Dad as my companion for home matches. With Al having decided to give up having a season ticket altogether that summer, largely due to the distraction of his first serious girlfriend, and me clearing off to the Trent End, Dad was left facing the prospect of having to sit on his own. And on that basis, he decided to call it quits and simply stop going.

I guess as teenagers we're all guilty of being a bit selfish and self-obsessed. Nevertheless, after all the efforts Dad had made over the previous five or six years to take me to games and indulge my passion for Forest, it was poor form on my part for me to be so thoughtless.

That said, in hindsight you could say it was good timing on Dad's part. There's an art in life in knowing the right time to walk away from something – and the third-place Premier League finish that Forest achieved in that final season where Dad, Al and I all sat together is a height that the Reds have never even come close to since.

And while Dad has maintained an interest in Forest over the years and been known to go along to the odd game, he certainly saved himself from many years of frustration and disappointment in stopping going week in and week out when he did.

Of course though, back in that summer of 1995, no-one had any idea that the next few years would see Forest on a downward trajectory. Far from it - the mood amongst the fanbase was actually one of great excitement.

After all, finishing third in the Premier League had earned Forest a place in the UEFA Cup for the following season – the first time they'd qualified for a European competition in over a decade.

It was time for me to make my maiden trip abroad to cheer on the mighty Reds…

11. Europe

"There were desperate scenes on the ferry to Denmark, with most of the inhabitants of our coach trying to cram as much booze down their gullets as they could during the 30-minute crossing. Despite the fact that it was 6am..."

Though too young to have experienced Forest's European successes of the late 70s and early 80s, I quickly began learning all about the triumphs of that era when I started getting into the Reds a decade or so later.

All those tales of dramatic victories against teams with funny names like Grasshoppers of Zurich and Cologne well and truly captured my imagination – and I'd be all ears whenever I got the opportunity to talk to older Forest supporters about trips that they'd made back in the day to watch the Reds on the continent.

As mentioned in an earlier chapter, my Uncle Stephen had been one of the thousands of fans who'd travelled to Munich to cheer on Forest in the 1979 European Cup final. Brilliantly, I actually ended up inheriting Stephen's programme and scarf from that trip, after his Mum – my Mommar – decided to clear out some of his old stuff that he'd left cluttering up her house.

I'm not sure my uncle was too happy about this when he got to find out – but he did at least still have his memories of a trip that has gone down in folklore within my family.

Though only 17 at the time, Stephen was already a seasoned drinker – and boarded the train to Munich armed with little more than his passport, scarf, match ticket and a case of beer.

Legend has it that all the beer was gone before the train had even made it to Peterborough, and there's also a hilarious story about Stephen attempting to find further liquid refreshment on arrival in Munich - only to discover the 'bar' he'd walked into was actually a brothel!

Fortunately there was a happy ending – although not *that* sort of happy ending! – with Forest beating Swedish champions Malmo 1-0 in Munich's famous Olympic Stadium, to win the first of their two back-to-back European Cups.

As soon as I got properly into Forest I always hoped there'd come a time when the Reds would get to compete in Europe again. However this was the late 80s - and English clubs were excluded from all European competitions at this point in time. It's a shame, as I think the Forest team of that era would've done well in Europe – and third-place league finishes in both 1987-88 and 1988-89 seasons would've presumably earned qualification for the UEFA Cup had it not been for the ban.

Still, all good things come to those who wait. By the time Forest achieved another third-place league finish, in the 1994-95 season, English clubs had been allowed once more to compete in Europe. Consequently, the summer of 1995 saw not only the usual excitement over possible new signings, but also eager anticipation at finding out which far-flung part of the continent we'd be visiting to cheer on the Reds.

For me personally though, the timing wasn't great. The 1995-96 season was my GCSE year - so if I was to travel abroad to go and watch Forest, it would mean taking time off school and missing vital preparations for my exams.

But important as my education was, there was no way I was missing the chance to go and see Forest in Europe. Indeed, I remember at the time thinking that it might be something I'd never get the chance to do again.

Of course, this is a scenario where you could imagine a lot of parents putting their foot down and refusing to allow their child to go – particularly in this day and age, where you can get fined if you allow your kids to miss school. My Mum and Dad had turned a blind eye in the past on occasions when I'd bunked off school in the name of the mighty Reds, whether it was to go and queue for tickets or to try and blag interviews with players for *Forest Forever*. However, those instances were only ever for one day, whereas an overseas trip to watch a UEFA Cup game was likely to take up the best part of a week - and would thus be taking skiving off to a completely new level.

Needless to say, it was a tense moment when I decided to broach the subject with my folks. As it turned out though, I needn't have worried – they knew how much Forest meant to me, and never tried to stand in my way.

Fair play to them.

That said, it was probably an easier decision for my Mum and Dad than it might have been – as I'd always done well at school, and I think we were all confident that I'd still cruise through my exams even if I missed a few days of lessons.

In fact, my decision to put Forest ahead of my own education became something of a running joke within our household. We were all big fans in my family of the comedian Billy Connolly, and throughout the 1995-96 football season I often found myself referred to affectionately as 'Woby Tide'. This was in reference to the Big Yin's famous monologue about his school days when teachers always used to use the phrase 'woe betide': "I thought they were talking about an actual guy called Woby! 'Woe betide the boy who goes to football instead of coming to school'. Good old fucking Woby, I used to think. He's got his priorities right!"

All that was left then was to wait for the draw for the first round of the UEFA Cup. And when that day came, there was a wonderful connection with the past, with Forest paired with Malmo – the very same team who the Reds had beaten in 1979 to win their first European Cup.

The first leg of the tie was to be away from home, and all of a sudden the big topic of conversation amongst Reds fans was how everyone was going to get to Sweden. Sadly though, I soon discovered that my usual method of transport for away trips - the charabanc otherwise known as the 'Gedling bus', as immortalised in the previous chapter - was not going to be an option. This was because Forest had announced that the only fans who were being allowed by the authorities to travel were those going via the club's own official travel packages – and that anyone ignoring that instruction would risk being arrested. This gave us two options – either an air package flying from East Midlands Airport, or a coach trip leaving from the City Ground.

Unsurprisingly, the coach trip was significantly cheaper – so myself and a number of other regulars from the Gedling bus took the plunge and booked our places at £129 a head.

Naturally we were all very excited, and the week before the game I arrived at school with a letter from my Mum - which explained that I wouldn't be in for most of the following week as I was off to Sweden to cheer on Forest!

As it turned out, school didn't give me any grief at all. Nevertheless, I enjoyed handing in that letter to my tutor. While I was generally quite a conscientious student, I've always had a quietly rebellious streak - so it felt good sticking it to The Man.

It was a bit of a shock though when we received our itinerary for the trip to Malmo. For a group of fans who regarded away trips to places like Newcastle or Southampton as a hefty journey, it was hard to comprehend just how long we were going to be sat on a coach for. We were due to arrive in Malmo on the afternoon of the game, which was taking place on a Tuesday night - and we were departing from the City Ground at 9am on the Monday morning.

Yes, our journey was expected to take a full 28 hours!

Not being seasoned overseas travellers, we'd assumed the easiest way to get to Sweden would have been to just get a boat straight across the North Sea. But apparently not. No, it had been decided that the best route was to head to Dover and get a ferry to Calais… and then drive all the way through France and Belgium to Germany. Here we would get another ferry to Denmark, drive a bit more, and then get *another* ferry from Denmark to Sweden.

Sadly, the organisation of the trip was pretty poor. Right from the off the coaches were nearly an hour late leaving the City Ground, which meant we were playing catch-up from the word go. This resulted in plans for a stop-off in Antwerp being jettisoned – and though we were getting to pass through a fair few different countries, all we were seeing of them was motorways and motorway service stations.

Inevitably, cabin fever began to set in fairly quickly. It wouldn't have been so bad if we'd been allowed to have a few drinks on board – but alcohol on the bus was a strict no-no. This led to desperate scenes on the ferry to Denmark when it was discovered that there was a bar open on the vessel, with most of the inhabitants of our coach trying to cram as much booze down their gullets as they could during the 30-minute crossing. Despite the fact that it was 6am!

There was one particular lad who became so immersed in the joys of German beer that he actually forgot to get back on the coach when we docked in Denmark – resulting in our driver leaving without him. We only made it about half a mile though before we had to stop at passport control – at which point our hapless hero suddenly reappeared, having bagged a lift off a Danish truck driver after realising he'd been left behind! Naturally, the lad in question was nicknamed 'Yorkie' for the rest of the trip.

After another ferry crossing from Denmark to Sweden, we eventually rolled into Malmo pretty much on schedule. It was a relief to have finally made it to our destination after such an arduous journey – and having survived since the previous morning on a diet consisting solely of various different types of foreign crisps, it was also good to get some proper food before we succumbed to scurvy!

We duly spent a pleasant afternoon in the sunshine wandering around the city centre - and groups of Forest fans seemed to be everywhere. Sharing war stories with our fellow Reds about our respective journeys, it very quickly became apparent that Forest had told a massive fib about fans only being allowed to travel if they made the trip via the club's official travel packages. Loads of those we met had made their way to Malmo under their own steam - and none of them had had any problems whatsoever.

Still, we were just happy to be there – and even happier when the realisation dawned on us just how stunning the local girls were!

Admittedly I was a hormonally-charged teenager at the time - but even so, as we sat in the main square in the centre of Malmo, it honestly felt like every blonde goddess who walked past was the most beautiful girl in the world. And it wasn't a case of beer goggles either – as plans to sample copious quantities of local ale had been immediately curtailed on arrival in Malmo, when we discovered that the going rate for a beer in Swedish Krona was equivalent to about £5.

Inevitably there were a fair few Forest fans keen to see if the local ladies were susceptible to a bit of Nottingham charm, although no-one really got very far. Hardly surprising really – after all, none of us were looking or smelling our best after 28 hours sat on a sweaty bus!

But what of the reason we'd actually made that arduous journey – the match?

Well the game was far from a classic. Forest took a first-half lead through Ian Woan, but the second half saw the Reds capitulate and end up losing 2-1.

It was disappointing not to get the UEFA Cup campaign off to a better start – and even more disappointing when it dawned on us that we were getting straight back onto the coach after the full-time whistle to commence the long journey home.

Still, it had certainly been an interesting experience – and a 1-0 win for Forest in the second leg back at the City Ground saw the Reds through to the next round on away goals.

Which meant we'd get to do it all again!

The second round of the UEFA Cup saw the Reds drawn against French side Auxerre – and with Forest's claims about fans only being allowed to travel on the club's official travel packages having been exposed as a load of nonsense, there were suddenly far more possibilities for how we might get there.

For me though, there was only one choice. The news had come through that the Gedling bus would be making its first foray overseas – and I immediately booked my place.

But there was a downside to this. While powerless to stop fans making their own travel arrangements, Forest were still dragging their feet over tickets for the match, only making them available to fans travelling on their official trips. Trooper though that she is, Joan Bakewell of the Gedling branch of the Supporters Club managed to work her magic – although the tickets she managed to acquire were for one of the home sections of the ground.

This meant we'd be attending to some degree incognito – and naturally there were plenty jokes about how we should all turn up at the match with baguettes and strings of onions to try and 'blend in'.

Thankfully Auxerre wasn't as far as Malmo – only a mere 15 hours or so. This time we got to France via the newly-opened Channel Tunnel rather than the ferry, which was a new experience for pretty much everyone. The enormous shuttle train that whisked us through the tunnel was pretty empty other than our bus – in fact, when we all got off for a leg-stretch during the crossing, we discovered that the next carriage along from ours was pretty much empty. With someone having had the foresight to bring a football with them, we ended up partaking in an impromptu kickabout some 40 metres below the bottom of the English Channel!

As with the trip to Malmo, we arrived in Auxerre around lunchtime on the day of the game – and thankfully, the beer prices were a bit more reasonable than they had been in Sweden.

That said, the toilet facilities left a lot to be desired. As seasoned travelling football fans, we thought we were hardened to awful loos. However, we were all quite bemused when the first bar we went in gave us our first experience of one of those strange bogs you see quite often in France - where it's pretty much just a hole in the ground as opposed to the customary porcelain throne!

Still, over the course of the afternoon the town was slowly taken over by Forest fans – and toilet horrors aside, an enjoyable time was spent drinking beer in the sun and chatting to our fellow Reds. One bloke who I got talking to turned out to be one of the members of the pop group KWS – who were Forest fans, and had enjoyed a 'one hit wonder' moment back in 1992 with the song 'Please Don't Go'. Legend has it of course that the band had recorded the track to try and persuade Des Walker not to leave the City Ground – although despite going to number one in the charts the plea fell on deaf ears, with Des clearing off to Sampdoria just a few weeks later.

During that afternoon in Auxerre we also bumped into Forest midfielder David Phillips, who had travelled with the Reds squad but not made it into Frank Clark's team – and thus decided to go for a look at the town. He was a nice bloke, and thanked us all for making the trip over to lend our support.

As the kick-off approached we made our way to the stadium, and were quite taken aback by the heavy police presence – with dozens of coppers with riot shields and guns. Clearly, the reputation that English football fans had acquired on the continent during the 70s and 80s was still fresh in the minds of the powers-that-be in France.

That said, the cops didn't seem too concerned about us entering one of the home sections of the ground – although even so, we figured it would be sensible to try and keep a low profile as we picked a spot on the concrete steps behind one of the goals.

As the match kicked off Forest immediately found themselves under intense pressure from the home side - and it was hard keeping our emotions in check.

For a while we did manage it. However, midway through the first half there was a test that was simply too great for our self-control, when the Reds launched a rare counter attack and Steve Stone was suddenly racing through with just the Auxerre keeper to beat.

The balding Reds midfield maestro decided to go for the cheeky lob - and it was one of those moments where it felt like the world had gone into slow motion.

The ball seemed to hang in the air for ages – although slowly it began to drop and eventually landed gloriously in the back of the net in front of us.

Needless to say, we all completely took leave of our senses and went absolutely bananas!

Brilliantly, it turned out we needn't have worried about keeping a low profile – as it became immediately apparent that most of the people sat around us were also Forest fans, and also in the process of blowing their own covers by celebrating the goal. Feeling now that we had safety in numbers, we ended up behaving for the remainder of the game like we normally would at an away match.

And to be fair, Forest needed every bit of vocal support they could get - as the rest of the game saw the Reds' goal under siege as Auxerre tried desperately to get back into the tie. In all my years as a Forest fan I can't remember a time when the Reds have had such a battering from an opposition team and yet still managed to keep a clean sheet. There were a fair few 'heart in mouth' moments, including at least two goalline clearances, but Forest to a man defended magnificently. We were certainly all very relieved when referee Pierluigi Collina finally blew the final whistle – and we were able to return back to England triumphant.

We also returned laden with booze. On the Malmo trip, buying of duty free when we passed through Calais on the way home had been strictly forbidden – but the rules were a lot more relaxed on the Gedling bus, and we were allowed to stop at a hypermarket on our way back to the Channel Tunnel. Inevitably, everyone took the opportunity to stock up on as much cheap alcohol as they could physically carry – and classy individual that I was fast blossoming into, I decided to blow my last few French Francs on a bottle of Baileys! When I went back to school the next day I decided to smuggle it in with me – and myself and couple of my mates ended up necking the whole bottle at lunchtime on the school field.

Maths that afternoon was certainly an interesting experience!

Happily, the second leg against Auxerre at the City Ground saw Forest defend their hard-earned lead – with a 0-0 draw enough to win the tie on aggregate and go through to the third round. It was exciting to know that another trip abroad was on the cards – and the feeling of jubilation was enhanced even further by the fact that all the other English teams competing in Europe had now been knocked out. Forest were now the nation's sole representatives.

It was back to France again in the third round, with the Reds drawn against Lyon. This time the first leg was at home – and Forest were able to travel to France with a 1-0 advantage, after Stuart Pearce missed a penalty but Paul McGregor tucked in the rebound. The one thing most fans remember about that goal more than anything else though was how Reds defender Colin Cooper went haring over to join his celebrating team-mates – only to run straight into one of the goal posts!

I made the trip to Lyon once again on the Gedling bus - and this time, we were actually allowed tickets to sit with the rest of the travelling Forest fans. It was early December, and after travelling through the night we arrived in France's second city around lunchtime of the day of the game to find it snowing.

With the stadium a fair way out of town, it had been decided to drop us off in the city centre so we could go for a mooch around – before returning to the bus an hour or so before kick-off for the drive to the ground. With Lyon boasting a Roman amphithéâtre and stacks of medieval and renaissance architecture, there was plenty of culture for us to go and get our teeth into – although it probably says a lot about the mentality of us Gedling bus regulars that one of the few photos I have from that trip was of a group of us posing with a Forest flag outside one of the city's sex shops!

To be honest, the degree to which we explored Lyon extended little further than visiting various bars – but we did also take a few minutes to send greetings to a couple of absent friends.

Yes, the previous summer had seen two of Forest's star players leave the City Ground in somewhat acrimonious circumstances – with Stan Collymore and Lars Bohinen clearing off to Liverpool and Blackburn respectively. On their departures, both players had talked in the press about how they were moving on because they felt they had a better chance of winning trophies at their new clubs – words which went down like a lead balloon with the Forest faithful.

Still, we got the last laugh, as both players' teams had crashed out of European competition very quickly that season – with Collymore's Liverpool eliminated in the second round of the UEFA Cup, and Bohinen's Blackburn failing to make it past the group stage in the Champions League. And with Forest's own European campaign still going strong, it seemed only appropriate then to send them both a postcard to say how much we were enjoying our continuing adventure, and what a shame it was that they couldn't be with us.

Needless to say, I have no idea whether those postcards actually made it to the intended recipients. We were very meticulous though in making sure we sent them to the right place – with Collymore's, we'd even written 'Stan Collymore, c/o the subs' bench, Anfield' as the address!

Of course, time flies when you're having fun and it was soon time to get ourselves back to the bus and make our way to the ground. During the journey we were stopped by the local police, who got on board the bus and warned us to have our wits about us - as Lyon had a well-known group of hooligans who were apparently very keen on a spot of aggro with their English visitors.

Unfortunately though for the local plod, these attempts to strike fear into our hearts failed dismally – as they went on to made an ill-advised decision to tell us what these Gallic ruffians called themselves. Not for Lyon the sort of sinister names associated with hooligan groups in England – from Birmingham's Zulus to Derby's Lunatic Fringe.

No, Lyon's top trouble-makers called themselves... le Flash Boys!

Naturally, the discovery that the local 'firm' had a name that made them sound like a bunch of male strippers was a source of enormous amusement.

On the whole though, I think the biggest danger to those of us on the Gedling bus was ourselves – as quite a few of our number were rather worse for wear having massively overdone it on the beer during the afternoon in Lyon. One of our resident nutters was so leathered that he actually ended up being sick on the bus during the journey to the ground. Fortunately someone managed to pass him a transparent plastic bag just in time – although he then proceeded to spend the rest of the journey proudly waving his bag of puke around, in the manner of a child who'd just won a goldfish at Goose Fair!

There was also a legendary Gedling bus stalwart who'd got so carried away in Lyon's bars during the afternoon that they passed out during the short ride to the ground. There was talk of trying to conceal this person's inebriated state and smuggle them into the ground in the style of the cult 80s film *Weekend at Bernie's* – in the end though they actually stayed on the bus and missed the game!

For those of us who did make it into the ground, we ended up being glad of our 'beer coats' – it was a freezing cold night, and when we got inside we discovered that we'd be sat on bare concrete steps with no roof to protect us.

The game was far from a classic, with Forest pretty much 'parking the bus' and defending their 1-0 lead from the first leg. Happily though this approach worked - with the Reds holding out for a 0-0 draw and securing their passage through to the last eight.

Sadly of course, the quarter finals proved to be as far as Forest's Europe adventure would go. However, just as the UEFA Cup run had started with a connection to the past, it also ended with one - with the Reds drawn against Bayern Munich, and the first leg away.

This meant I'd get to follow in the footsteps of my Uncle Stephen – with Bayern's Olympic Stadium being the very arena where he'd watched Forest lift the European Cup back in 1979.

The trip to Germany was just one part of what was a pretty epic week of away travel for us Reds fans. The game in Munich was on a Tuesday night – and that was sandwiched between away trips both the Saturday before (Sheffield Wednesday in the league) and the Saturday after (Tottenham in the FA Cup). For me then, this meant pretty much a whole week of my life on the Gedling bus. And if anything has ever completely epitomised the saying 'You can have too much of a good thing', then this situation was probably it!

That said, the trip to Munich was superb. In organising our itinerary, Joan Bakewell from the Gedling branch of the Supporters Club had decided to push the boat out – and rather than just arriving on the day of the game as we had done with previous European trips, she'd arranged for us to get to Munich the day before and stay overnight in a hotel.

This was great, as it meant we got to spend much more time in Munich – where we mastered the Metro system, and enjoyed an excellent drinking session in the city's famous Hofbrabaus.

There was also a highly amusing incident when we were checking out of the hotel on the morning of the match – when it became apparent that one of the regulars on the Gedling bus who we'd always regarded as a respectable sort of bloke had clearly got carried away watching the adult TV channels, and landed himself with a hefty bill!

Matchday saw us head for the Olympic Park, where there was a carnival atmosphere and thousands of Bayern fans in double denim and scarves tied to every limb. With its famous canopy roof the Olympic Stadium was a spectacular setting, and around 5,000 Forest fans had made the trip to cheer on the mighty Reds.

We all knew though that Bayern would be the biggest test of the UEFA Cup run so far, with the Germans having a host of big name players such as Jurgen Klinsmann and Jean-Pierre Papin. And when they took the lead through Klinsmann after just 16 minutes, I think many of us feared that a pasting was on the cards.

But what happened just a minute later remains one of my favourite ever moments as a Forest fan.

After restarting the game, Forest went forward, attacking the far end of the stadium from where we were sitting, and won a free-kick on the left-hand side. David Phillips took the kick and floated the ball into the Bayern penalty area – and of all people, big defender Steve Chettle arrived at the far post apparently from nowhere and nodded the ball into the back of the net.

Steve Chettle.

The one Nottingham-born player in the team.

The man who'd visited my primary school when I was a kid.

He'd only gone and bloody scored!

And not only that, he'd headed the ball from practically the same spot where Trevor Francis headed his winning goal in the 1979 European Cup final!

On that night in Munich, Chet's goal was one of those ones where there was a slight pause of disbelief among the travelling Forest fans while everyone tried to work out whether or not they'd just been seeing things. As soon as it had properly registered with everyone though that the ball really had hit the back of the net, there were scenes of absolute pandemonium – one of those moments of utter delirium, where you find yourself hugging complete strangers and falling into a heap.

To be honest, you would've struggled to write a better script. In fact, probably the only thing I would go back and change if I had the power to rewrite history would be the awful yellow away kit that Forest were wearing on the night.

Of course, speaking to the media some time later, Chet revealed that he hadn't actually meant to score at all – and that his intention had been to try and head the ball back across the box for one of his team-mates to try and get on the end of.

But we won't let that get in the way of a good story!

Naturally, the euphoria created by Chet's goal was dampened slightly when Bayern took the lead again just before half-time. However, Forest managed to contain their hosts during the second half – and when the final whistle blew with the score still only 2-1, it was the fans of the team that had lost who were by far happiest.

By the time we got back to the Gedling bus and began the long journey back to Nottingham, we were very much daring to dream. Though clearly a good side, Bayern hadn't seemed all that special – and all Forest needed was a 1-0 win at the City Ground and they'd win the tie on away goals and be through to the semi-finals.

Such a scoreline certainly didn't seem at all beyond the realms of possibility. In fact, with the novelty of long coach journeys across Europe having very much worn off by this point, some of us even started talking about how we'd splash out and fly to the away leg if the Reds managed to get through to the semi-finals.

As is often the way though in football, it's the hope that kills you.

Yes, a couple of weeks later, Bayern came to the City Ground for the second leg - and walloped Forest 5-1.

The UEFA Cup dream was over. It was absolutely gutting – and following the final whistle, not even the sight of Jurgen Klinsmann trudging off the pitch wearing Forest colours, after the two sets of players swapped shirts, could come anywhere near to quelling the deep sense of disappointment that we all felt that night.

What's more, further salt was rubbed into the wounds when the draw was made for the semi-finals, and it turned out we'd missed out on a trip to Barcelona.

The thought that'd we'd never get to witness the sight of Jason Lee gracing the hallowed turf of the Nou Camp was hard to take.

As things turned out, Bayern went on to beat Barca, and then Bordeaux in the final – so I suppose there was some consolation in going out of the competition to the eventual winners.

And looking back, there's no sense of 'what if?' at all really. Given how they'd struggled throughout the 1995-96 season to score goals, I think that Forest team punched massively above its weight to get all the way to the quarter finals of the UEFA Cup. Not only that, they gave us fans some brilliant adventures along the way - adventures that we've not been able to have since and may not ever get to have again.

Of course, in the grand scheme of the club's history, Forest reaching the last eight of the UEFA Cup pales in significance compared to those back-to-back European Cups of 1979 and 1980. Nevertheless, us Reds fans of a certain age will still look back on those trips to Malmo, Auxerre, Lyon and Munich with great fondness.

Oh, and despite missing a total of 12 days of school to potter around Europe watching Forest, I'm happy to say that I passed all nine of my GSCEs during the summer of 1996 – including four A grades.

What's more, part of the coursework I submitted for my English GCSE was a lengthy account of the trip to Malmo that I'd written for *Forest Forever* – so what more proof do you need that bunking off school to go and watch football can have a positive effect on your education?

---

12. Confessions of a teenage fanzine editor - part two

"I immediately understood why centre forwards would soil their breeks at the mere sight of Larry Lloyd back in his playing days..."

By the time of Forest's UEFA Cup run during the 1995-96 season, I was into my fifth year as editor of *Forest Forever* - and I think it's fair to say that the fanzine had come on in leaps and bounds by this point in its existence. Each edition now had a full-colour front cover, and the trusty typewriter had been jettisoned in favour of proper desktop publishing on a PC.

But you can never please everyone – and there were a few naysayers around this time who said the fanzine had betrayed its cut and paste roots and become a bit too slick.

To be honest I never really understood that view. As far as I was concerned, *Forest Forever* remained as irreverent and belligerent as it ever was in terms of its content. I was just keen to provide my readers with something that had a bit of quality about it. There was even one particular issue of the fanzine around this time where the front cover was printed with actual gold!

This was a special edition published in September 1995 to coincide with Forest's return to European competition. I wanted to do something special to mark this achievement, so dreamed up the idea of creating a front cover that looked like an old-fashioned British passport. Amazingly, rather than dismissing this as another of my ridiculous flights of fancy, our long-suffering printers Trish and Chris actually worked out a way to achieve the exact result that I wanted – which involved embossing the passport coat of arms on the front cover in gold leaf.

The end result looked brilliant – although ironically we actually ended up with loads of unsold copies, quite possibly because it looked so different to a normal issue that a lot of our regular readers maybe didn't recognise it as *Forest Forever*. In fact, the lower-than-usual sales combined with the not inconsiderable cost of the gold leaf led to that particular issue making a significant loss. It was *Forest Forever's* equivalent of New Order's 'Blue Monday' single, which famously saw the band lose money each time someone bought a copy due to the exorbitant manufacturing costs of the fancy design they'd decided upon for the 12-inch.

That same edition of *Forest Forever* contained an annual feature that was always hugely popular with the readers – namely, the results of the previous season's end-of-season poll. This would always start out as a questionnaire included in the final edition of the season, which would ask readers to give their opinion on everything from player of the season to best goal of the season. Usually, a hundred or so folk would be good enough to take the time to send in their answers, and I'd then spend hours manually calculating the results for each category. The fans' verdicts on the 1994-95 season offer a fascinating snapshot of that particular era - with Forest's 7-1 win away at Sheffield Wednesday unsurprisingly getting the most votes for best match of the season, and Eric Cantona narrowly pipping Paul Ince in 'Biggest prat of the season'.

It's interesting how use of language evolves over the decades - does anyone actually still use the word 'prat'?!

By this point in time *Forest Forever* was as popular as it ever would be, with its circulation having grown to 1,800 copies per issue. It was always quite exciting when a new edition came back from the printers. The hallway in my Mum and Dad's house would be piled high in boxes, each containing bundles of 20 copies.

That said, these would soon be straight out of the door again – either dispatched to the various shops that stocked the fanzine, loaded into holdalls ready to sell on the next Forest matchday, or stuffed into envelopes and sent out to our 100+ postal subscribers – most of them in the UK, but a few in places as far flung as Scandinavia and Canada.

Usually, each new issue of the fanzine would be launched to coincide with a Saturday Forest home game. I was still at school until the summer of 1996, so on the Monday after a new edition had come out, it was fairly common for me to turn up at Arnold Hill Comprehensive with six or seven hundred quid in cash stashed in my school bag from the weekend's 'takings'... much of it made up of pound coins and fifty pence pieces. Sensibly, the fact that I had so much money on my person was something I kept quiet from my peers – and as soon as the bell went for lunchtime, I'd be straight off to the bank to get it all safely deposited into the *Forest Forever* bank account.

Of course, any amount of money going into the hundreds of pounds is an absolute fortune when you're a teenager. Contrary to what some people might think though, I wasn't exactly living the life of a teenage playboy – the reality was that most of the proceeds from each issue of *Forest Forever* went to pay for the printing of the next one. And besides, there was a sort of ethic within the world of football fanzines at that time that the publications were a labour of love and not produced for a profit – and I stuck to that principle quite strictly. I did dip into the fanzine bank account to subsidise the cost of trips to away games – however, given that I'd be going home afterwards and writing a match report for the next issue, I felt that that could be justified as a 'business expense'.

As well as being ploughed back into the fanzine, any surplus cash generated by *Forest Forever* was always given back to Nottingham Forest Football Club in some shape or form. And one of the ways we did that was by becoming Jason Lee's official kit sponsor!

Most people will remember Jason Lee for the famous 'pineapple' hairstyle that he sported during his time at the City Ground, which became something of a national talking point after Frank Skinner and David Baddiel began to make endless jokes about it on their enormously popular TV show *Fantasy Football*. Jason Lee himself has gone on record since as saying that he felt all the attention he got as a result of Skinner and Baddiel's jibes had a negative effect on his career. He even ended up shaving his head to try and regain a bit of anonymity – although this in itself became a national news story. In my capacity as *Forest Forever* editor I actually got a phone call about it off a journalist from *The Sun*, and was inevitably misquoted when the story appeared in the paper the following day.

But revenge was sweet for Jason Lee in September 1996, when Forest were trailing 1-0 in injury time away at Chelsea – David Baddiel's team – and the big striker came off the bench to bag a late equaliser for Forest!

It was of course Jason's Lee's 'super sub' tendencies that led to him becoming a massive cult hero at the City Ground. During the spring of 1995, he had a purple patch in which he kept coming on and scoring late and important goals – with opposing defences seemingly unable to deal with his imposing physical presence.

Around this time, I happened to notice on the page in the official Forest matchday programme that listed all the players' kit sponsors that Jason didn't actually have a sponsor – so it seemed only right for *Forest Forever* to step in. It was a bit of a feather in the cap, being able to say that we were Jason Lee's official kit sponsor – and best of all, as part of the 'deal' when you sponsor a player's kit, you get to go down to the City Ground and have lunch with them. I'm happy to say that Jase was as nice a bloke as you could wish to meet – and at the end of our first season as his kit sponsor, he very kindly gave me one of his match-worn shirts. This very much remains one of my most cherished Forest-related possessions.

Lunching with Jason Lee was just one of many interesting opportunities that came about as a result of publishing *Forest Forever*. With the 90s being the age before electronic communication, the fanzine would receive dozens of letters through the post every week – and more often than not, these would be articles sent in to be published, or cheques from people wanting to take out a postal subscription.

Every now and again though, something more obscure would arrive. At one point, sometime around 1996, I got a letter from Cherry Red Records – a London-based record label best known for releasing punk music. At that time they were releasing a series of football compilation albums focusing on particular clubs – and were wanting to know whether enough Forest songs had been released over the years to scrape together an album.

Being something of an anorak when it comes to all things Forest, I was able to provide the Cherry Red guys with a long list of tracks that I knew of. This list included everything from the one Forest song that everyone knows – 'We've Got The Whole World In Our Hands' by Paper Lace and Forest's league title-winning squad of 1978 - to a frankly painful version of 'You'll Never Walk Alone' that was recorded as a duet in the early 80s by Reds legends Viv Anderson and Trevor Francis. Given that neither player ever played for Liverpool, quite why this recording even exists is anyone's guess. If anyone can tell me I'd love to know!

But anyhow, armed with the intelligence that I provided them, Cherry Red were able to acquire rights to pretty much all the songs – and later that year, their Forest album was released. It was a proud moment for me to get a namecheck in the sleevenotes, and the album includes everything from Brian Clough's attempts at rapping to a bizarre prog rock number called 'Nottingham Forest is My Rock'n'Roll' by some Norwegian dude called Njall Helle. Unsurprisingly 'We've Got The Whole World In Our Hands' was chosen as the opening track – I can only hope that the royalties that this generated for Paper Lace helped to sooth the rage of their bass player's son following his angry submission to the *Forest Forever* letters page as described in an earlier chapter!

Over 20 years on, the entire Forest album is still available to download on iTunes – though if anyone doesn't think that's necessarily a good thing, I can only apologise for the part I played in its existence! To be fair, there is one absolute stone-cold classic track on that album – a proper full-on punk anthem called 'You Reds!' by a band called Resistance 77. It's such a good song that I actually attempted once to start a petition to get Forest to start playing it at home matches as the players ran out of the tunnel – but sadly, that campaign was met largely with indifference.

Meanwhile, another interesting letter that arrived in the *Forest Forever* mailbag was when a computer game company got in touch. The company in question were making a new football game called *Championship Manager*, and to ensure it accurately reflected the teams of the time, they were contacting fanzines up and down the country and asking them to give ratings out of ten for their team's players' various attributes – everything from pace to heading ability. With *Forest Forever* being Jason Lee's official kit sponsor, it seemed only right to give our man tens across the board – and amusingly, this was taken at face value because our pineapple-headed hero was brilliant when the game eventually came out.

Of course, *Championship Manager* has gone on to become hugely popular. I became quite a big fan myself – there was a period during my teenage years where if you added together all the hours I spent playing the game, it'd probably equate to several entire years of my life.

You always knew you'd been playing the game a bit *too* much when the lines started to blur between the game and real life. I remember one time in the mid-90s having a vehement disagreement with a friend about Chris Waddle, who I was adamant had had a brief spell at the City Ground during his career. It was only later on I realised my mind had clearly been addled by the fact that I'd signed the mulleted former England winger for Forest myself a few months previously while playing *Championship Manager*, and he'd gone on to become one of my star performers!

Further interesting correspondence came in the summer of 1997, when Forest agreed a sponsorship deal with Pinnacle Insurance – and a letter from the company's marketing director arrived in the *Forest Forever* mailbag. The chap in question was called Graham Bolton and he'd got in contact to ask if I wanted to write a story for the fanzine about the club's new sponsors.

Initially I was sceptical – after all, would the readers of *Forest Forever* really care about what the club's official sponsors had to say?

However, when I went to meet Graham one evening at a pub in Nottingham city centre, it turned out he was a top man who had pulled off a pretty epic blag – basically, he was a lifelong Forest fan, who'd somehow persuaded his bosses to sponsor the club. What's more, as part of the sponsorship deal Graham had secured use of a private lounge at the City Ground to entertain the company's clients. So he was basically getting to go to the match in style with a free bar every other Saturday - all in the name of work!

You can only admire a bloke who can wangle something like that – and unsurprisingly, Graham and I got on like a house on fire. We kept in touch for the next few years, and there were several occasions when he invited me along to enjoy the full experience of 'The Pinnacle Lounge' on a matchday – the only times I've ever gone to a Forest game wearing a suit.

Being someone who's not very good at knowing how to behave in formal situations, I was a bit unsure whether I'd actually enjoy watching Forest with the 'prawn sandwich brigade'. I was worried I'd be surrounded by a load of posh people, all yoffing away amongst themselves and looking down their noses at a scruffy oik like myself. As it was though, I found that I thoroughly enjoyed the hospitality experience.

As part of the sponsorship deal that Graham had struck with Forest, his guests for each home game were allowed to vote for a man of the match. The chosen player had to pop down to the Pinnacle Lounge to chat with Graham's guests and pose for photos as soon as they'd showered and changed - and on one of the occasions that I was there, the Reds' big goalkeeper Dave Beasant received the majority of the vote. This was particularly amusing for me, because a few months earlier I'd had a drunken conversation with the veteran shot-stopper – on live television, no less!

This episode came about one fateful evening when Beasant had appeared as a studio guest on *Under The Moon* – a late night programme that was on TV for a few years in the late 90s, where sport fans could phone in and share their views.

Now that night I'd been out drinking with a couple of mates who were both Forest fans. After closing time, one of them invited everyone back to his place to continue the merriment - and when we flicked the telly on, we were naturally delighted to see the Reds' keeper holding court.

Given the format of *Under the Moon*, a conversation was quickly started about how funny it would be if one of us were to phone in – and for reasons lost in the mists of time, it was decided that the responsibility should fall on my shoulders.

I found myself dialling the number then – and despite the fact that I was clearly battered, I somehow managed to convince a member of the show's production team that I deserved a few seconds of airtime.

I then had to wait on the phone for a few minutes – before suddenly my cue arrived.

"Our next caller is Rich from Nottingham," said presenter Danny Kelly. "And he's got something to say to Dave Beasant…"

"'Ello Dave, I'm a Foresht fan," I seem to remember slurring, "and I jusht wanted to shay that you're 'the man'!"

Sadly that was just about all I managed to say before the programme's production team clearly realised - better late than never – that I was a drunken idiot and they should really be moving on to their next caller.

Unsurprisingly my mates found the whole caper absolutely hilarious – and a few months on in the Pinnacle Lounge, I sheepishly asked Dave Beasant if he remembered the barely coherent drunk bloke who'd phoned up *Under The Moon* when he was on. Amusingly, he did - and said that he'd found it very funny.

All in all, Beasant was a thoroughly nice bloke. He even humoured us when someone decided to bring up the subject of a certain moment from his pre-Forest days, when he arrived at the City Ground in 1991 as part of a Chelsea team - and endured a torrid afternoon in which he picked the ball out of the back of his net no less than seven times.

And it wasn't just present Forest players that I was getting to rub shoulders with either during my visits to the Pinnacle Lounge - there was also a time when I got to meet a legend from the Reds' past in the burly shape of Larry Lloyd. The man who'd worn the number five shirt in Brian Clough's all conquering team of the late 70s and early 80s was working for Forest at the time in the club's PR department - although wasn't very happy when I was introduced to him and it dawned on him that a member of the fanzine mafia had managed to infiltrate the club's inner sanctum. "You hypocrite!" he boomed, bringing his right arm crashing down onto my shoulder. "I thought you fanzine people were supposed to be against all this corporate hospitality? I thought you spoke for the man on the terrace, with his flat cap and his Wagon Wheel?"

I immediately understood why centre forwards would soil their breeks at the mere sight of the man back in his playing days!

Of course, spending the afternoon in corporate hospitality isn't something I'd want to do all the time – however, it's an interesting and enjoyable experience if you ever get the opportunity to do it. I certainly got to meet some interesting people – and not just Forest players past and present. On one of my visits to the Pinnacle Lounge Forest were playing Portsmouth, and I ended up chatting to several members of the Pompey board. One of them was a gentleman who was about 70 but was very much 70 going on 20 – as he gleefully told me how he'd travelled up to Nottingham the previous day and enjoyed a night out around the city's bars, "having a few beers and checking out the crumpet"! He even gave me his business card and told me to get in touch if I fancied meeting up with him for drinks down in Portsmouth prior to the return fixture – although I never did as I was worried that I would've cramped his style!

As well as offering me all sorts of interesting experiences, there came a point when *Forest Forever* started to kick quite a few doors open for me career wise. During my final year at secondary school, myself and my peers were all required to find ourselves a week's work experience – and having decided by this point through my experience of publishing the fanzine that I wanted to pursue a career in journalism, I decided to write to the *Nottingham Evening Post* to see if they'd be willing to offer me a placement.

Happily, having been impressed with the copies of *Forest Forever* that I'd included with my letter, the editor agreed that I could come and spend some time with the *Post*'s sports team. He also kindly turned a blind eye to the fact that many of the photos we used in the fanzine were actually stolen shamelessly from the pages of his newspaper!

A few weeks later then I spent a week at the *Post*'s old offices on Foreman Street in Nottingham city centre – and that time offered me an invaluable insight into the inner workings of the press. All the staff were tremendously encouraging and supportive, particularly sports editor Mick Holland and photographer Steve Mitchell.

Overall, my one abiding memory of my placement at the *Post* related to the build-up to Forest's next game. During the week I was there the Reds were due to play against Manchester City on the Saturday – and as part of the paper's pre-match coverage, one of the sport reporters did a phone interview with Alan Ball, who was City's manager at the time. Even though I was sat on the other side of the office, I was still able to hear faint traces of the former England legend's high-pitched voice squeaking out of the telephone receiver!

Meanwhile, *Forest Forever* continued to open doors for me after I left school at 16 in the summer of 1996.

Being still keen at this point to pursue a career in journalism I'd decided instead of staying on at sixth form to apply to go to Clarendon College in Nottingham, to do a BTEC qualification in media studies – and when I was invited for an interview for a place on the course, I took along a few copies of *Forest Forever*. The tutors must have been impressed, because I was offered a place pretty much immediately.

That said, I actually decided not to tell any of my fellow students that I published a fanzine. Much as I still loved putting *Forest Forever* together, by this point in my life I felt like I'd been well and truly pigeonholed by a lot of people as being that kid who published a magazine – and knowing that starting college would involve meeting a load of new people, I was keen to be judged on who I was as a person rather than what I happened to get up to in my spare time.

I spent much of the next two years drinking in the Grosvenor, the pub round the corner from the college - although I did actually do quite a bit of work as well. And with one of our lecturers being an experienced former journalist who'd spent years working on tabloid newspapers, the quality of my writing improved dramatically.

Some of the guys who I got to know from that course actually remain great friends to this day - including a Forest fan called John Newton.

As I got to know John, I discovered that his whole family were massive Reds fans, and were actually related to Henry Newton – who'd been one of Forest's key players back in the late 60s. What's more, at the time when John and I were studying together at college, his Dad was running his own business fitting TV aerials and satellite dishes - and brilliantly, had actually done jobs for various members of the Forest first team squad.

With brazen disregard for any notion of customer confidentiality, John would take great delight in sharing the little nuggets of information that his Dad managed to glean from the times he spent carrying out installations round at players' houses. This included, most memorably, a revelation that a particular Reds striker had had a huge satellite dish installed in his garden, for the specific purpose of ensuring he'd be able to pick up every porno channel on the planet!

There did come a time when John's Dad's impressive client list actually came in useful for our college course. One week we were given an assignment where we had to film a TV interview with someone – and it just so happened that John's Dad had recently fitted a satellite dish for Pierre van Hooijdonk, who was by far and away the Reds' star player at the time.

You can probably guess what's coming next – yes, John shamelessly rifled through his Dad's contact book to find the big Dutchman's number… and rang him up to ask if he'd be willing to answer a few questions!

Amazingly, van Hooijdonk actually agreed - so John and one of the other lads off the course trooped off down to the Forest training ground armed with a camera and a boom mic.

By all accounts Pierre gave a fascinating interview – although the rest of us had to take John's word for that, because the footage he returned to college with was a ten-minute silent movie. Sadly, it turned out him and the other lad had been so excited to get an audience with the Reds' leading scorer that they'd neglected to actually check whether the mic was switched on before they started filming!

Just like at school, there was a point during the college course where we all had to go and do a week's work experience – and after once again sending off a letter with a few copies of *Forest Forever*, I managed to bag a placement at a national magazine that was around at the time called *Total Football*.

The magazine was based down in Bath – and much like the week I'd spent at the *Nottingham Evening Post*, my time there proved really useful. Rather than doing the sort of menial tasks you usually end up doing when you're on work experience, the editorial team actually got me doing some proper work – including phoning up every Premier League football club and asking to be put on hold, so I could write a light-hearted story about which teams had the best and worst 'on hold' music.

Sadly I'm unable to reveal what Forest's on-hold music was at that time, as they'd just been relegated from the Premier League and thus weren't on the list of clubs that I rang. Everton were the undoubted winners though, with their use of the rousing theme music from the 70s Scouse cop show *Z Cars*. Meanwhile it was 'nul points' for Aston Villa, who at the time were subjecting their fans to a dreadful compilation CD of powerballads called 'Unforgettable Love'!

I went on to write regularly for *Total Football* over the next year as a paid freelancer, including a feature on Notts County – for which I did an interview with Sam Allardyce, who was manager at Meadow Lane at the time.

I did the interview with Big Sam at the Powerleague five-a-side football pitches in Nottingham, as Notts used to do some of their training there back then. After we'd finished our chat, I traipsed off to get the bus back into Nottingham city centre – although I wasn't waiting at the bus stop for very long before the man I'd just interviewed pulled up in a plush BMW and offered me a lift!

Of course, I had no idea at this time that I was about to accept a ride from a man who would one day become the England manager – albeit very briefly. Bless him though, Big Sam drove me all the way back into town and dropped me off at the back of the Broadmarsh shopping centre. The gesture was appreciated, although he did make it known during the short car journey that there'd be repercussions if I wrote anything negative about Notts in my article.

Don't mess with Big Sam!

As part of my research for the same piece I also went to watch a Notts County match at Meadow Lane, blagging a ticket in the press box in order to do so. As it turned out, sitting just a few seats away from the legendary Colin Slater for the full 90 minutes while he did a live commentary for BBC Radio Nottingham proved far more entertaining than the actual game.

Ultimately, my experience of publishing *Forest Forever* provided me with a springboard that has enabled me to go on and find employment as a wordsmith for most of my working life.

There are also several other people who wrote for the fanzine back in the 90s who have gone on to enjoy successful careers in the media. So I guess myself and others have a lot to thank *Forest Forever* for really.

But for all the positives from my years as a teenage fanzine editor, there were also one or two moments that I'd really rather forget – most notably when I nearly got sued for libel! This happened in 1994, when I published an article by one of our regular writers – in which he had a bit of a dig at a certain individual who used to work for Forest 'behind the scenes'.

The piece in question had passed the usual editorial controls and made it into print – however, the next thing I knew, I had the very gentleman who was the subject of the article on the phone, making it very clear that he was very unhappy with what had been written.

I did the only thing you can do in this type of situation, and apologised profusely. And hoped that would be that.

But no – a few days later I received a letter through the post from a solicitor representing the subject of the article, basically threatening to sue.

Being only 14 years old at the time, I was properly cacking myself – I actually had visions of ending up in jail. Fortunately, we had a family friend who was a solicitor who was kind enough to offer us free legal advice – and he suggested we might escape a court case by offering to publish a grovelling apology in our next issue and pay half of their legal costs.

Happily this offer was accepted, and a few days later I turned up at the offices of the offended party's solicitor to pay up. Having dashed straight from school I was still in my uniform, and handed over the couple of hundred quid that I'd agreed to stump up largely in coins – the takings from pre-match *Forest Forever* sales the previous Saturday.

An expensive lesson had been learned, though the excruciatingly awkward atmosphere as I sat and waited for the staff at the solicitors to count the money so they could give me a receipt was quite amusing.

Another low point meanwhile was when I tried to sell a few copies of *Forest Forever* outside White Hart Lane prior to a Forest game away at Tottenham – and ended up having to talk my way out of getting arrested for illegal street trading. But by far and away my worst moment from all my time publishing the fanzine was a major falling out that I had with Sanjay, my partner in crime who I'd started it with in the first place.

A lot of people say you should never go into business with friends – and though *Forest Forever* wasn't really a business per se, it did lead to a complete breakdown in the relationship between Sanjay and I, leaving me as sole editor from issue eight and the two of us not speaking for the best part of a decade.

Looking back, it was really sad - Sanjay and I had been really good mates for years, ever since we'd first met at infant school.

There is a happy ending however. By the time Sanjay and I reached our twenties I think the two of us had grown up enough to realise how silly it had all been - and after bumping into each other by chance, we managed to put our differences aside and rekindle our friendship.

By this time though *Forest Forever* had long since ceased to exist – as after 41 issues, I decided to call time on it in April 1998. I'd published the fanzine for a total of just over six years – a period which had seen me grow from a 12-year-old boy into an 18-year-old man.

The previous couple of years had seen *Brian*, *The Tricky Tree* and *The Trent Times* all fall by the wayside too. So suddenly, after the glut of fanzines in the 90s, Forest now had none.

And it was much the same all over the country. Some fanzines continued to hang on in there – indeed, there are actually a few publications that have survived to this day that date back to the 'fanzine boom' of the late 80s and early 90s, such as *City Gent* (Bradford) and *The Square Ball* (Leeds).

Generally though, fanzines were starting to dwindle in numbers by the late 90s. In fact, there are a lot of folk who believe that the publications peaked way before then, and way before *Forest Forever* even existed– as early as 1989 or 1990, which was the period when the number of titles up and down the country suddenly exploded from the dozens to the hundreds. It was during this period, so it's said, that the quality began to get diluted – a bit like in music in the mid-90s when bands like Oasis and Blur became massive, only for a load of poor imitators to follow in their wake.

Meanwhile, the quality of football fanzines was further diluted by a not inconsiderable number of chancers who attempted to cash in on the phenomenon by throwing together half-baked publications in a bid to make a quick buck – which went totally against the grain of what fanzines were all about. All in all, like a lot of good things, it's probably fair to say that fanzines ended up becoming a victim of their own success to a degree.

As it happens, there were actually numerous attempts made by various different folk to start a new Forest fanzine following the demise in 1998 of *Forest Forever*. There was one called *Everywhere We Go*, one called *Rambusters*, one called *Psycho*, and one called *Red Raw*. None of them lasted any more than a few issues though, and it wasn't until 2001 that anyone managed to come up with a new publication that lasted any sort of distance. This was *Blooming Forest*, which I actually ended up becoming a regular writer for from 2001 to 2005.

However, the writing was undoubtedly on the wall for fanzines by the beginning of the new millennium. I guess most things have a natural lifespan - and ultimately, the one main factor that would do more than anything to sound the death knell for fanzines was this new-fangled phenomenom called the internet. All of a sudden there were these things called forums, where fans could rant and rave and see their words published for all to see pretty much instantly – whereas with a fanzine, you often had to wait for weeks to see your words in print.

Naturally, there were still those fanzine purists. This internet thing is all well and good, they would say - but you can't sit and read it at half-time when you're at the match, can you?

Of course, rapid advances in mobile phone technology would eventually prove otherwise.

———
139

Personally though, much as I love technology, I've never had much time for the various Forest internet forums. There's no denying that they're great in terms of their immediacy – but I can't help but feel we've lost something in this modern world of instant gratification, where everything's always available at our fingertips. Call me old fashioned, but back in the days of the fanzines I used to really enjoy the anticipation of knowing that a new issue of *Brian* or *The Tricky Tree* was coming out. When the day finally came and I got my hands on a copy, I'd truly savour each page – and then, when I'd finished reading it from cover to cover, I'd immediately begin the process all over again in looking forward to the next one.

I'm sure I'm not alone in having felt that way – but I'd be amazed if any of the online Forest outlets that exist in the throwaway world we live in today are held in the same sort of reverence.

I also think the immediacy of the forums is their biggest weakness as well as their greatest strength. As we all know, kneejerk comments made in the heat of the moment often don't make for the most rational of views – and providing a potentially large audience for such views only seems to create an unhealthy echo chamber.

What's more, we live these days in the age of the keyboard warrior - and while I'm all for a bit of reasoned debate, things seem to get far too venomous far too often from what I've seen on the various forums.

To be fair, this appears to be a wider problem with the internet in general, in this strange modern world in which people are constantly falling over themselves to be upset or offended by seemingly everything. On the Forest forums, I've witnessed some poor sods hung out to dry just because they didn't subscribe to the popular view of what formation the Reds should be playing.

Some folk really need to live and let live.

The sort of nastiness that I've seen on the forums also seems to have manifested itself even further since Twitter became popular with football fans. And don't even get me started on the sheer amount of attention-seeking 'in the know' types out there in Forest cyberspace. We all know them - the ones who claim they know which player the club are about to sign, just because their cousin's neighbour's babysitter's work colleague knows someone who knows someone who has a trusted inside source at the club...

My brother Al and I have always differed though in our views on the online Forest forums. In fact, he actually ended up helping run one of them for a good few years, posting under the username Winnits - a pseudonym that will bring a wry smile to anyone who's familiar with the brilliant *Viz* book *Roger's Profanisaurus*.

Over time Al's friendships with many of the fellow Reds that he got to know online spilled over into real life, when he began meeting up with some of them for a few drinks before Forest home games. I'd often tag along with him - and much to my amusement, there were many occasions while in one of the pubs near the City Ground when he'd get random blokes sidling up to him and awkwardly asking "'Scuse me mate - you're not Winnits are you..?" in a conspiratorial tone.

Most of the forum guys were brilliant people, and there are some of them who I've ended up becoming really good friends with. I've just always preferred chatting to them in the pub rather than from behind a keyboard.

To each their own I guess.

All in all, the time I spent publishing *Forest Forever* is a period of my life that I remember with a great deal of affection. Sure, I don't think my little publication was ever held in quite the same esteem as *Brian* and perhaps also *The Tricky Tree* by a lot of Reds fans. But it's certainly no disgrace merely being the Buzzcocks, as opposed to the Sex Pistols or the Clash – and I do still get people coming up to me at the City Ground every now and then and telling me how they used to buy every issue of *Forest Forever*.

All these years later as I approach middle-age, it's quite strange to remain defined in the eyes of a fair few folk by something that I did as a kid. A bit like how those guys from the 90s pop group Hanson will probably never escape the association with the song 'MmmBop'! It's all good though, and it's always particularly flattering when people make a point of telling me that they still have all their old copies of the fanzine stored away in a drawer or up in the loft. They might actually be sitting on a goldmine – as past editions occasionally appear on eBay listed at vastly inflated prices.

A few people have even said that there should be a book of best bits of *Forest*

Forever and the other Reds fanzines. I've certainly heard of worse ideas. I still have the occasional flick through my old copies of them all, and they offer a great snapshot of that particular era.

That said, like anything you did when you were a teenager, there are certain things about *Forest Forever* that make me cringe when I look back.

Not least the name.

All these years later I can't remember whether it was me or Sanjay who came up with it, but there did come a point relatively early on in the fanzine's existence when I started to feel conscious of how banal a title *Forest Forever* was – especially in comparison with some of the witty and surreal monikers around at the time within the fanzine world, such as QPR's *A Kick Up the R's*, or Gillingham's *Brian Moore's Head Looks Uncannily Like London Planetarium*. By the time this realisation dawned though, the fanzine was fairly established - so we were stuck with the title.

To be fair, the phrase 'Forest Forever' does seems to have remained as part of the lexicon of the Reds faithful over the years. To this day I occasionally spot fans at the City Ground who have even had it printed onto the back of a Forest replica shirt – 'FOREST' at the top where you'd have a player's name, then a number four underneath that, and then 'EVER' underneath that.

As for the actual content of the fanzine meanwhile, sometimes when I look back through old copies of *Forest Forever* it feels a bit like reading an embarrassing teenage diary – only an embarrassing teenage diary that was available in the public domain for all to see. And even with the mitigating circumstances of how young I was, I think it's fair to say that the first ten issues were pretty terrible. Much as I had noble intentions of giving the readers maximum value for money by cramming as much content as possible into each issue, just looking at how the pages were laid out gives me a headache now!

In addition, there were far too many rambling articles in those early editions – probably because they were written on a typewriter, meaning much of the content was essentially a stream of consciousness. It was only when the fanzine went computerised that I was able to start fine-tuning and honing articles until they were a bit more intelligible.

And it also amazes me when I look back at my old copies of *Forest Forever* at just what an angry young man I was. For instance, there'd be times where I'd be spitting bile about people calling the Reds 'Notts Forest' – something that I tend to just shrug my shoulders about now.

I guess most of us mellow a fair bit as we get older.

For all my reservations though, I do genuinely think *Forest Forever* grew over the years into a decent magazine. Fanzines were such a big deal in the 90s that there was actually a fanzine about fanzines for a while – a publication called *Fanzine Collector* – and in 1995 its readers voted *Forest Forever* eighth best football fanzine in Britain.

But beyond the fact that it ended up being a decent publication, the one thing I'm most proud of about all my years of publishing the fanzine is quite simply the fact that *Forest Forever*, along with the likes of *Brian* and *The Tricky Tree*, gave Reds fans a voice. Several decades on, this is something that has a solid legacy through the creation in recent years of the Nottingham Forest Supporters Trust, the Forza Garibaldi initiative that aims to improve the atmosphere at Forest games, plus some brilliant fan-produced podcasts.

And the various online forums I suppose!

And who knows – rather than being something largely confined to the past, maybe there will come a time when fanzines become a common sight once again at the nation's football stadiums?

For quite a long time I was strongly of the opinion that this would never happen - a view that I formed based on my experiences in 2005, when I was part of a group of Forest fans who tried to get a brand new fanzine off the ground. Called *Lost That Loving Feeling*, this new publication was launched as a print offshoot of the successful LTLF.co.uk website. However, despite us producing something that was (in my opinion) far better than *Forest Forever* ever was, we struggled to sell any copies. Quite simply, it seemed the City Ground faithful no longer had any appetite for a fanzine - so reluctantly, we made the decision to pull the plug after just four issues and accept that the paper fanzine was a dead medium.

More than a decade has passed though since then - and while the internet is unlikely to go away any time soon, it's become such a dominant part of modern life that folk seem to increasingly have a love-hate relationship with it. You hear people talking about craving non-digital things – and we've certainly seen it in music, with the revival of vinyl in recent years.

Could a return of fanzines follow in the wake of this? After all, what goes around comes around, as the saying goes.

The beginning of the 2016-17 season did see the launch of a new publication for Reds fans called *Bandy and Shinty* – a curious name that references the two hockey-like sports that the founders of Forest played back in the 19th century, before they decided to settle on just football.

And funnily enough, one of the lynchpins behind *Bandy and Shinty* is a lovely fella called David Marples, who actually wrote a few bits and bobs for *Forest Forever* back in the day.

As brilliant a read though as it is, the *Bandy and Shinty* crew have deliberately distanced themselves from the idea of being a conventional fanzine. You won't find match reports from recent away games lamenting the quality of the half-time pies, or letters ranting about the ineptitude of the Forest ticket office. Indeed, rather than focusing on 'current affairs' at the City Ground, *Bandy and Shinty* is more a vehicle for talented writers to eulogise about the club's past – both glorious and inglorious – and their wider experiences of following Forest.

So the void that was left when Forest fanzines finally died out altogether very much remains - although all it would take to fill it would be for another couple of young bucks to come along with fire in their bellies and illicit access via sympathetic parents to a work's photocopier.

If there are any such Reds fans out there – consider the gauntlet laid down...

13. Drifting away # 1

"Watching a bunch of millionaire manbabies strutting around in their increasingly lurid-coloured boots, it felt to me like football was losing its soul..."

So, the story so far probably gives the impression that my formative years as a Forest fan were an exciting time to be supporting the Reds.

And looking back, they were.

Yes, there were a few kinks in the road, with the Reds twice losing their place in English football's top tier – and the 1993 relegation also marked by the sad end of Brian Clough's 18 years at the City Ground.

However, the Reds bounced straight back the following season on both occasions – and when you throw in a few trips to Wembley and a foray into Europe, it wasn't a bad period on the whole.

It was certainly a far better decade than any era that us Red types have had since!

But even so, as we started to reach the end of the 90s I'd begun to feel a bit disenchanted – with not only Forest, but also football in general.

In hindsight, it's fair to say that my formative years as a football fan occurred during a seismic time of transition for the beautiful game – with a lot of the changes arguably not for the better. The launch of the Premier League in 1992 saw the game becoming increasingly money-orientated - and the Bosman ruling in 1995 enabled players and their agents to start demanding ludicrous wages.

Suddenly, the time during his early days at Forest when Stuart Pearce used to supplement his modest salary by advertising his services as an electrician in the club's matchday programme began to feel like a very long time ago. And of course, it was us fans getting the raw end of the deal – with rising ticket prices and an increasing sense of disconnection from the players, who were starting to earn as much in a week as the average punter was in a whole year.

Watching a bunch of millionaire manbabies strutting around in their increasingly lurid-coloured boots, it felt to me like football was losing its soul. And this, coupled with the fact I had a lot of major distractions in my life, prompted me at the end of the 1997-98 season to make the decision to not only call time on *Forest Forever,* but also to give up my Forest season ticket and take a step away from the Reds as whole.

Not unusually for an 18-year-old lad - as I was at the time - those distractions that were diverting my attention away from Forest included the holy trinity of music, alcohol and girls.

However, the biggest distraction of all was a decision to move away from Nottingham, when I was offered a place at Liverpool John Moores University to study for a degree in journalism.

Now Merseyside was perhaps a strange choice of destination for a young Forest fan. After all, during the Reds' glory days of the late 70s and early 80s, Brian Clough's team had developed a bitter rivalry with Liverpool.

As it turned out, Forest never really sustained their status as serious long-term rivals to the Kopites – and a fateful day in the spring of 1989 brought the worst possible reminder to everyone associated with the two clubs that sporting rivalries are just a load of nonsense really in the grand scheme of life and death.

Nevertheless, resentment remained on both sides of the divide. Only two years after the awful events at Hillsborough, I'd sat with Dad and Al at the City Ground watching Forest play Liverpool in the penultimate league fixture of the 1990-91 season – a game that the visitors needed to win to keep their hopes alive of winning the title.

Forest, on the other hand, were cruising towards a mid-table finish and thus had very little to play for – but the antipathy towards Liverpool was such that the game was played at a ferocious pace. The atmosphere was electric, and I remember everyone taking great pleasure in Forest killing the Scousers' title hopes with a brilliant 2-1 win – with the winning goal scored, ironically, by the Reds' Merseyside-born winger Ian Woan.

So why choose to spend three years of my life up in Liverpool?

Well like a lot of the best things in life, it was a bit of an accident really. At the point when I'd decided I wanted to go to university, I actually had my heart set on doing my degree in Sheffield. This was mainly because that was where one of my best mates at the time was looking to go, and also because it was far enough away that I could leave home and enjoy the student lifestyle... but not so far that I couldn't easily nip home to Nottingham whenever I fancied.

In hindsight these were probably the wrong reasons to choose a place to go and study – but what do you know when you're 18?

Now at this point in my life I'd never really failed at anything – and with the arrogance of youth, I just blindly assumed that I'd get a place at Sheffield without any problems. As such, I didn't even bother doing any research on the various other journalism courses available elsewhere in the country. I just filled the remaining spaces of my UCAS application form with four chosen pretty much at random – Liverpool, Lincoln, Teeside and Edinburgh.

Oh, and I also took a punt on studying English at Cambridge, just because I thought it'd be funny if I actually got in.

Of course, you can guess what's coming next – yes, the very first response I got was... an outright rejection from Sheffield!

As things turned out, I ended up with a straight choice between Teeside and Liverpool - and at the time, having visited both places previously during my travels with Forest, neither were prospects that massively enthused me. Teeside had always struck me as a grey, depressing sort of outpost, while the area around the two football grounds in Liverpool always carried a lingering whiff of violence.

I always remember one particular trip to see Forest at Anfield when we parked up by the side of Stanley Park – and within seconds of getting off the coach, a group of scallies sat on top of a nearby wall greeted us with menacing cries of "Welcome to hell!"

That said, if any of us had felt intimidated the tension was quickly diffused by a blunt retort of "Fook off, Speccy!" from one of the lads off our coach, directed at a glasses-wearing member of the would-be Scouse hoodlums!

You probably had to be there.

You should never judge a city though by the area where its football grounds happen to be – and keen to keep an open mind, I decided to go and spend a couple of days up in Liverpool during the spring of 1998. And I'm glad that I did – as from the friendliness of the locals to the peerless musical heritage, I discovered there was actually an awful lot to love about the city.

That was it then, I was sold. I didn't even bother going to look at Teeside – and by the time the autumn of 1998 began to loom large, I was chomping at the bit to get up to Merseyside and begin my higher education adventure.

The fact that I'd stopped publishing *Forest Forever* only a few months earlier might have been a big void in my life, but university soon filled that. I was dropped off by Mum and Dad at my halls of residence one Sunday afternoon in early September 1998, and I immediately took to the uni lifestyle like a duck to water. I quickly made a brilliant group of friends - who all appeared just as eager as I was to drink dry Liverpool's many bars.

During the summer before I'd headed to uni, I'd actually made quite a bit of money by spending a few weeks working in a temp job doing admin at Radford Road police station in Nottingham. To this day that job remains in some ways my favourite job I've ever had – with every day feeling like being in an episode of *The Bill*. Meanwhile, further funds had also been gathered that summer by selling pretty much my entire collection of Forest matchday programmes – which by that point numbered around 2,000, including quite a few rare ones.

I'm not particularly proud to say that all of the cash that I'd made was gone by the end of my first term in Liverpool – largely spent on alcohol.

Nevertheless, I still maintain that it was money well spent. Liverpool is a great city and a fantastic place to be a student, and I enjoyed all sorts of hi-jinks with my new friends. My escapades during those first few months ranged from a drunken night out at a rock club where we randomly ended up hanging out with Lemmy from Motorhead, to getting busted for flouting the strict 'no pets' rule in halls of residence after a perhaps ill-advised decision to buy a hamster!

During my time at uni some of my new friends and I also enjoyed a great day out at the Grand National – which is of course held just a few miles down the road from Liverpool. The one thing I remember the most about this day was when we were hanging around near the entrance to one of the VIP areas, and we suddenly spotted Alex Ferguson arriving.

Fergie is of course quite well known for his interest in racehorses, and as he made his way through the enclosure there was a hush of reverence. This was quickly punctuated though when a pimply-faced scally scaled the fence that was separating the Manchester United boss from the proles such as ourselves, and brazenly shouted in a broad Scouse accent "HEY FERGIE, YER FOOKIN' WANKER!"

It was a priceless moment – even Fergie himself looked quite amused!

Looking back, I was guilty of quite a lot of clichéd 'studenty' behaviour during my three years at uni – though the time wasn't entirely spent just drinking and dossing about.

By the time of my foray into higher education, the government had abolished student grants and started to introduce tuition fees. The amount that my course cost was peanuts compared to what students have to pay nowadays – however, it was still a significant outlay at the time for my Mum and Dad. As such I made sure I never lost sight during my time up in Liverpool of how privileged I was to be there. My parents had certainly never had the option of getting a university education themselves as young people – in fact, I think I was the first person in my whole family to go away to university. So I was always determined to make the very most of the opportunity I'd been given.

Fortunately for me, the journalism degree that I did was a brilliant course, and one which has acted as a springboard over the years for many successful careers in the media. There was one particular girl on my course who ended up down in London working as a reporter on various national tabloids – and three years after we all graduated, she was actually the 'honeytrap' used to expose Stan Collymore's infamous dogging habit!

I think on the whole I'm happy about the fact that my own journalistic adventures have never put me at the heart of a tabloid scandal – however, my degree did enable me to build significantly on the skills I'd already developed through publishing *Forest Forever*. Along with all the academic side of studying, the course provided me with loads of opportunities to gain hands-on experience – including a broadcasting module where I got to work in real TV and radio studios. These studios were located in the Liverpool Institute of Performing Arts – the very building where a pre-fame John Lennon had studied art.

Over the three years of the course I also did numerous work placements at newspapers in and around Merseyside, as well as writing music stuff for the student union magazine. Through all of this I was able to massively improve my journalistic abilities - in particular my interviewing skills. My involvement with the student union magazine gave me the opportunity to put questions to numerous bands who were quite famous at the time – everyone from Kula Shaker to Reef – although it's fair to say that most of them are names that have faded into relative obscurity over subsequent decades.

Probably the musical equivalents of Forest players like Chris Bart-Williams or Thierry Bonalair in that respect!

Other well-known names who I interviewed meanwhile included the legendary broadcaster Sir John Peel, the author Nick Hornby and the comedian Mark Lamarr. Nick Hornby is of course probably best known for his debut book *Fever Pitch*, a memoir he had published in 1992 about his life as an Arsenal fan. It's a tome that many people regard as a landmark one - in the sense that it helped intellectualise football and turn it into something that was talked about by the types of people who read *The Guardian*, as well the traditional fanbase of working class oiks.

Rather than all that though, Hornby and I ended up talking mainly about Kevin Campbell - a player we'd both spent many hours watching, with him having played for both Forest and Arsenal. Amusingly, the author told me he always used to think of Campbell and his Arsenal strike partner Ian Wright as an old married couple – with Campbell the henpecked wife.

As for my interview with Mark Lamarr, that all came about because he was doing a load of press to promote a stand-up tour he was doing – and when making the arrangements for our chat with his 'people', we'd agreed that the comedian would call me at home on one particular evening at 8pm. At 7.30pm then on the designated day, I sat down to start writing a list of questions – only for the phone to start ringing. And yes, it was Mark Lamarr – the journalist he was meant to ring before me hadn't picked up, so he'd decided to move straight on to me.

It was good practice though in the art of completely blagging it – and despite having no prepared questions, it actually ended up being quite a good interview. We spent a significant portion of my allotted 30 minutes talking about the years he spent presenting the early 90s TV Show *The Word*, and in particular the time when they had MC Hammer on as a studio guest. This was the infamous occasion when the baggy-trousered rap goon clearly wanted to kill Lamarr by the end of the episode, after he kept interrupting him by going "Stop. Hammertime!"

All in all, those years up in Liverpool studying for my degree were an exciting time. However, preoccupied though I was with drinking and honing my journalistic skills, and disenchanted as I'd become with football, I never forgot Forest completely…

14. In exile...

"In 2015 when Dougie Freedman returned to Forest as manager, it made me laugh to think that he'd nearly gotten me beaten up by a load of Scousers some 17 years earlier..."

For much of the time I spent living up in Liverpool whilst studying for my degree, I found it quite hard work being an exiled Forest fan.

Things would probably be very different now with the advances in technology of recent years – but back in 1998 the web was still in its infancy, and being up in Merseyside there was no way I could pick up BBC Radio Nottingham.

All in all then, information on the Reds was pretty scant - and for my three years at university, I survived largely on a meagre diet of occasional text message titbits off my Dad, and a postal subscription to the *Nottingham Evening Post's* weekly *Football Post*.

That said, the spectre of football still loomed large throughout my time away at uni. Liverpool is of course home to two of England's biggest clubs – and Liverpool and Everton fans are among the most passionate supporters you'll find anywhere.

During my time up in Merseyside, it wasn't actually an uncommon occurrence to spot members of the Liverpool or Everton teams while out and about. I remember once being on a night out with some friends in a city centre club when it suddenly dawned on me that a flamboyantly-dressed man throwing some impressive shapes just across from us on the dancefloor was none other than Everton's Portuguese full-back Abel Xavier!

Most of the new friends that I made at uni were also massively into football. I'd learned by this stage in my life that the beautiful game can be a great icebreaker when it comes to meeting new people – and allegiances among my new social circle ranged from Manchester City to Plymouth Argyle.

Within this group there were three guys called Paul, Jon and Ed, who I lived with in halls of residence during my first year. Among many other things, we bonded over a shared love of *Scorer* in the *Daily Mirror* – a slightly tongue-in-cheek daily cartoon depicting the ongoing adventures of a fictional footballer called Dave Storey, who was prolific both on the pitch and off it. At one point we even started cutting out the cartoons from the paper every day and sticking them up on the wall in our hallway. After a while it started stretching up the stairs, resembling some sort of low-rent version of the Bayeux Tapestry.

I even cheated on Forest on a number of occasions during my uni days, by tagging along with Jon to a few Plymouth games - and if nothing else, those outings to places like Halifax, Macclesfield and Rochdale are part of the reason why I'm less than ten grounds away from having visited all 92 of England and Wales' football league stadiums. Over the years I've actually become quite partial to a day out at the football as a neutral – it's amazing how much you can relax and enjoy a game for what it is when you don't really care either way who wins.

But I did make the odd Forest game as well during my uni days – either when I made the 112 mile journey to go home to Nottingham for the weekend, or if the Reds happened to be playing within striking distance of Liverpool.

The shortest distance I ever had to travel was when Forest played Liverpool at Anfield – a fixture that fell just a month after my arrival at uni. My first few weeks up in Liverpool had seen me fall into a relationship with a girl who was actually a Liverpool fan, so I went to the game with her and sat with the natives. Naturally, I had a wry smile to myself when they started singing "We hate Nottingham Forest" – with the travelling Forest fans to our right immediately shouting them down with the obligatory cry of "AND NOTTINGHAM FOREST HATE YOU, YOU BASTARDS!"

Of course, when Forest went a goal down after only a few minutes there was a certain sense of inevitability about the afternoon – after all, it's a well-known that Forest never bloody win at Anfield.

But against the odds, the Reds went up the other end and got an unlikely equaliser, with striker Dougie Freedman bundling the ball into the back of the net in front of the Kop. Given that I was sitting with the home fans, I'd been sensibly trying to keep a lid on my allegiance to Forest – however, the sheer novelty of seeing the Reds actually score at Anfield saw me momentarily forget where I was and leap to my feet in celebration.

In 2015 when Dougie Freedman returned to Forest as manager, it made me laugh to think that he'd nearly gotten me beaten up by a load of Scousers some 17 years earlier!

As it was though, any animosity that the Liverpool fans felt towards me quickly turned to pity. Yes, the foothold Forest had gained back in the game was only very brief, and Liverpool ended up cruising to a comfortable 5-1 win.

And such a thrashing was nothing out of ordinary during that season....

Having just climbed back to the Premier League, there had been high hopes that the Reds would kick on during the 1998-99 season and re-establish themselves as a household name in the top flight. But the club hierarchy clearly had other ideas, and before the start of the season decided to weaken the team that had gained promotion by selling Kevin Campbell and Colin Cooper, both key players – and not provide any money for manager Dave Bassett to buy replacements.

As you would expect, fans were outraged.

But one man who was seemingly more outraged than anyone was Forest's talismanic Dutch striker Pierre van Hooijdonk. Furious about the club's blatant lack of ambition, he went on strike and buggered off back to Holland – weakening the Reds' team even further. Naturally these actions didn't endear himself to many people – but it was hard to disagree with his gripe.

In spite of everything Forest did bag three points in their opening league game of the 1998-9 season. Alas though, this was anything but a sign of things to come – as following that opening day victory against Coventry, the Reds were terrible and didn't win again until January.

And it was pretty depressing stuff. Without the strikeforce of van Hooijdonk and Campbell, who had hit the back of the net some 60 times between them the previous season, goals were few and far between. In fact, it probably says everything that Steve Chettle of all people ended up becoming Forest's penalty taker around this time. Don't get me wrong, Chet is a player from my years as a Reds fan who I have huge affection for – but previously he was someone more associated with hoofing the ball into row Z than coolly sending keepers the wrong way from 12 yards!

Inevitably the long run without a win led to Dave Bassett getting sacked, with Ron Atkinson brought in as manager for the remainder of the season. The fact that Big Ron insisted on finishing a holiday in Barbados before getting to work though didn't exactly fill anyone with hope that he was the man to keep the Reds up.

Nor did the fact that he plonked himself in the wrong dugout when he finally arrived in Nottingham to take charge of his first game!

That said, Big Ron did manage to achieve that elusive win within his first few weeks in charge – and ironically for me, the long awaited victory actually occurred up in Merseyside, with Forest grinding out a 1-0 win away at Everton. I remember throwing caution to the wind that day by going out in Liverpool after the game proudly wearing my Forest shirt - and getting absolutely hammered to celebrate a rare three points. Having had months of derision from my new uni friends, who all thought it was hilarious that my team hadn't won a single match in the entire time that I'd known them, I felt that I'd earned the right.

Alas though, that win at Goodison Park failed to kick-start anything. A few weeks later Forest had a home game against Manchester United – and I decided to spend the afternoon keeping tabs on the score on Teletext. Early in the second half the Reds were still very much in the game at 2-1 down, when I nipped out to the local shops buy some milk.

Having completed my errand I rushed back hoping to see news of an equaliser – but sadly, the reality was more stark. Yes, though I'd only been gone for about 15 minutes, Forest were now losing 7-1 – and I barely had time to come to terms with that when United stuck in an eighth! Hilarious comedy figure that he is, Big Ron tried to make light of the result after the game by describing it as a "nine-goal thriller" – but nobody was really laughing.

Around this same time the Liverpool legend Alan Hansen had just released his autobiography – and was doing a series of book signings around Merseyside to help promote it. And being a fan of sporting autobiographies and having a grudging respect for Hansen in spite of his association with Liverpool Football Club, I decided to go along to one of these signings to meet the man and get a copy of his tome.

By this time it was a good few years since Hansen had retired from playing, but he'd since established himself as a pundit on *Match of the Day* – where he'd developed a reputation for his outspoken and sometimes quite cantankerous opinions. When I eventually got to the front of the queue though, I actually found him to be a thoroughly lovely bloke – and after I told him about my own footballing allegience, he even referenced one of his famous *Match of the Day* catchphrases when signing my copy of his book.

"Dear Rich," he wrote, "shocking defending from Forest! Best wishes, Alan Hansen."

The Liverpool legend's comment was quite apt really. After all, the Reds conceded a total of 69 goals that season – more than any other team in the Premier League.

With such a leaky defence, it was no surprise when Forest were relegated at the end of the campaign – and at the time of writing, they've never returned to the Premier League since.

The Reds slipping into the footballing wilderness also meant there would be no repeat for me of those short journeys to Anfield and Goodison Park in my second and third years at uni.

In all honesty though, Forest losing their place among English football's elite didn't really upset me too much at the time. After all, there'd been a grim sense of the Reds being doomed for months.

What's more, I'd been pretty busy with the distractions of university life and only been to about three games throughout the whole season – so I didn't feel like I was too emotionally involved.

In fact, far worse than suffering relegation from the Premier League, the low point of my entire time as an exiled fan came the following season.

At the time Forest were languishing in mid-table in English football's second tier – and inexplicably, Sky Sports had decided that the Reds' home league game against Huddersfield midway through the season was worthy of live coverage. It was a Sunday lunchtime kick-off - so I dragged myself out of bed, pulled on my Forest shirt, and went up to the student union bar to watch it.

A couple of hours later I was wishing I hadn't bothered – as Forest slumped to a dismal 3-1 defeat. And to compound my woes, the other five people who'd made the effort to get themselves to the student union to watch the match in an otherwise empty bar were all Huddersfield fans!

By this point in time David Platt was in charge as the Reds' manager. And to begin with, things had looked promising – with the former England midfielder pulling off the inspired coup of bringing in his old mate Ian Wright on loan.

But sadly, that was pretty much Platt's only success in the transfer market. Most of the other players he brought in at huge expense turned out to be complete and utter wastes of money – and his Forest team played some of the most lacklustre football I've ever seen.

All in all then, you wouldn't have thought there was much chance of me getting sucked back into the world I once occupied any time soon, where Forest matches were the main event of my week.

But sucked back in I was…

15. Sucked back in

"The travelling Forest fans proceeded to heap further requests on the veteran shot-stopper – who even complied with a request of "Beasant, show us yer arse!" by gleefully 'mooning' the away end!"

During the first two years of my time away at university up in Liverpool, I only went to watch Forest a total of about half a dozen times. And given that I'd had a season ticket at the City Ground for the previous nine seasons, I think it's fair to say this sporadic level of attendance represented a drastic decline in my level of support for the mighty Reds.

Of course, I might have made a bit more of an effort had Forest been doing a bit better. As documented though in the previous chapter, my first year at uni was marked by the Reds getting relegated from the Premier League; while my second year coincided with the first of David Platt's two hugely underwhelming seasons as manager.

It's also quite lonely supporting a team when you don't have anyone to share your passion with – and throughout my first two years up in Liverpool, I didn't meet a single other Forest fan. With the rise of social media over the last couple of decades I imagine it's a lot easier these days for young people to meet folk with the same obscure interests when they go away to university. Sadly though, the only Instagram we had during my student days was the dodgy lad who used to lurk in a dark corner of the student union bar selling drugs.

As they say though, all good things come to those who wait. And shortly after I began my third and final year up in Liverpool, a fellow scholar sidled up to me one evening in that same student union bar - and uttered a string of words that have remained permanently etched on my consciousness ever since.

"This might sound strange," said the stranger, "but did you go and watch Nottingham Forest play away at Crewe last season?"

As a chat-up line, it was irresistible. Indeed, it came as no surprise later on when this guy came to be known by the nickname 'The Lothario', due to his winning way with the ladies.

Yes, I had been at Crewe.

And so had he.

And in those few seconds, a great friendship was born...

My new friend, I discovered, was called Andy Best. He was also a massive Forest fan, and – like me – was also embarking on his final year at Liverpool John Moores University. And a few months previously, he'd made the short trip down from Liverpool to go and watch the Reds play away at Crewe.

I'd also gone to the same game – one of those few occasions when I'd actually made the effort to go and watch Forest during my first two years up in Liverpool. And during the afternoon, Andy had spotted me across the crowd and recognised my face from the fact that we'd been studying in the same building for a good couple of years. He'd made a mental note to collar me next time he saw me around the university – and I was glad that he did.

Finally, I had someone in Liverpool I could go for a beer with and share my despair over the idiocy of David Platt!

What's more, Forest fans exiled in Liverpool proved that they are rather like buses – in the sense that you wait for ages for one to turn up... and then two come along seemingly within a matter of minutes!

Yes, just days after making acquaintance with Andy, another Reds fan came into my life – a lass called Rachel Hardy.

Sadly there's no devastating chat-up line in this story. However, it is still quite a cool story as to how I met Rach – as we actually got chatting on a platform at Stockport station... where we'd both found ourselves stranded due to the fecklessness of Central Trains.

A bit of polite smalltalk while we waited for a replacement train had revealed that Rach, like me, was in her final year at university in Liverpool... and, like me, was on her way back there after a visit home.

But most excitingly of all, she was also a Forest fan!

Interestingly, my two new friends both had similar back stories, both of them being Forest fans despite the fact that neither had grown up anywhere near Nottingham – with Rach from Norwich and Andy from Sussex. Rach did have family roots in Nottingham, hence her supporting the Reds. With Andy though, his decision was borne simply out of the fact that the first ever football match he'd watched on telly when he was a kid was a Forest game.

Inevitably, it wasn't long before arrangements were made between Andy, Rach and myself to meet up and go and watch Forest together. And conveniently, the Reds had an away match in a few weeks' time just a short train ride from Liverpool – at Stockport, funnily enough.

Much like the Three Musketeers then, Andy, Rach and me set off from Liverpool. It wasn't a particularly good game, and it poured down with rain for most of the afternoon – which meant we got absolutely drenched while standing on the open terrace behind the goal. But it was all worth it – as with the match looking like it was heading for a 1-1 draw, Jack Lester popped up with a decisive goal to bag the three points for the Reds just two minutes from time.

As we all know, late winning goals are always the greatest winning goals of all – and when we arrived back in Liverpool after the game, it seemed only right to embark on an epic drinking session to celebrate. Randomly, our night out saw us bump into much-reviled D-list celebrity Darren Day, who was appearing on stage in the city in a musical at the time. I seem to recall that we got the infamous tabloid love rat to autograph one of our Stockport v Forest tickets – though with none of us having a pen, he ended up using some girl's lipstick.

Probably as niche a bit of Forest memorabilia as you're ever likely to find!

Needless to say, such japes are the bedrock upon which lifelong friendships are built. What's more, I suddenly had a reason to start going to watch Forest again – and over the remainder of the 2000-01 season, Andy, Rach and myself continued to squander our precious student funds on further trips to cheer on the mighty Reds. Our various adventures included a relatively 'local' outing to see the Reds at Tranmere, where I witnessed one of my favourite things I've ever seen at a football match – namely, a player starting a song!

The player in question was goalkeeper Dave Beasant, who was a popular figure with Forest fans at the time. During the first half of the game at Prenton Park, Beasant was guarding the goal in front of the away end – and during a point in the proceedings where he wasn't having a lot to do, the travelling Forest fans started singing "Beasant, giz a song, Beasant Beasant giz a song!"

Now I've already talked in an earlier chapter about what a nice bloke I'd found Beasant to be on a previous occasion when I'd met him. Well on this afternoon at Tranmere, he went up even further in my estimation, because he actually accepted the challenge from the travelling Reds fans – turning round and imploring everyone to shush before bellowing a rendition of "Forest 'til I die! I'm Forest 'til I die! I know I am, I'm sure I am, I'm Forest 'til I die…"!

A brilliant moment – and given that Beasant was clearly up for anything, the travelling Forest fans proceeded to heap further requests on the veteran shot-stopper – who even complied with a request of "Beasant, show us yer arse!" by gleefully 'mooning' the away end!

To be fair, it was all probably pretty tame compared to some of the stuff Beasant got up to earlier on in his playing career back in the 80s, when he was a member of Wimbledon's infamous 'Crazy Gang'. Nevertheless, it's always refreshing when players don't take themselves too seriously – and Beasant is clearly someone who relishes a bit of a laugh and a joke with the fans. Indeed, I heard a hilarious story about a time only a few years ago when he attended a Chelsea home game as guest of honour, with the Londoners being another of his former clubs. As is customary in these situations, he was brought out onto the pitch before kick-off to be introduced to the fans, and generally got a welcome reception. I say 'generally' though, because Chelsea happened to be playing Liverpool that day – so as well as the warm applause of the home fans, he also found himself being serenaded by the Scouse fans with a chorus of "Who the fucking hell are you?"

Beasant's response to this however was absolutely brilliant. Most football fans will remember the famous moment from Beasant's playing days when he saved a penalty in Wimbledon's shock victory over Liverpool in the 1988 FA Cup final at Wembley. That afternoon then at Stamford Bridge, Beasant took the opportunity to remind the Scousers exactly who the fucking hell he was - by turning to face them, and cheekily re-enacting his famous save.

Priceless!

Probably my funniest memory though from all the Forest games I went to with Andy and Rach over the 2000-01 season came during an away trip where Forest's Norwegian centre half Jon Olav Hjelde hadn't been picked to be part of the Reds squad - but had decided to come and watch the game anyway, and sit in the away end with the travelling fans.

Alas, I can't remember who the Reds were playing that day. But wherever it was, it caused a ripple of excitement through the travelling fans when word began to spread that we had one of the players sat among us. And at half-time I actually ended up standing only a few feet away from the big defender, when I found myself just a few places behind him in a large queue of people making their way into the toilets.

Now this scenario could have resulted in me acquiring one of those 'the time I stood next to someone famous in the bogs' stories that us blokes are fond of telling. However, rather than use the urinals when he got to the front of the queue, Hjelde instead opted to hang back and wait for one of the cubicles to become free. And brilliantly, a bloke with a foghorn voice quickly clocked this – and immediately started singing "Hjelde needs a shit, Hjelde needs a shit… ee-aye-addio, Hjelde needs a shit!"

Inevitably, loads of other fans waiting for the bogs quickly began to join in with the song – with Hjelde looking a bit embarrassed but amused on the whole.

Eventually the big defender was able to escape into a vacant cubicle, although even then there was little chance of him being able to enjoy a nice peaceful poo – with the words of the song simply changing at that point to "Hjelde's *having* a shit!"

One bloke even made a point of banging on the cubicle door and shouting "Keep it tight at the back, Jon!"

A hilarious moment – who said terrace wit has slowly died out over the last couple of decades?

That said, the assumption that Hjelde was having a number two was very much a case of two and two being put together. After all, there could have been any number of other reasons why he actually opted for the cubicle that day. Perhaps it was simply a desire for privacy? Or maybe he didn't want to run the risk of any 'splashback' on his immaculate suede brogues if he joined the throng at the urinals?

If he had indeed gone in to take a dump, he was clearly a braver man than I. I'm quite proud to say that I've never once been for a poo at a match during my entire 25-plus years as a football fan – with my determination to avoid doing so entirely down to the grim toilet facilities at most grounds up and down the country.

For all the amusing shenanigans though such as mooning goalkeepers and pooping centre-halves, the actual football that Forest were playing under David Platt was still pretty terrible. However, my new friends and I were having such a laugh together on our various trips to see matches that it hardly seemed to matter. Rach and me even made a solemn vow at one point that we'd both get Forest tattoos if the Reds got promoted. It's perhaps just as well that they didn't!

And as I got to know them better, my friendships with Andy and Rach quickly moved beyond just football. It turned out we were also all into similar music, which led to regular trips to see live bands as well as Forest – not to mention numerous nights out on the sauce. At the time Andy was working a few nights a week in a legendary grothole of a club in Liverpool called the Blue Angel, so we'd usually end up there.

Of course, one thing you're probably wondering as I recount my blossoming friendships with Andy and Rach is whether there were any romantic goings on within our little group.

Now for those of you hoping for a bit of sex in this book, I'm afraid you're going to be disappointed. That said, with Andy being widely known at the time as The Lothario, it's perhaps no surprise that there was a point when he tried to work his silver-tongued charm on Rach during a particularly drunken night out in Liverpool – although she rebuffed his advances with a classic line that's gone down in legend among the three of us.

"Stop it Andy," she said, "I don't think David Platt would approve!"

To be fair, we didn't really approve of David Platt either.

But despite the questionable job that Platt was doing at the time as Forest's manager, the fact that I now had two people with whom I could share my passion meant I was suddenly far more enthused about the Reds than I had been for a good couple of years.

What's more, things stepped up even further when I headed home from Liverpool at the end of the year 2000 to spend the Christmas break back in Nottingham with my family.

That year Forest had a home fixture on Boxing Day against Crewe – and with my interest in the Reds having been rekindled, I decided on the day to head down to the City Ground to watch the match.

As was pretty much customary under David Platt, the game was terrible. It goes down in history as a 1-0 win for Forest, but I struggle to recall a single thing about what happened on the pitch that afternoon.

What I do remember though is an advert on the scoreboard at half-time, announcing that the club were offering half-season tickets for the remainder of the season for just £44 for under-21s.

Now at this point in the season there were still a dozen or so home games left – so £44 for a half season ticket worked out at less than four quid per game. In fact, even if I only made it to half of them, it would've still represented pretty good value for money. And so it was then that I traipsed round to the ticket office as soon as the final whistle went, in order to do the deed and resume my status as a Forest season ticket holder after a two-and-a-half year sabbatical.

There was the small matter that I'd actually turned 21 a few months previously – however, the staff at the ticket office didn't ask me for any proof of age, and I absolved myself of any guilt for my fraudulent behaviour on the basis that Forest were better off getting 100% of £44 than 0% of whatever the full price was. And anyhow, I think Forest would've happily taken the hit in hindsight – as I would go on to keep that seat for the next 14 seasons.

After returning to Liverpool then following the end of the Christmas break, I began embarking on regular trips back to Nottingham to attend home matches. Passing as it did all manner of sights from Old Trafford to Warrington's delightfully-named Cockhedge Shopping Park, the two-and-a-half hour train journey quickly became as familiar as the back of my hand. For Saturday games I'd usually make a weekend of it in Nottingham and catch up with my family; while for midweek games there was no choice but to make it an overnight trip, as the last train back to Liverpool left well before the full-time whistle.

There was always a major drawback with midweek games if I had to be in uni for lectures the following morning – as it meant getting up at silly o'clock to get an early train back to Liverpool in order to be there in time. But such are the lengths that all of us football fans go to in the name of supporting our beloved teams.

Naturally there was always an open invitation to both Andy and Rach to join me on these trips down to Nottingham whenever they felt like a dose of Forest. Of the two of them, Andy in particular was often game – or glutton for punishment - and for most of our trips to the City Ground we found he was able to buy a ticket on the same row, meaning we could sit together.

My seat was on the front row of the upper Bridgford End, pretty much in line with the corner flag – and I'd chosen that particular spot for a very simple reason. Yes, having previously had seats in the Executive Stand, the Trent End and the Main Stand, it meant I'd now had a season ticket on all four sides of the City Ground.

One thing that I quickly learned to love about sitting in the upper Bridgford was the fact that there was presumably a bat's roost tucked away somewhere in the rafters – as you'd often see the small flying mammals soaring through the sky near the roof of the stand during evening matches.

Perhaps more importantly, my new vantage point also offered a great view of both what was happening on the pitch, and also the away fans in the lower tier below. Sadly it was usually the latter that afforded the most entertainment, with David Platt's Forest continuing to flounder. It probably says everything that, when looking at the list of fixtures and results for the second half of that 2000-01 season, I can barely remember a single thing about any of the games.

With a squad featuring forgotten men such as Keith Foy and Tony Vaughan, Forest eventually stuttered to a bang-average eleventh place finish in the league. But there was some hope for the future for us Reds fans – as the summer saw David Platt depart the City Ground, with the FA having inexplicably decided that he was the right man to run the England under-21 team. As far as most Forest fans were concerned, it was good riddance.

That summer of 2001 also saw Andy, Rach and I all complete our degrees –

in my case with a 2:1 honours degree in journalism.

Of course, graduating from university tends to represent the end of a chapter – and Rach bade farewell to Liverpool to head back to her home town of Norwich as soon as we'd all handed back our caps and gowns.

Like those people though you get at every party who never know when it's time to leave, Andy and I decided to stick around in Merseyside – with both of us landing jobs and ending up living together in a shared house in the posh-sounding-but-not-actually-that-posh-at-all Liverpool suburb of Kensington. Flush with the novelty of actually having money in our pockets, I also splashed out on a car!

One of the best things about suddenly having wheels was that it opened up even further possibilities for Andy and I to travel to Forest games. I'd bought my trusty white Metro for the princely sum of £800 – and it actually cost more than that to insure it for a year, such was the dodgy nature of the neighbourhood that we lived in. But aside from the expense, it was glorious no longer having to rely on public transport to get our fix of the mighty Reds.

As the 2001-02 football season approached then, there was never really any question as to whether or not I'd be renewing my season ticket. And not only did I renew my own seat, I also snapped up a second season ticket for the seat next to mine. This meant Andy was always guaranteed a spot next to me whenever he wanted to come to a game. He gave me some cash in return each time he joined me on the 112-mile pilgrimage to the City Ground – and whenever he wasn't able to make it, my brother Al would generally claim the seat.

At this point Al had barely been to any games for the previous five or six years. However, those games where he bagged my spare ticket saw him lured back into the world of the Reds – to such an extent that he claimed the spare ticket as his own the following season, and would go on to keep it for the next 12 seasons.

And to be fair, those first few seasons of Al's rekindled love affair with Forest weren't a bad time. Following David Platt's departure in the summer of 2001, Forest had given the manager's job to Paul Hart - who had previously been running the club's academy. And the man was a breath of fresh air.

With the club now in financial difficulty as a result of the millions that Platt had squandered on terrible players, there was no money to spend in the transfer market - and no-one had huge expectations about how well Forest would do in the 2001-02 season. But Harty did a great job on a shoestring budget, moving on some of the dead wood and building a team around some of the talented young academy players such as Jermaine Jenas, Michael Dawson, Gareth Williams, Andy Reid and David Prutton. This was the first time in my life when players who were actually younger than I was were starting to get into the Reds' first team, which felt a bit strange. Not that I was complaining – after all, even though Forest were losing as many games as they were winning, it felt incredibly refreshing after the torture of the Platt era to watch an exciting young team who were clearly giving their all and proud as punch to be wearing the shirt.

Favourite memories of following Forest from around this time include a weekend when all the stars seemed to align – with a Saturday afternoon home game and a gig by one of my favourite bands both falling on the day of my 22nd birthday. I couldn't have asked for a better way to mark the occasion – a day in which Andy and I drove down from Liverpool to watch a 1-0 win for the Reds against Burnley, before jumping back in the car and hoofing it back to Merseyside to see a brilliant gig by Mancunian indie rock types Elbow.

During this same period there was also a Forest home game against Manchester City – which gave me the very odd experience of watching Stuart Pearce playing *against* Forest, what with Psycho having ended up at Maine Road at the very end of his playing career, following spells at Newcastle and West Ham. To this day, that game remains the only time where I can remember an opposition player being cheered by Forest fans every time he touched the ball – although to be honest I found it a bit painful watching my childhood footballing hero playing for the other team. It felt a bit like one of those times when you're out and about and you bump into an ex-girlfriend who you're still not really over, and she's arm in arm with another bloke.

Still, at least Psycho had the decency not to leather one of his trademark free-kicks into the back of the Forest net.

As well as home games meanwhile, I was also taking in the odd Forest away trip around this time - including a very eventful visit to Millwall during the October of 2001. With Liverpool to London being a fair old distance, Andy and I had decided to drive to Nottingham the night before the game and stay overnight at my Mum and Dad's - before making the rest of the journey to the game via one of Forest's official travel coaches.

As we arrived in London, it seemed like the trip was going smoothly, and it appeared that we'd be arriving at the New Den in plenty of time for kick-off. However, a few miles from the stadium, our coach was pulled over by the local police – who informed us that another coach full of Reds fans had arrived at the stadium and immediately had pretty much all of its windows put through by Millwall fans.

To reduce the risk of further similar attacks, the cops had decided to make our coach and a load of other Forest coaches wait in a lay-by until after the match had actually kicked off – the idea being that the coast would hopefully be clear by then, and they could quickly escort us all to the ground as one big convoy with minimal trouble.

As you can imagine, we were a bit annoyed that we'd be missing the kick-off – and even more annoyed when we finally arrived at our seats about ten minutes into the game to find already Forest 1-0 down. It felt like it was going to be 'one of those afternoons' – but happily Paul Hart's team had other ideas and fought their way back into the match. By the time we entered the last few minutes of the game the Reds were 3-2 up, thanks to a hat-trick from the brilliantly-named Trinidadian striker Stern John.

It was a great game, and made even more entertaining by the fact that we were sat next to Forest's infamous German 'superfan' Ebby - who practically dry-humped a slightly terrified Andy in celebration as each Forest goal flew into the back of the Millwall net!

Contrary though to the jubilant scenes among the travelling Forest fans, the Millwall faithful were not at all happy - and reacted to the Reds' third goal by launching a firework into the away end. Unsurprisingly this caused outrage among those who were lucky not to have been seriously injured – although the stewards pretty much just shrugged their shoulders as if to say "What do you expect? This is Millwall!"

That afternoon remains the one occasion when I've actually felt quite glad to see the Reds concede a late equaliser – as it genuinely felt like we'd probably get killed leaving the ground if Forest had taken all three points. Indeed, I discovered some time later that a film crew had attended the game that day to make a documentary about hooliganism at Millwall - and if you type 'Forest Millwall violence' into YouTube, you can still see harrowing footage of some of the scenes outside the ground after the match. In the clips hundreds of

Millwall fans can be seen running amok through the streets, throwing bricks and anything they can get their hands on at anyone who looks like a Forest fan, while a police helicopter buzzes overhead and coppers with riot shields try in vain to control the situation.

Goodness knows what it must be like when they play West Ham!

Fortunately Andy and I made it out of south east London unscathed - and aside from that slightly terrifying afternoon at Millwall, our adventures following the mighty Reds around this time were largely trouble-free. It was a brilliant time which we both still reminisce about often, and we clocked up thousands of miles in my trusty white Metro, obligatory red and white scarf flapping out of one of the back windows.

Many of those hours on the road were soundtracked by a cassette of Cherry Red Records' Forest album, and also a 'driving rock' compilation tape. The latter was one that Andy and I had compiled ourselves, after we crashed at my Mum and Dad's house in Nottingham following a Forest home game - and came in really drunk and decided it'd be hilarious to ransack some of the dodgier fringes of my folks' CD collection. Over the next few months, the two of us felt truly heroic over on our various trips to go and cheer on the Reds, as we thundered along the A50 or the M6 with classic guilty pleasures like 'Africa' by Toto or 'Gimme All Your Lovin' by ZZ Top blaring out of the car's tinny speakers.

Alas though, all good things invariably come to an end – and one fateful day I poked my head out of our front door in Liverpool to find an empty space where the white Metro was normally parked. Yes, some robbing scumbags had gone and nicked it – and it was later found written off. And to cap it off, the thieving gits had also lifted mine and Andy's 'driving rock' tape.

I think we were actually more gutted about that than the car!

The sad demise of the white Metro felt like the end of an era – and it was the end of an era in another way too. Having both decided to stay up in Liverpool after we graduated from uni, Andy and I actually both lasted less than a year before we eventually moved back to our respective home towns.

For both of us, the decision was partly career-orientated. In my case, I'd bagged a new job back in Nottingham – something I'm convinced I have Forest to thank for, given that the bloke who interviewed me for the role and who became my manager was a massive Reds fan. In fact, during the couple of years that I spent in that job, my boss even let me skive off work to go down to the City Ground to queue for tickets for a big cup game – providing I got his as well while I was down there!

But as well as advancement of my own career, I think it's fair to say that my decision to move back to Nottingham was driven in no small part by the fact that Forest home games would suddenly be much more accessible.

Many folk would tell you that it's ridiculous to allow your support for a team to have such a bearing on major life decisions – and they'd probably have a point.

But such is the mindset of the football fan...

Above even Forest though, there was one reason above any other why I needed to get out of Liverpool and get back to Nottingham.

Yes, I was getting a Scouse accent!

Joking aside, Merseyside remains a place that I have huge love for – and I feel lucky that I moved away from Nottingham to get a degree but also ended up finding myself a home away from home as part of the bargain.

It always amazes me when I compare my experiences with other people I know who moved away from their home town to go to university. I actually have several friends who completed their degrees and have never once returned to the city where they studied.

On the other hand, even though it's a good few years since I graduated, I still try and get back up to Liverpool at least once a year. Having stayed on in the city and worked for a while after I finished uni, I made quite a few friends from outside the student bubble who were locals – and as such, I still know a fair few people up there. This includes a group of lads I refer to affectionately as the 'Orrible Scrotes' – all big football fans too, although being native Scousers they're a mixture of lifelong Liverpool and Everton fans.

As it happens, Forest have never actually played Liverpool or Everton in the entire time I've known the Scrotes, although over the years I've dragged most of them along with me to see the Reds at some point - usually when there's been an away game up in the north west, and I've used it as an excuse to go and visit my old Merseyside stomping ground. A couple of the gang still laugh to this day about the time they joined me for what is widely regarded as one of the dismal Forest games of modern times – a 3-0 away defeat at Chester City in the FA Cup back in 2005, during the dark days of Gary Megson's tenure as manager. As well as the comically bad game of football my friends were forced to endure, the afternoon has also stuck in the memory for a hilarious episode when we were making our way back to the car after full-time, and found ourselves threatened by the local 'firm'. I use the term loosely though – they were actually a bunch of spotty Herberts, whose idea of intimidating a group of six foot-plus blokes was to address us with possibly the least convincing battlecry ever unleashed in the history of football violence.

"Come on then you Forest nuggets!"

Rather than soiling our kecks like our deluded assailants presumably hoped we would, we all just fell about laughing at the ludicrousness of it all. Bless 'em, they didn't quite know what to do from this point, and after a few seconds of standing there awkwardly they eventually just scuttled off sheepishly into the shadows. For me it was a much-needed dose of hilarity after what had been a tough afternoon to be a Reds fan – and over a decade on, the Scrotes still sometimes refer to Forest in a tongue-in-cheek fashion as 'The Nuggets'!

Of all the friendships though I made during my time up in Liverpool, it's Andy and Rach who can claim by far the biggest part in my Forest story. Nearly two decades on I'm happy to say that the two of them both remain really good friends – and despite living fair distances from Nottingham, they both still make the effort to get up to the City Ground every now and then. Naturally it's always great to see them when they do. That said, the fact that Forest always seem to lose whenever Andy is in attendance has seen him develop a reputation over the years as something of a bad luck charm - in that slightly arrogant way that us football fans think our actions, whether it be simply being there or going for the time-honoured 'tactical piss', have any effect whatsoever on the outcome of a game.

Of course with the passing of years life has changed a fair bit for all of us since our student days. We're all married now – yes, even people known as The Lothario settle down eventually - and we all have families and sensible jobs.

In fact, the chain of events that ultimately led to Rach's marriage can be traced all the way back to that fateful afternoon when her and I met for the first time on that railway platform in Stockport.

Had I decided to get an earlier or later train that day, I probably wouldn't ever have met Rach.

But meet we did – and a couple of years later, a Forest-supporting friend of mine called Andy Cross got a new job that involved him moving out to East Anglia.

With him not knowing anyone in that part of the world, I decided to put Andy C in touch with Rach, who by that point was happily settled back in Norwich. The two of them immediately became friends – and over the next few years, Rach ended up getting married to Andy C's best mate… while Andy C ended up getting married to Rach's best mate.

So far then, one chance encounter on a railway platform has led to two marriages and three children - it's mind-boggling really how relatively trivial choices that we make in our day-to-day lives can sometimes go on to have a butterfly effect later down the line. Brilliantly, with Rach and her fella Drei having written their own vows, part of their wedding in 2015 involved Drei having to make a solemn oath never to support Derby County!

As for the other Andy, I can't take any credit for his marriage – however, I did manage to subject a large group of his mates to some pretty terrible football in early 2008 by organising a trip to see Forest play a League One fixture away at Leyton Orient as part of his stag do.

I also managed to orchestrate a bit of a Forest-related surprise for him on the day of his actual wedding…

Now Andy committed the heinous crime of not only getting married during football season, but also on a Forest matchday - with him and his partner Amanda choosing to tie the knot on the same day Forest were playing Cheltenham Town at the City Ground.

With Andy being a close friend there was no question of where I'd be that afternoon – so in the run-up to the wedding I made arrangements to give my season ticket away for the day.

As it turned out, I would not only be missing the match, but also the opportunity to meet a member of Forest's all-conquering team of the late 70s and early 80s. Yes, Larry Lloyd had just released his autobiography - and it was announced on the week of the game that he'd be appearing in the club shop prior to kick-off to sign copies.

Holding no grudges against the big defender after our little run-in during my days publishing *Forest Forever*, I decided I'd very much like to get my hands on a copy of his book. Good egg that he is, my brother Al agreed to go along to the book signing and pick up a signed copy for me – and when he texted me on the day to confirm that he was in the queue for the signing session, I decided to push my luck and ask my esteemed sibling for one additional favour.

"Al," I asked, "when you get to the front of the queue, any chance you can quickly ring Andy's number on your mobile, pass your phone to Larry Lloyd – and get Larry to offer him his congratulations on his wedding day?"

Luckily for me, Al is usually happy to go along with my daft ideas - and Larry was also game.

Now with the book signing taking place only an hour or so before Andy was due to get married, it was far from certain whether he would actually answer his phone.

But answer it he did…

"Hi Andy, this is Larry Lloyd," the big man said down the phone in his distinctive rasp. "I've heard you're a big Forest fan and that you're getting married today, so I just wanted to offer my congratulations…"

However, the call had actually flashed up on Andy's phone as 'Al mobile' – and so it was that one of Forest's all-time greatest players found himself being berated with a bemused cry of "Fuck off Al, I know it's you – your Larry Lloyd impersonation is shit!"

From my one and only previous encounter with Larry Lloyd , I knew that he wasn't a man to mince his words – and I was slightly worried about how he might react to being told to fuck off. Fortunately though, he saw the funny side!

All in all, Andy and Rach stand testament to what I regard as the one of the most important things about being a football fan – namely, the wonderful friendships you make through your team. Though in some ways, I still haven't quite forgiven the two of them for the part they played in getting me back into watching Forest again, given how terrible the Reds have largely been in the years since!

That said, getting sucked back into the dark web of my beloved team did lead to me making another great friendship…

16. The Bloke Who Sits Next To Me Who Looks Like Gordon Ramsay

"There were times during the first decade of the 21st Century when it felt like Forest were on some sort of perverse kamikaze mission and constantly trying to outdo themselves to achieve new levels of awfulness…"

Now when you buy a season ticket for your football team, it's a bit of a lottery in terms of who you'll end up sitting next to for the whole season.

I've certainly been stuck with some pretty dubious people at the City Ground over the years – not least a moaning guy who looked like Elton John, and a bloke who had the grim habit of unleashing sudden involuntary burps throughout the game.

They always say you should keep a healthy distance from your neighbours - and the same probably applies to football.

Indeed, in over two decades as a season ticket holder at Forest, I sat next to dozens of different people, some for quite a few years - and while most of them have seemed perfectly pleasant folk, my interactions generally went little further than exchanging a few banal bits of chit chat.

But there has been one exception…

Following my decision mid-way through the 2000-01 season to buy a half season ticket, I quickly got back into the ritual of going to every Forest home game again - and after a few matches, I started sharing the odd exchange with the bloke who sat in the seat next to me.

Initially I only knew him as The Bloke Who Sits Next To Me Who Looks Like Gordon Ramsay.

Gradually though, I learned that his name was Graham.

Now friendships come and go in all walks of life - and this has very much been the case with people who I've met through Forest. In fact some of the friends mentioned in this book are folk who I've pretty much lost touch with, as lives have gone in different directions.

But Graham has proven over the years to be one of the most enduring friends I've ever made through the mighty Reds.

As well as a shared love of Forest, it turned out as Graham and I got to know each other that we were very much on the same wavelength when it came to humour. It turned out both of us shared a similar palette of leftfield comedic reference points, ranging from the *Viz* cartoon Billy The Fish to the obscure veteran indie rock band Half Man Half Biscuit – and we began having a right laugh together on matchdays.

We also discovered over time that we were from the same part of Nottingham, and had both enjoyed the dubious pleasure of having our secondary education at Arnold Hill Comprehensive. Subsequently, many a dull afternoon at the City Ground was spent reminiscing about old teachers we had known, such as 'Pebble Head' Smith and 'Well 'Ard Woollard'. A sentence that sounds more like something from a Billy Bunter story than I'm strictly comfortable with!

When my brother Al started coming along to matches again, he also got on with Graham like a house on fire. Before long, the three of us started spending time together outside the confines of the City Ground - everything from five-a-side football kickabouts to trips to watch Forest play away. To this day, the colour still drains from Graham's face when I remind him of a time when we went in my car to see the Reds away at Hartlepool – and the journey up saw me pull a death-defying manoeuvre across several motorway lanes after it had suddenly dawned on me that we were about to miss our exit. That said, some of Forest's defending later that afternoon was a far greater potential cause of heart failure than any of my driving!

The greatest test of any friendship though is when the chips are down – and in the run-up to the 2007-08 season, Graham very much came through for me.

That summer, money was tight for me for a variety of reasons – so much so that I decided with great reluctance that I had no choice but to give up my Forest season ticket.

Bless him though, Graham immediately offered to pay for my seat – telling me I could pay him back whenever I could afford it. It was a wonderful gesture, and one I will never forget.

And needless to say, I eventually paid him back every penny.

I honestly think the laughs that Al and I had with Graham were the main reason we kept renewing our season tickets year after year. It certainly wasn't the quality of the football that Forest were laying on! Indeed, there were times during the first decade of the 21st Century when it felt like Forest were on some sort of perverse kamikaze mission, and constantly trying to outdo themselves to achieve new levels of awfulness.

Most notably, the Reds managed at the end of the 2004-05 season to get themselves relegated to League One – becoming the first European Cup winners to plummet to the third tier of their own domestic league. And as if that wasn't bad enough, there was also a time during the League One years when Forest managed to get knocked out of the League Cup by a team who, thanks to a certain late-80s TV advert for milk, will always remain the epitome of atrociousness for English football fans of my age.

Of all the players that represented Forest that night at Accrington Stanley's Crown Ground, big Wes Morgan cut a particularly hapless figure as Forest slipped to a dismal 1-0 defeat. Who would have guessed at that point in time that he'd go on to become a Premier League winning captain – and for Leicester of all teams…

That said, it's not all been terrible for us Forest fans during the 21st Century. There have been the occasional good times too amid the general diet of mediocrity and disappointment – not least the 2007-08 season, when the Reds finally managed to escape out of English football's third tier.

As achievements go, getting promoted from League One obviously pales in significance compared to some of Forest's other triumphs over their history. But the smash and grab manner in which the Reds did it on the very last day of the season made it incredibly memorable - not to mention the sheer jubilation of knowing that we'd finally escaped English football's wilderness after three seasons.

There have also been no less than three seasons - 2002-03, 2009-10 and 2010-11 – when Forest have even been good enough to make us fans dare to dream about a return to the Premier League. Alas, the only thing anyone really remembers now about those seasons was that the Reds ended up choking in the play-offs on each occasion. But the 46 games that it took to actually get to the play-offs in each case saw some great football.

Those three or four seasons aside though, it's been a largely forgettable time for us Forest fans since the turn of the century. In fact, there have been more seasons than I'd care to remember where more pleasure has been gained from Derby's failings than anything Forest have actually achieved.

Which is pretty sad really.

But they say that laughter is the best medicine. And as I've said, I still look back fondly on those times in spite of all the disappointments - largely because of the laughsthat Al and I shared with Graham.

Football is of course a ridiculous game on so many levels, and it's never too hard to derive humour from it.

Sometimes we laughed about what was happening on the pitch. One time there was a home game against Leicester when a marketing stunt saw free Cadbury's Boost chocolate bars given out to fans outside the ground. It probably wasn't the best idea in hindsight – as Forest fans sat in the A Block filled their pockets with the things, and then took great delight in pelting Leicester's former Reds defender Alan Rogers with them when he came over to take a throw-in.

Now I know one can't condone lobbing missiles at players – but this particular incident *was* pretty funny!

Meanwhile other moments on the pitch that brought tears of mirth to the three of us included an inexplicable own goal scored by MK Dons' Trent McLenahan right in front of us; while off the pitch, regular amusement was also provided by the travelling fans of whatever team Forest happened to be playing.

Sitting near the front of the upper Bridgford directly above the visitors' enclosure, Al, Graham and I would find ourselves targeted quite regularly by some of the gobbier away fans - and of the three of us, Al in particular would often rise to the bait. However, rather than giving them a load of verbals in response, he would generally react calmly by stroking his chin or blowing kisses - something that would wind up the visitors even more.

Best of all was when Al's antics would lead to him being subjected to what we called 'glasses face', where the away fans would taunt him for being a spectacle wearer by holding their fingers round their eyes in the shape of a pair of specs - in scenes of staggering maturity rarely seen this side of a primary school playground!

Something else that brought Al, Graham and I a great deal of entertainment – and which also never failed to rile the away fans - was during Radoslaw Majewski's time as a Forest player from 2009 to 2014. During that time, the Polish playmaker would regularly take corners for the Reds – and he was a bit of a sod for giving himself a slight advantage when doing so by placing the ball just outside the corner quadrant. Whenever he did this at the corner flag in 'our' corner, the away fans below us would invariably spot what he was up to and go ballistic in the hope of getting the attention of the ref. This became such a source of hilarity to Al, Graham and I that we started beating them to the punch each time the Reds won a corner, by throwing mock fits of outrage ourselves before they'd even had a chance to!

Our own fellow Forest fans also provided a regular source of matchday mirth for Al, Graham and I. Football matches are brilliant for 'people watching' – and for a couple of years we had a bloke who sat on the same row as us who bore an uncanny resemblance to Italian football legend Gianluca Vialli, which brought us a huge amount of amusement. There was also a point during Joe Kinnear's time as Forest manager when we became aware of an old guy who sat in the next block of seats who always brought an old briefcase with him to matches. In that classic way that you invent names for people when you don't know their actual name, the chap in question was christened, imaginatively, Briefcase Man – and with little excitement on the pitch to distract us, his battered brown leather receptacle became a huge subject of fascination to the three of us.

What was particularly intriguing was that Briefcase Man never seemed to actually open his briefcase – and as our imaginations went into overdrive, we started coming up with increasingly outlandish ideas as to what might be inside it. Probably the most ludicrous theory was that he was a prolific serial killer, and that his briefcase contained body parts of his victims that he'd dump in the Trent on his way home from the match!

Sadly, the truth turned out to be somewhat more mundane. Yes, at a home game a good year or so after we'd first become aware of Briefcase Man, I was stood by our seats chatting to Graham during the half-time interval, when suddenly my mobile started ringing. It was Al, who'd disappeared a few minutes earlier to go to the loo – and his tone of voice was one of excitement.

"Rich, you and Graham need to get yourselves down here right now," he said. "Briefcase Man has got his briefcase open!"

The two of us immediately made straight for the stairs and rushed down to the concourse. Alas though, the sight before us was distinctly underwhelming. While Pandora's Box had finally been opened, it turned out that it contained nothing more than a flask of soup and some sandwiches!

Perhaps inevitably, Briefcase Man kind of lost all his mystique after that. But Al, Graham and I soon found a new source of intrigue – a chap who sat a few metres away from us, who became known to us as Mr Angry!

Now Forest fans have had quite a lot to get angry about in recent years. But the thing that was funny about Mr Angry was that it always seemed to be the smallest things that would send him over the edge. Forest could implode and concede three sloppy goals in quick succession – and whilst clearly hacked off at the situation as any fan would be, Mr Angry would remain in full control of his emotions. A few minutes later though the Reds would commit a relatively minor crime like giving away a throw-in - and without warning he'd explode into an apoplectic torrent of unadulterated rage. It was something that never failed to bring Al, Graham and I a bit of light relief on the (many) afternoons when things weren't going so well on the pitch.

The City Ground's stewards were also an endless source of comedy gold for the three of us – not least the constant running battle that's been raging for years in the upper Bridgford of the yellow jacketed ones trying in vain to get fans to sit down. In addition, we also derived literally hours of laughter for a few years during the very early part of the 21st century from a couple of stewards who were usually on duty in the visitors' enclosure on matchdays - who we imaginatively christened Right Said Fred, on account of their ridiculous steroid-pumped physiques and matching bald heads.

Of course, stewards tend to get a lot of flak from fans – and though I wouldn't want to tar them all with the same brush, the brothers Fairbrass would spend the match strutting around like a pair of absolute wallies, clearly buzzing from the enormous sense of power that their high-vis jackets and walkie talkies gave them.

Inevitably 'Right Said Fred' quickly became cult figures to Al, Graham and I – and on days when the football wasn't much cop, we'd even spend more time watching them than the actual game. At one point Graham even had the hilarious experience of seeing one of the brothers Fairbrass somewhere other than the City Ground, when he went on a trip to Ilkeston Fair with his family and spotted one of them on duty and patrolling the site. Naturally he immediately texted Al and I to share the exciting news of this sighting!

Sadly there came a point when the brothers Fairbrass seemingly disappeared – presumably they either got proper jobs, or were perhaps redeployed to a different part of the ground. Or maybe they took the plunge and finally started that Right Said Fred tribute band?

Finally, another long-running source of amusement for Al, Graham and I was the increasingly elaborate attempts in our little corner of the City Ground to generate a bit of festive spirit each season. This all started one year when Forest were playing at home a few days before Christmas, and some of the other guys who sat a few seats from us brought mince pies to the match with them, and started passing them down the row midway through the game.

It was an excellent gesture – and a much-loved annual traditional on our row was duly born, with everyone getting into the spirit and bringing festive goodies along to whichever home game fell nearest to Christmas.

Being the sorts of idiots that we are though, Al and I were always keen to up the ante each year – and one year we ended up somehow smuggling a massive chocolate Yule log into the City Ground, which caused a great deal of laughter as we proceeded to carve it up midway through the game and pass the pieces down the row on disposable paper plates!

On Boxing Day 2008 I even brought along a box of Christmas crackers. As it turned out though, no-one was really in the mood to pull them, as Forest killed all feelings of festive joy by getting thrashed 4-2 by Doncaster Rovers - a grim defeat that led to the Reds' manager Colin Calderwood getting sacked just a few hours after the final whistle.

Like many things that are borne of camaraderie, a lot of the things that Al and I spent many an afternoon at the City Ground laughing about with Graham are the sorts of things that are hard to explain to anyone else.

Even our own families!

There came a point after we'd known him for a few years when Graham started bringing his two daughters to matches - and I can recall plenty of occasions when even Megan and Connie clearly thought the three of us were completely off our rockers, as we laughed ourselves silly over the various in-jokes we've accumulated over the years.

The crusty sweatshirt.

Smoulds.

The wasted Isaac Hayes birthday present.

The Steve Cotterill Memorial Bike Horn.

Dog man.

The cheese terrorists.

The loomer.

"Where's your tool?"

The swordsman.

70s man.

Peter Ndlouv and the case of mistaken identity.

Fat Digester.

Old Fothergill.

The Curly Wurly thief.

I only have to mention any of these things to Graham, and I can guarantee he will crack up. But if I try to explain them to anyone else, I'm more likely to end up being sectioned under the Mental Health Act!

There was one in-joke that probably brought greater mirth into mine, Al and Graham's matchday experience than any other – and that was the birth of a mysterious character known only as 'Carl From Carlton'.

More of which later…

17. The Church of Stuart Pearce

"Picking fault with Stuart Pearce for his use of the Queen's English is a bit like criticising William Shakespeare for his inability to scythe down tricky right wingers..."

So then, the Church of Stuart Pearce.

It's a tall tale that's given this book its title – and having waded your way through over 60,000 words to get this far, you could be forgiven for wanting to know by this point what the story is.

Or you may have just flicked straight to this chapter.

Either way, the Church of Stuart Pearce was founded entirely by accident in 2003 during a trip that summer to the Glastonbury festival.

Now ever since I was 15 and made an illicit underage trip to the legendary Nottingham music venue Rock City to see a solo gig by Iron Maiden frontman Bruce Dickinson, I've always loved going to see live music. In fact, I've often thought over the years that going to watch a football match and going to see a band are strikingly similar experiences on many levels – from the sense of anticipation you get beforehand, to the feeling of being part of a crowd, to the way you end up losing yourself amid a visceral battering of the senses.

It's perhaps no surprise then that folk who are really into football often tend to be really into music too. That Bruce Dickinson gig certainly put me well onto the path of becoming one of those sorts of people - and after getting a few gigs under my belt, I decided at the age of 16 to take things to the next level. Yes, armed with a £29.99 Argos tent, I headed off to my first ever music festival.

The event in question was a four day-long bash called the Phoenix Festival, which took place in Warwickshire during the summer of 1996 - and over the weekend I got to see all sorts of bands from the Prodigy to the Sex Pistols.

It's funny, as music festivals seem to be regarded as cool nowadays - with the blanket coverage of Glastonbury on the BBC, and backstage areas crammed with A-listers.

But back in the mid-90s, you were generally considered a bit of a strange fish by most of society if you chose to go to them.

Still, even as a teenager I was never one to worry too much what other people thought – and having had a brilliant time at the Phoenix Festival, such events became an annual summer ritual for me. There were even numerous times when Forest had to play second fiddle to the irresistible prospect of spending three or four nights kipping in a field and immersing myself in wall-to-wall live music. Glastonbury was always safe territory because it happens every year in June, and thus there was never any chance of an awkward clash with the fixture list. However, the Reading Festival has always been held over the August Bank Holiday – and as such there was more than one year as a teenager when I chose rock over Reds.

Thanks to the wonders of modern technology, it's quite easy these days to keep up-to-date with how your team is getting on if you happen to be away at a festival. Back in the late 90s though most people still didn't have mobile phones, so there was a ritual at Reading at around 5pm on the Saturday when all the afternoon's football scores would be read out over the PA system. It was always quite an amusing experience being in a field among thousands of people all carefully listening to try and hear how their team had got on – and seeing reactions ranging from ecstasy to despair as each score was read out.

Happily, I was on the right side of that particular fence at Reading '97, when the news came through that Forest had bagged a 1-0 win away at Oxford United.

There have also been a few occasions over the years when my two passions of Forest and live music have dovetailed quite neatly – perhaps never more so than the summer of 2005, when one of my favourite ever bands, R.E.M., played a massive outdoor show at the City Ground.

Sadly it chucked down with rain for most of the evening – nevertheless, the combination of band and location made it pretty much my dream gig. What's more, the football season that had just finished had been a long and turgid one for Forest, ending with the Reds being relegated to League One – so it was the first time in a while I'd gone to the City Ground and actually enjoyed myself!

In the context of the Reds' woes, it actually felt strangely appropriate standing somewhere around the halfway line on the covered-up pitch and watching Michael Stipe sing 'Everybody Hurts'. Though for reasons that have never been made clear as far as I know, Forest never again hosted any live music after that.

A few years before that R.E.M. gig meanwhile, in the summer of 2001, I went on a European road trip with a couple of friends to go to Germany's Rock Am Ring festival – and during the weekend we actually ended up chatting to the Manic Street Preachers, who were one of the bands performing.

Now despite having grown up in Wales, the Manics' singer James Dean Bradfield is well-known for being a Forest fan – and in the brief chat we had with him I asked him his views on David Platt, who at the time had just completed a second underwhelming season as the Reds' manager. As someone who never had much time for Platt, I was quite surprised by Bradfield's view that the club should "give him another season" – although it was all immaterial just a few weeks later, when the former England midfielder decided to leave the City Ground on his own accord.

The Manics were on the bill again in 2003 when myself and some friends decided to go to Glastonbury – and as we were loading my car with our camping equipment, we decided on a whim to take Stuart Pearce with us.

Although when I say Stuart Pearce, I of course mean a lifesize cardboard cutout of the great man...

Now I'd owned this effigy of Psycho since I was 12 years old, back in the early 90s. At that time the Forest left-back and captain was very much in his pomp – and the club had decided to cash in on his popularity by marketing a limited edition run of Psycho cardboard cutouts for £20 a pop.

Naturally, I had to have one – and brilliantly, Forest launched them by arranging a signing session where you could get your cardboard cutout autographed by the man himself.

Ever willing to indulge my love of all things Forest, my Mum had agreed to take me along – and we arrived at the City Ground to find ourselves in the rather surreal situation of standing in a room with loads of Stuart Pearces!

In two-dimensional form, Psycho was wearing full Forest kit, and his face bore the slightly awkward expression of a man who hadn't been wholly comfortable with having his photo taken for the purpose of creating a lifesize cardboard cutout. His trademark blonde bowl cut had a slight side-parting, and looked suspiciously blow-dried. The Reds skipper was also posing with his hands behind his back, which was a bit disappointing - as I'd been hoping the existence of the cardboard cutouts would allow a closer look at something that at the time had long been a source of great intrigue to us Forest fans.

Yes, Psycho's tattoo…

It seems funny now when you look back, because in the modern era the majority of professional footballers seem to have entire 'sleeves' of tattoos covering both arms. But back in the early 90s it was quite rare for players to be 'inked' – and what exactly it was that Psycho had branded on his right arm had been a hot topic of debate among Forest fans for quite a few years…

For anyone who is still intrigued, I learned some years later that Psycho's tattoo is an eagle accompanied by the word 'Stuart'. That afternoon at the City Ground though it remained a mystery as Mum and I joined a long line of fellow Forest fans snaking its way towards a table where, excitingly, the actual Stuart Pearce was sat. The great man seemed to be in good spirits as he happily signed away – although when I think back to that day, I can't help but wonder whether he must have inwardly found the whole experience slightly creepy, as he watched dozens of fans walk away with cardboard cutouts of himself tucked under their arms.

At this point in my life as a Forest fan I'd never previously met Psycho – so I was a quivering wreck by the time we got to the front of the line. I'd brought a couple of other bits and pieces with me for him to sign - but as we stepped forward to approach the table where he was sitting, I ended up dropping everything all over the floor

"Do you have this effect on everyone?" I remember my Mum asking the Reds skipper as I scrabbled round on the floor picking up my stuff.

"I have the same effect on myself!" came the instant reply.

And that was about as far as our conversation with Psycho went. Looking back, I suppose I should've really taken the opportunity to ask him if I could have a look at his tattoo – although I was barely able to string a sentence together in the great man's presence.

Still, it was mission accomplished as we shuffled back to the Main Stand car-park – where it took us several minutes to successfully manoeuvre the cardboard cutout into the back of Mum's car.

Of course, owning a lifesize cardboard cutout of your footballing hero seems like a brilliant idea at the time – however, it's not long before you find yourself thinking "Okay, so what am I actually going to do with this now?" Initially, we had Psycho stationed looking out of one of the windows at the front of my Mum and Dad's house – the idea being that he'd do a great job of scaring away burglars.

Over time though, Psycho perhaps inevitably ended up being unceremoniously chucked in the loft – so after a decade or so of gathering dust, he probably welcomed the opportunity come the summer of 2003 to spend a weekend down in Somerset watching loads of top bands.

Indeed, of all the footballers who we could have taken to Glastonbury with us in 2D form, Psycho was probably the best fit for the situation - after all, he was well known for his love of live music. There was actually an album released in the late 70s by London punk group the Lurkers which, on its inner sleeve, featured a photo of a mosh pit from one of their gigs - with one of those pictured pogoing away none other than a teenage Psycho.

Over the weekend at the festival, Psycho became a sort of mascot for my friends and I as we enjoyed the sights and sounds of the festival. We also quickly discovered that a lifesize cardboard cutout of Stuart Pearce is a pretty useful thing to have at such an event. We'd mounted Psycho on a wooden pole so he could be carried around easily, and this proved handy whenever any of us wandered off to buy a drink or whatever – as we could easily find our way back to the rest of the group by simply looking out for Psycho hovering above the crowds. One member of our group who'd decided to spend the weekend smoking himself into oblivion also reported that our cardboard hero was great for skinning up on! He even made a hole in Psycho's mouth, so the former Forest and England number three could relax and enjoy the odd 'jazz cigarette' himself.

Being a national hero and all, Psycho attracted a lot of attention from our fellow festival-goers. He even had a few celebrity encounters, as at one point during the weekend me and one of the other guys managed to blag our way backstage - where we got Psycho to pose for comedy photos with various famous folk including Lawrence Lewellyn-Bowen and Steve Lamacq. There was a bit of a hairy moment though in the backstage bar, when we were approached by one of Glastonbury's drug casualties – a man who not only seemed utterly convinced that our cardboard cutout was actually a living breathing Stuart Pearce, but also that Psycho was offering him out for a fight. Bizarrely, this potential altercation was actually diffused by a physical intervention from Gruff Rhys, singer with Welsh rockers the Super Furry Animals!

But it was only when we were approached by a journalist that 'Psycho-mania' truly kicked off.

The journo in question wanted to know why we'd brought Psycho with us – and with the truth being a bit mundane, I decided for a laugh to tell him that we were the founders of the Church of Stuart Pearce, and that we were at Glastonbury to recruit disciples!

Hilariously, this story was taken at face value and was reported the following day in the official Glastonbury daily newspaper – and as word spread around the festival site, we quickly found that it was by no means just Forest fans who had big love for Stuart Pearce. Wherever we went we found ourselves mobbed by people with all manner of different footballing loyalties – with all of them loving the idea of the church and wanting to pledge their allegiance.

And why not? After all, there's said to be an African tribe who pray to Bryan Ferry and even an island in the Pacific where the entire population worship Prince Philip – so the Church of Stuart Pearce was far from the strangest idea in the world.

As we made our way around the festival with our cardboard hero, we were getting stopped by so many people that it took us ages to get anywhere. Sadly we had to disappoint quite a lot of people by breaking it to them that the Church of Stuart Pearce wasn't actually a real church – although the more people we spoke to, the more we found ourselves thinking that starting it properly might not be a bad idea. We even gave ourselves titles – I became First Minister of the church, while my mates Simmo and Zippy became Archdeacon and Bishop respectively!

One thing in particular that amazed us was how so many of the people who came and talked to us had their own Stuart Pearce story. There was one guy who told us that he lived in a house that used to belong to Psycho in the Nottinghamshire village of Ruddington; while another bloke claimed he was a friend of Psycho's wife, and that he'd been a guest at their wedding.

It was all very entertaining – and by the time we reached the last night of the festival, we decided there was just one thing left to achieve: to get Psycho on the telly.

In terms of how we intended to make this happen, our plan was pretty straightforward. We'd simply get ourselves down the front when a band was playing on Glastonbury's main Pyramid Stage, and hold Psycho aloft above the crowd.

Given their singer's Forest tendencies, the Manic Street Preachers seemed the obvious band – and brilliantly, the crowd parted like the Red Sea as we made our way closer and closer to the stage shortly prior to the start of their set, to the sound of cries of "Make way for Psycho!"

And it was very much a case of mission accomplished. Much of the Manics' set was shown on TV as part of the BBC's Glastonbury coverage - and my mobile phone began vibrating in my pocket like a randy bee as I suddenly started getting inundated with text messages from friends back home, who had spotted Psycho bobbing about above the mosh pit whenever the cameras panned onto the crowd. Sadly, the band made no reference during their set to Psycho's presence – they couldn't have not spotted him though, and I like to think they would've been amused.

Perhaps unsurprisingly, Psycho was a bit battered by the time Glastonbury drew to an end and my friends and I packed up our tents and prepared to return to the world of The Man. But it's fair to say that our cardboard hero had made a bigger mark on the festival than any of us had ever imagined he would - and there were numerous mentions of the Church of Stuart Pearce in the national media over the next few days.

But the funniest part of the whole episode actually occurred a few weeks later. A few days after we'd got back from the festival, it dawned on me that word of our exploits may have got back to Stuart Pearce through all the media coverage - and that he might be wondering what on earth had been going on in his name. As such, I decided it was only fair to write to him to explain the whole saga.

I sent the letter care of Manchester City Football Club, as that's where Psycho was coaching at the time. I must say, I was reasonably confident that he'd see the funny side of it all – after all he'd always come across over the years when giving interviews as someone who had a good sense of humour and didn't take himself too seriously.

But at the same time, it wasn't without some trepidation that I popped my letter into the postbox. An entire generation of English right-wingers would testify that Psycho wasn't really the sort of character to get on the wrong side of – so what if he read my letter and decided he wasn't happy about the idea of having a church founded in his name?

A few weeks later though I received a reply from Psycho – and much to my relief, it seemed that he was highly amused by it all.

"Dear Rich," he wrote.

"Many thanks for taking me to Glastonbury in the summer. It has been a while since I enjoyed some body surfing at a festival, but to many drunken events like this will see the end of me I fear!

"I did manage to go to the Guildford Festival this year, where I saw Madness and the Stranglers, but kept a lower profile than Glastonbury."

He then went on to say that he wished Forest all the best for the forthcoming season, before signing the letter 'Stuart Pearce (Cardboard Cutout and Coach)'.

Naturally, receiving this letter absolutely made my day. Probably the greatest thing about it though was the fact he'd clearly sat down and bashed it out himself, rather than dictating it to a secretary as you may expect – as rather than being on official Manchester City headed paper, it had been typed in block capitals and printed out onto a blank piece of A4.

And as the more eagle-eyed among you will have noticed, there is actually a minor grammatical error in Psycho's letter – with him having used 'to' instead of 'too' in his second sentence. Not that I'm wanting to get all grammar Nazi on the man – after all, picking fault with Stuart Pearce for his use of the Queen's English is a bit like criticising William Shakespeare for his inability to scythe down tricky right wingers.

You won't be surprised to know that Psycho's letter remains a cherished possession – and while a fair amount of time has passed since the summer of 2003, the tale of the Church of Stuart Pearce has taken on a life of its own over the years.

The story certainly seems to follow me around. For instance, when Psycho returned to the City Ground in 2014 to be the Reds' manager, I was summoned onto BBC Nottingham to tell it again.

But best of all was a scenario a year before that, one lunchtime when I was sat listening to TalkSport on the radio. At that time there was a daily programme on the station presented by Colin Murray, who would choose a different topic each day and invite listeners to phone in and talk about it – with the person judged as having the spun the best yarn winning a hundred quid's worth of vouchers for the DIY store Wickes.

And yes, on that particular day, listeners were being asked simply to share their Stuart Pearce stories…

I couldn't resist phoning in – and as soon as I'd finished telling the tale of the Church of Stuart Pearce, I knew that those Wickes vouchers weren't going anywhere else.

When they arrived in the post a few days later I used them to buy a new light fitting for my living room.

With Psycho having of course earned a living as a sparky before he made it as a professional footballer, it seemed only appropriate!

18. Living the dream # 1

"I'd fulfilled my childhood dream of burying the ball into the back of the Trent End net in front of a packed City Ground – and no-one can ever take that away from me..."

Like most young people growing up as a football fan, I used to dream all the time when I was a kid about one day playing for my beloved team - and would regularly imagine myself pulling on the Garibaldi red and scoring spectacular goals in front of the Trent End.

Alas though, any chance I may have had of making it as a professional footballer were largely kiboshed fairly early in life by... Forest, ironically enough.

Yes, when I started getting into football as a kid, my parents had found out about a local kids' team where I lived called Parkdale Rovers. They played in Nottingham's Young Elizabethan League – a local grassroots breeding ground that has borne numerous stars over the years, most notably Andy Cole.

I duly signed up to play for the Parkdale under-11s team, and started going along to their training sessions – and it was quite exciting playing for a proper team who had their results published each week in *The Football Post*.

But there was one problem – the fact that Parkdale played their matches on Saturdays. Given that I had a Forest season ticket by this point, I was left with a straight choice between either playing for Parkdale or watching the mighty Reds. And probably not for the last time in my life, I decided that Forest were a bigger priority than something that many would argue was a much better use of my time...

I still got the occasional game for Parkdale on weeks when Forest were playing away or didn't have a game – I quickly realised though that playing for a football team wasn't really something that could be done by halves, and eventually jacked it in.

And that was that really.

That said, I did manage to force my way into the school football team during my final year at primary school, where my goalhanging tendencies led to me forming a lethal strike partnership with my mate Stewart Green. Which was quite an achievement really on my part, given that I spent the whole season wearing a pair of football boots that were three sizes too big – with Mum and Dad having bought me a pair that I could 'grow into', as parents did in those days.

Bless him, during my time playing for the school team Dad would come and watch every game home or away - sneaking off early from work in order to do so. Our home ground probably wasn't the imposing fortress that we hoped it would be though - we didn't even have proper goals, and had to improvise with rounders posts covered in cardboard tubes. Embarrassingly, these would often blow over in the wind.

That said, I can actually still picture some of the goals that I scored whilst wearing the light blue nylon of Mapperley Plains Primary – my favourite being an audacious last-minute lob away at Richard Bonington Primary that dramatically earned us a 4-4 draw.

But my competitive footballing career never really progressed any further. I did continue playing the beautiful game when I moved on to secondary school and started at Arnold Hill Comprehensive – and we had something to aspire to there, as England striker Mark Hateley was a former pupil. At that time the big striker was playing his football up in Scotland, although he allegedly still owned a massive house on Plains Road in Mapperley, not far from his alma mater.

However, I never really made much of an effort to try out for the Arnold Hill school team - as most of the other lads who I'd be vying with for a place were a bunch of jocks. For me, that stopped it from being enjoyable – and playing football *should* be enjoyable.

Indeed, the sheer love of playing football has never ever gone away for me. Even now as I write these words as a man approaching my 40s, I still play five-a-side regularly - although I find I'm increasingly more and more of a liability to my team-mates with each passing year!

But while my footballing career never really got going on any serious level, I can still claim to having fulfilled my footballing dreams to some degree – as I have graced the hallowed turf of the City Ground.

And I'm not just referring to various end-of-season pitch invasions I've been part of, having braved the cordon of red and white plastic tape that the stewards unleash in such situations, in the hilariously deluded belief that it's going to stop anyone.

No, I've actually strutted my stuff on the very same turf that I've spent so many hours watching my heroes perform on – and not once but twice. Come to think of it, that's more times than some actual Forest players – though admittedly, only those odd few like John Sheridan, who take their place in that strange elite club of footballers who only made a single appearance for the Reds.

But how did these opportunities to play at the City Ground come about?

Well the first one came in 2004, when I discovered the existence of a charity called Football Aid.

Each year, Football Aid get clubs to give up their ground facilities for a day – and then host a match, with each of the 22 playing positions auctioned off to the highest bidder. Having heard in 2004 that the charity were doing a match at the City Ground, I couldn't not get involved – and after a furious bidding war, I successfully acquired the number nine shirt for one of the two teams.

I paid a silly amount of money - but it was worth every penny.

The whole day when it finally arrived was fantastic. Not only did I get to turn out on the field of dreams, I also got to park in the players' car-park, walk through the players' entrance, and use the away team dressing room.

In reality, the dressing room facilities at the City Ground at the time were actually pretty basic - and also had the same curious hum of sweaty goalkeeper gloves and Deep Heat that'll be familiar to anyone who's spent any amount of time in a football team changing room. But even so, it was very exciting to walk in and find a boxfresh white Forest away kit hanging ready on my peg, complete with my name and number printed on the back of the shirt.

Naturally the atmosphere in that dressing room was buzzing – with ten other men of varying degrees of fitness also present, and also eagerly anticipating the opportunity to fulfil a lifelong dream. I hadn't met any of my team-mates before, but they seemed a good bunch – and as we lined up in the tunnel ready to take to the pitch, I remember thinking that I didn't really care what happened as long as I managed to bag myself a goal at some point.

So what of the match?

Well over a decade since my starring role in my primary school football team, my Dad was still my biggest fan – and thanks to him coming along to the City Ground and bringing his video camera, I actually have an old VHS cassette with some pretty wobbly footage from the day. Watching it back now, what immediately stands out is how the game was played at a tediously pedestrian speed compared to the frenetic pace of proper professional football – although it didn't feel like at all when I was actually out there and struggling to catch my breath!

With the team that I was playing for being the 'away' team, we'd started off attacking the Trent End in the first half. To be honest though I spent much of those 45 minutes just ambling aimlessly around the lush turf, which was far superior to any surface I'd ever played on, and gazing up at the stands in a bit of a daze. In some ways then, my performance probably wasn't that dissimilar to those dark days when Ishmael Miller used to wear the Forest number nine shirt!

That said, I did have a few half chances - but all in all I didn't really manage to get into the game, and my team went in at half-time 2-1 down.

Still, there was plenty of time left – and by the time the second half began I think I'd just about come to terms with my surroundings and was starting to focus a bit more on the task in hand. I began to wonder though whether it simply wasn't going to be my day, when I received the ball in space about 25 yards out and hit a peach of a shot - only to see it smash against the crossbar of the Bridgford End goal.

But a few minutes later, a loose ball fell to me just outside the six yard box - and I'm proud to say that I thumped it emphatically into the back of the net to level the scores before wheeling away in celebration!

That moment was one of pure nirvana. To those of us who play football, the novelty of scoring a goal never wears off - even if it's just in a casual five-a-side kickabout. So to put the ball i n the back of the onion bag on the very same pitch where I'd watched so many of my heroes do the same was really special.

Sadly Dad didn't manage to capture my big moment on his video camera, but I can still close my eyes and picture the moment like it was yesterday. It certainly wasn't the prettiest of goals – and from Archie Gemmill against Arsenal in 1978 to Ian Woan in the FA Cup against Tottenham in 1996, I can think of dozens of better strikes that have been dispatched into the same net by Forest players over the years.

But even if the ball had bounced in off my backside from a yard out, I'm pretty sure The Day I Scored At the City Ground will forever remain one of my favourite moments as a Forest fan.

As it happened, my goal was also a key turning point in the match – because having hauled ourselves level, my team went on to win 7-4. A ridiculous scoreline, obviously – but as time wore on legs were starting to get more and more tired… so goals began flying in left, right and centre at both ends.

An unforgettable experience then – although the one thing that stopped it from properly feeling like I was living the dream was the fact that I played in front of a crowd that was nearer 20 than the usual 20,000 or so that you'd expect at a Forest home game.

Ten years later however, I actually got another chance to show off my shooting skills at the City Ground – and this time in front of a near capacity crowd.

This second instance of gracing the hallowed turf was all in the name of half-time entertainment – something which I think football clubs have always found a tough nut to crack. Forest have certainly experimented over the years with quite a few different ideas, with most of them eventually brushed under the carpet after being met with derision or just plain indifference.

One piece of half-time entertainment that seemed to enjoy unprecedented popularity though amongst Forest fans in recent years was the Garibaldi Golden Goal Gamble. This was a ritual that ran for a number of years, and which basically involved fans coming out onto the pitch and attempting to kick a ball into the Trent End goal from a series of increasing distances.

For some time whilst attending Forest home matches, I'd watched this spectacle with increasing amusement. There was an element of 'stick or twist', as scoring from each distance earned those fans taking part a prize - and if they chose to 'stick', they could immediately call it a day and walk away with that prize.

But of course, the more tempting option was to 'gamble' and have another go at scoring from further out - for the chance of winning an even greater reward. Indeed, I can't remember a single instance of someone scoring from 18 yards and deciding to 'stick' and settle for the vacuum cleaner - which was on offer each week to those who succeeded in putting the ball in the net from that distance.

That said, I don't actually remember a single instance of anyone winning *anything* in the Garibaldi Golden Goal Gamble!

Generally, most fans taking part would easily stroke the ball home from 18 yards, and then again 25 yards – for which the prize was a DVD player. Emboldened though by having succeeded in the first two challenges, they'd usually then gamble again - but invariably fluff their effort from 40 yards and end up empty handed.

A select few fans did manage to succeed from 40 yards, for which the prize was a football signed by the entire Forest squad. And if you did get that far, I think you'd be tempted on many levels to 'stick'.

However, most people would inevitably be seduced by the next level of challenge - with the prize of a massive telly up for grabs to anyone who could score from the halfway line.

After a good year or so though of Forest running the Garibaldi Golden Goal Gamble, not a single person had succeeded in this ultimate bid for glory – and with each passing home game, I found it puzzling me more and more. I mean, kicking a football in a reasonably straight line over a distance of 55 yards couldn't be that hard, surely?

There was only one way to find out – yes, I ended up going online and putting myself and my brother Al forward to have a crack at the Garibaldi Golden Goal Gamble ourselves!

Unsurprisingly it took a while for our names to be pulled out of the hat – but eventually, in December 2014, I got a call from someone at Forest asking if we fancied showing off our shooting skills at the Reds next home game, which was against Leeds.

Naturally Al and I were both very excited. Forest hadn't been playing particularly well in the preceding weeks – so when the big day arrived, we made our way down to the City Ground knowing that the first shot on target that afternoon from someone in a red shirt could well be from one of us!

There'd been a fair bit of rain on the day of the match - and with visions of falling over on a slippery surface and making a total idiot of myself, I'd decided to play it safe and bring proper football boots with me to change into. Given the Reds' form at the time, this led to quite a lot of jokes when Al and I nipped to the pub for a pre-match drink to calm the nerves – with more than one person telling me that if I reported to the players' entrance with my trusty Mitre size nines I'd probably end up getting a game!

As part of the whole deal for taking part in the Garibaldi Golden Goal Gamble, Al and I had agreed with the club to trade our usual seats in the upper Bridgford End for tickets in the Main Stand, to enable us to get down to the side of the pitch quickly as soon as the half-time whistle went. On arriving at our seats we settled down to watch the match - although I think we both struggled to concentrate on the first half, focused as we were on basically not wanting to make ourselves look like an absolute pair of tools!

But the two of us did make a pact whilst watching that first half that there'd be no 'sticking'. If either of us got the chance, we'd definitely be going shit or bust and attempting to score from the halfway line. After all, surely it's always better to be a glorious failure than a moderate success?

So how did we get on?

Well after making our grand entrance onto the hallowed turf and being introduced to the crowd by Forest's tannoy man Mark Dennison, we both managed to score without too much trouble from 18 and 25 yards.

However, if I'm about to sound like I'm making excuses for what happened next – well, it's probably because I am!

Looking back, I think I'd probably gone into the Garibaldi Golden Goal Gamble with far too much confidence in my own shooting ability – a confidence based on the fact that I was playing five-a-side regularly at the time, and most weeks would generally score a screamer from well outside the box.

Of course though, 'well outside the box' on a five-a-side pitch is a completely different kettle of fish to 'well outside the box' on a full-size pitch. I hadn't actually played any football on a full-size pitch for quite a few years - and as I limbered up during the Garibaldi Golden Goal Challenge to make my third attempt from 40 yards, I distinctly remember looking up at the Trent End goal and suddenly thinking "Bleeding hell, that looks a long way away!"

I immediately realised that taking the sensible approach and trying to sidefoot the ball home as I had done from 18 and 25 yards was out of the question – and that I'd need to simply put my laces through it and hope for the best.

And yes, I promptly went and spannered the ball about five yards wide of the left-hand post, to a chorus of groans from the crowd…

Al also blew it from 40 yards – amusingly, he blazed his effort so high and wide that he even got a chorus of "How wide do you want the goal?" from the Trent End!

So, no big telly then for either of us, and we went away empty-handed like a pair of woebegotten *Bullseye* contestants having failed miserably in an attempt to win the obligatory speedboat.

Nevertheless, taking part in the Garibaldi Golden Goal Gamble had been a very funny experience - particularly for all of our friends who were at the game, who got to laugh at our dismal efforts!

What's more, Forest's game that afternoon was being televised live on Sky – and as such, I discovered later that my attempts from 18 and 25 yards could be seen clearly in the background during the pundits' half-time analysis. For quite some time afterwards, Al and I were also able to lay claim to having put the ball into the back of the Trent End net more recently than any Forest player – as the next few games saw the Reds go on a poor run where goals were few and far between.

Inevitably, this proud boast eventually came to an end when the Reds finally managed to get their act together.

But all the same, I'd fulfilled my childhood dream of burying the ball into the back of the Trent End net in front of a packed City Ground – and no-one can ever take that away from me.

And realising how hard it actually is to hit the target with a dead ball from 40 yards – even without a keeper in the goal – has made me develop all the more respect for the players like Stuart Pearce and Pierre Van Hooijdonk and Lewis McGugan, who did it for fun during their time as Forest players.

19. Statue

*"Mike chased Kenneth Clarke across the Main Stand car-park -
showing a lightning pace over ten yards not seen since Franz Carr
donned a Forest shirt in the late 80s!"*

They say that all good things come to those who wait – and though I'd spent years growing up as a young Forest fan with Brian Clough as my hero, it wasn't until nearly a decade after he retired that I finally got to properly meet the great man.

It all happened in 2002, when it was announced that Cloughie was releasing a new autobiography called 'Walking On Water'. A series of book signings were duly arranged around Nottingham, including one at the Forest club shop – and knowing that going along to one of these would pretty much guarantee me a long-awaited audience with my idol, I decided to book a day off work and head down to the City Ground.

On arrival at the club shop it became immediately apparent that I'd have a bit of a wait, as there was already a massive queue. This was no hardship though, as for much of the time I spent stood in line I was in earshot of Cloughie - who was sat at a table signing away, and providing great entertainment simply by being Brian Clough. He was very much in that sort of mood we'd all seen so often in interviews over the years, where he was a strange mix of incredibly charming but also slightly cantankerous. A bloke who was a few places in front of me in the queue had asked Cloughie to write 'To Steve' in his copy of the book, only for the great man to make a point of writing 'Stephen' instead – a little idiosyncrasy many of his players will have been familiar with over the years, from Kenneth Burns to Edward Sheringham. Meanwhile, another punter found himself accused of being a villain, for no apparent reason other than he had a strong London accent!

There was also more than a touch of downright eccentricity about Cloughie's behaviour – not least a point where he suddenly burst into song for reasons I couldn't quite fathom, with a rendition of Frank Sinatra's 'Let's Face The Music and Dance'. It was brilliant to see him in such good form though – and when I finally got to the front of the queue, the great man made it a memorable encounter by subjecting me to one of his stock-in-trade tirades. "Look at the state of you!" he immediately bellowed at me as I sidled over to him. "You need to get yourself a haircut!"

And to be fair, looking back at the photo I had taken with Cloughie that day, he probably had a point!

The advice to get myself to a barber did catch me a bit off guard though, and ensured that I completely forgot all of the things that I'd planned to say to Cloughie. But it was magical to spend a few brief moments in the company of someone who I'd revered for so many years. My copy of his book, which he signed with his trademark 'Be Good', remains a cherished possession – although I'm always puzzled by the strange photo of the great man chosen for the front cover, where he's stood on the touchline wearing what appears to be a pair of three-quarter length trousers. Not exactly a 'look' I'd generally associate with Cloughie.

But strange sartorial choices aside, I'm glad I grabbed the opportunity to meet Cloughie when I did – because just two years later, he was gone.

The day when it was announced that Cloughie had passed away after succumbing to stomach cancer is one that I'll never forget. People always talk about how they remember exactly where they were when they heard that John Lennon had been shot – and for me, the death of Brian Clough was just as profound an event.

For the record, I was actually coming towards the end of a family holiday in rural France when the news broke. It was quite strange – obviously it was a huge talking point back home in Nottingham and indeed across the whole of the UK, but being where I was I felt a bit disconnected from it all.

Nevertheless, I was absolutely gutted.

Of course, Cloughie's sad demise came only seven years after the loss of Princess Diana – an event that, tragic as it was, has been widely pinpointed as starting the national trend in the UK of excessive outpourings of grief following the death of people who we never actually knew.

To me though, the loss of Cloughie did genuinely feel like a proper bereavement.

The great man had passed away on Monday 20 September 2004, and everyone always remembers the emotionally charged occasion six days later - when Forest played at home against West Ham and fans packed out the City Ground to pay their respects.

That game against the Hammers wasn't actually the first Forest game to take place though in the immediate aftermath of Cloughie's death - as before that, the Reds had a League Cup tie at home against Rotherham on the Wednesday evening. My family and I were booked onto a ferry back to England that day – and prior to the holiday I'd been planning on giving the Rotherham game a miss, mainly because I didn't think I'd get back in Nottingham in time.

During times of sadness however we always draw comfort from being among our own – and reeling as I was from the shock of Cloughie's death, I suddenly began to feel a strong urge to be there at the City Ground. As such, some *Smokey and the Bandit*-style driving from Dover saw us make it back to Nottingham just in time for me to be dropped off on Trent Bridge - where I managed to buy a ticket and get myself into the ground with a few seconds to spare before kick-off.

It was a strange occasion. History will record that Forest ground out a 2-1 win thanks to two goals from big striker Gareth Taylor, but my mind was never really on the game. While it had been more than a decade since Cloughie had taken his bow as Forest manager, his presence at the City Ground still loomed large – and I found it hard to shake the feeling that life just wouldn't be the same any more without him around.

Over the next few weeks I paid my respects to Cloughie by attending memorial services in both Nottingham and Derby - and slowly but surely, life got back to normal.

For a while at least, anyway.

For in early 2015, around six months after Cloughie's death, I received an email that would have a massive impact on the next couple of years of my life – an email in which I was asked if I'd be interested in being part of a campaign to have a statue of Brian Clough erected in Nottingham.

The idea for the statue campaign had been instigated by a fellow Forest fan called Marcus Alton – who, back in the year 2000, had founded the tribute website brianclough.com.

Through the website, Marcus had been running a high-profile crusade to get a Knighthood for Cloughie – with his efforts including hand-delivering a petition of 7,500 signatures to Parliament.

Sadly, Cloughie's death pretty much ended any possibility of the great man ever becoming Sir Brian – as it turned out the Government only gives out posthumous honours for gallantry.

Undeterred though, Marcus and his partner Sarah Clarke started thinking of what else they could do to build upon the momentum that they'd already started with the Knighthood campaign – and hit upon the idea of raising money for a statue of the great man to be located in Nottingham city centre.

The Clough family gave the idea their blessing – and having looked into the logistics of actually getting a statue made, Marcus and Sarah learned it would probably cost somewhere in the region of £60,000. Needless to say, raising such a large amount of money would be a massive challenge - and as such, they decided it might be an idea to get a few more hands to the deck.

Which is where I came in...

At this time I was writing regularly for a Reds fanzine called *Blooming Forest*, which existed for a few years during the noughties. Marcus and Sarah had felt it'd be useful to have someone on board from what was, at the time, Forest's only fanzine. This led to the aforementioned email – and after a few messages back and forth, I was invited to attend a meeting on the evening of Monday 28 February 2005.

The purpose of the meeting was twofold. First and foremost, it was an opportunity for myself and others who Marcus and Sarah had invited to attend to find out more about their proposals for the statue. In addition, arrangements had been made for representatives from Nottingham City Council to be there, in the hope that they'd formally agree to support the campaign.

The meeting was held in the Council House in Nottingham city centre – in the elegant surrounds of the Deputy Lord Mayor's Room. It all felt very official – on arrival I discovered that we'd had tea and coffee provided for us and posh china cups to drink it out of, along with fancy biscuits!

Along with Marcus and Sarah and myself, others who had come along with a view to potentially getting involved with the statue campaign were Paul Ellis, who at the time was Chairman of the official Forest Supporters Club; and a chap called Mike Simpson, who had been heavily involved in Marcus and Sarah's Knighthood campaign. I was already on nodding terms with Paul, as I'd actually known his son Chris since I was a teenager.

We duly got the meeting underway – and part of it was attended by the Leader of Nottingham City Council, Councillor Jon Collins. He was fantastic, basically giving us his personal assurance that if we could raise £60,000, he would ensure co-operation from the council in finding a suitable site for a statue somewhere in Nottingham city centre. He also agreed that the council would act as a 'bank' for the fund – and that people would be able send in cheques payable to 'Nottingham City Council – Brian Clough Statue Fund'. This was important in terms of giving the statue campaign legitimacy. It meant people would be able to send us money in confidence, knowing that we weren't a bunch of fly-by-nights likely to disappear any time with all the cash!

It was all quite exciting - and having received Councillor Collins' backing, it was unanimously agreed that a committee should immediately be formed to start working out exactly how we were going to go about raising £60,000.

Being completely sold by this point on the idea of a statue of Cloughie, I volunteered straight away to be part of this committee – although I don't think I quite realised just how much this thing that I'd agreed to be a part of would dominate my life for the next couple of years!

The Brian Clough Statue Fund was officially founded then with all of us who had attended that original meeting with Councillor Collins as members. Well, all of us but one – as though he'd been the driving force behind the whole idea, it had been decided that Marcus wouldn't formally be part of the group. This was because we knew that getting media coverage would be vital as a means of sharing information with the public about what we were doing - and with Marcus employed in his day job as a journalist for BBC Radio Nottingham, there was a danger of his involvement being seen as a conflict of interest.

Over time though, while Marcus didn't sit on the official committee, it was pretty much an open secret he was very much at the heart of what we were doing.

The four of us who initially made up the committee were quickly joined by two additional members – Mick Mellors and Paul Lowe – and I think it's fair to say that the six of us made a diverse team in terms of ages and backgrounds. At 25 I was the youngest member of the group; while Mike probably won't thank me for pointing out that he'd been around long enough to have seen Brian Clough as a player back the 50s!

Across the team we brought a diverse mix of different skills to the table. Most of us had never really been part of any sort of major fundraising activity before, but Paul Lowe had a strong background in events management; Sarah was all about ideas, organisation and drive; Mike was blessed was a shameless brazen cheek; while Mick simply seemed to know absolutely everyone in Nottingham.

Paul Ellis meanwhile was an experienced accountant, so his skills would prove invaluable. Through his involvement in the Forest Supporters Club he also had considerable experience of being part of a committee, so it was a no-brainer really for him to take on the role of Chair of the statue fund committee.

As for me, I'm not quite sure what I brought to the party – you'd have to ask the others. For all our variety though, the one thing we shared was a passion for the idea of creating a lasting tribute to Cloughie – and after several further meetings to thrash out ideas, the Brian Clough Statue Fund officially came to life in June 2015 with a media launch on board Nottingham's Brian Clough tram. Brilliantly, this was attended by the actor Colin Tarrant - a man who was probably most famous for appearing in TV cop show *The Bill*, but who had also done an amazing job earlier in the year when he starred as Cloughie in a play at one of Nottingham's theatres.

Pleasingly, the launch event generated loads of publicity, and the idea of a statue of Cloughie gained a very positive response from people in Nottingham and beyond – with numerous cheques arriving through the post within days. However, while it became very apparent that a lot of folk were prepared to back the campaign, we knew we couldn't sit back and expect £60,000 to just come rolling in. We knew we had to actively raise the cash – and having got the fund up and running, our first major piece of fundraising was to create a limited edition metal pin badge in the shape of Cloughie's famous green sweatshirt.

We first put the badges on sale at an official Forest open day held at the City Ground shortly before the start of the 2005-06 season – and happily fans flocked to our stall in order to stump up £2 to buy one. This was a relief, because getting 3,000 badges made had involved a bit of a risk – as with no way of paying for the manufacturing costs, we'd actually taken out a £1,500 loan from the Forest Supporters Club. Fortunately we were able to pay this money back pretty much straight away – and over the next few months the badges continued to sell in steady numbers after Forest agreed that we could have a stall on matchdays in the Education Centre in the Main Stand car-park. There was one memorable occasion whilst manning this stall when Mike spotted the MP Kenneth Clarke arriving at the City Ground, and managed to sell him a badge after chasing him across the Main Stand car-park - showing a lightning pace over ten yards not seen since Franz Carr donned a Forest shirt in the late 80s!

As well as the badges, other fundraising initiatives that we organised over the remainder of 2005 included a bucket collection outside the City Ground prior to a Forest home game against Hartlepool – who, of course, were the club where Brian Clough started out as a manager. Once again, this showed us the depth of feeling that fans had for Cloughie and the idea of the statue, with many fans throwing in not just coins but £10 and £20 notes. The total amount raised that day was over £4,000.

We also followed the success of the badges by launching our second piece of merchandise – green Cloughie style sweatshirts at £20 a pop. We got these on sale in the run-up to Christmas, which in hindsight was great timing as many of the hundreds of people who snapped them up were buying them as presents. The sweatshirts ended up being a complete sell-out and became collectors items – something that I found out about the hard way, when I lost mine and ended up paying over the odds on eBay to replace it!

By Christmas 2005, six months after the fund had been launched, the total amount of money raised was in the region of £20,000 – which myself and the rest of the committee were very happy with. That said, there was never time to stop and pat ourselves on the back – as we were too busy working on our big plans for 2016. These plans included more merchandise - with a second badge design and also keyrings.

As well as generally mucking in with all the efforts to try and flog our various wares, something that became a significant part of my involvement in the statue fund was maximising use of the internet to help with our fundraising efforts. This included getting an online shop set up on LTLF.co.uk, an unofficial website for Forest fans, which enabled fans to buy our badges, sweatshirts and keyrings online – or simply make a donation. This was a significant development, as suddenly it was easy for fans anywhere in the world to support what we were doing.

The greatest niche that I carved for myself though in my efforts to harness the benefits of the world wide web was becoming the statue fund's 'Mr eBay' – something which all began when Nottingham City Council allowed us to have the giant banners that had been hung around Market Square as part of the memorial service held shortly after Cloughie died. Each banner featured a photo of the great man and one of his famous quotes – and after deciding to test the waters and list one of them on eBay, we were amazed to see it go for a whopping £970 following a furious bidding war.

Further banners went for similar amounts – and having seen how effective eBay could be as a tool for bringing in money, myself and the rest of the committee all began making a concerted effort to lay our hands on anything we might be able to auction off to raise some cash. One success we had on that score was when I sent a begging letter to the Nottingham-born fashion designer Sir Paul Smith, and he sent us some signed footballs that he'd designed - which went on to fetch decent amounts.

Meanwhile other items that we acquired and successfully auctioned off included no lesser an artefact than Brian Clough's old desk, which was given to us by Forest when they were having a clear-out of old furniture. We also ended up eBaying one of the commemorative runners-up tankards that the Reds players had presented to them after their defeat in the 1980 League Cup final. This was a piece of memorabilia donated by a gentleman called Ken Smales – a name that will be familiar to Forest fans of a certain age, with him having worked at the City Ground as club secretary for many years.

There were also numerous items we managed to acquire to sell on eBay that had nothing to do with Forest or Brian Clough – or in some cases, nothing to do with football whatsoever. We weren't fussy – if it was likely to have some sort of value, we were happy to have it! At one point I even managed to get a dartboard signed by the *Bullseye* presenter Jim Bowen, which fetched £60. I also made contact during the height of our eBay activities with the *Guardian* football writer Danny Taylor, who is well known for being a Forest fan. At the time Danny was covering Manchester United a lot, and promised to get us a signed shirt from one of the United players.

"Great," we thought, "let's hope he can bag us Giggs, Ferdinand, Scholes or Ronaldo…"

Alas, we ended up with Gary sodding Neville.

Still, I guess it was the thought that counted.

As with everything we were doing to raise money for the Cloughie statue, we went to great lengths to try and get as much local media coverage as possible of all the eBay auctions – and with me being the one pulling the strings in terms of getting all the items listed on the site, I'd often get invited to talk on local radio about whatever the latest bits and pieces were that we happened to be selling.

Now given some of the previous media appearances already documented in previous chapters that I made during my misspent youth – being part of a group of Forest fans who were responsible for an exuberant utterance of the word 'sheepshaggers' on *Soccer AM*, and phoning in to *Under the Moon* to chat to Dave Beasant after consuming a small lake of beer – it's perhaps questionable that I was ever entrusted with the responsibility of being a spokesperson for the statue fund. Despite this, I like to think that I acquitted myself reasonably well in the role – in fact I still occasionally get contacted to this day by people from the local media in Nottingham whenever they want to talk to a Forest fan about something.

There was one time though when I perhaps wasn't at my best when talking to the media – when I gave a live interview on the Trent FM breakfast show.

I'd made all the arrangements with Trent FM the day before, and left it with them that they'd call me on my mobile at the agreed time. Usually in this sort of scenario I'd set an alarm to ensure I was awake in plenty of time, but on this occasion I'd forgotten. On the day then, I was woken up from a deep sleep by the call from Trent FM, and immediately informed that they were putting me on the airwaves in about ten seconds! Somehow I just about managed to string a few sentences together.

With all the different fundraising activities that we had going on, the total amount of money raised for the statue kept creeping up with each passing week – and lots of interesting people kept getting in touch to offer to help the campaign. One such person was a chap who lived up the road from my Mum and Dad in suburban Nottingham, a plasterer called Mick Somers. It turned out that Mick had been a professional footballer in the 60s, including a spell at Hartlepool – a part of his career that had given him the claim to fame of having been one of Brian Clough's first ever signings. I duly went to meet Mick, and he shared some great Cloughie stories and also agreed to give his public backing to the statue campaign. This made a great story for the local media, and thus helped keep what we were doing in the public eye.

Another interesting character who got in touch was a Yorkshire-based businessman called Simon Clifford, who sent us an email saying that he'd like to be able to support the statue fund in some way. I volunteered to follow this up – and after responding to Simon's email, he invited me to go up to Leeds to meet him.

Now I must admit, I hadn't really done my homework on Simon – and travelled up to Leeds on a Sunday afternoon for what I expected would be a fairly formal meeting, probably lasting no more than an hour or so.

As things panned out though, Simon and I hit it off famously and proceeded to embark on an eight hour drinking session – and over the course of this I got to know some of his absolutely fascinating life story.

It turned out that Simon had grown up in Middlesbrough, which was also of course where Brian Clough was from - and the place where Cloughie first made his mark on the world by scoring a hatful of goals for Middlesbrough FC. By the time Simon started to get into football as a kid in the 70s, Cloughie had long since hung up his shooting boots. Nevertheless, the tales of his goalscoring exploits were still widely talked about – and Simon began following the managerial career of his home-town hero with interest.

Fast forward then to the late 90s, and by this time Simon was working as a P.E. teacher - while Middlesbrough FC, after years in the doldrums, were back in the Premier League and going through a bit of a renaissance following the signings of Brazilian duo Juninho and Emerson. Having always been a 'Boro fan, Simon decided to get his fill of all the excitement by taking the plunge and getting a season ticket – alas though, the team were doing so well that the only seats available were the expensive hospitality ones. Simon decided to throw caution to the wind and splash out on one anyway – and spent an entire season sat next to Juninho's Dad!

In hindsight, the money Simon spent on that costly season ticket would prove to be a shrewd investment. Getting to know Juninho's Dad offered him a gateway into the world of Brazilian football – and coupled with his skills as a P.E. teacher, this led to him founding a football training programme called Brazilian Soccer Schools, which over time became so successful that he eventually franchised it all over the globe.

Simon's success with Brazilian Soccer Schools also led to all sorts of interesting opportunities. To name just a few of the ventures he's been involved in over the years, he worked as a choreographer on the cult British film *Bend It Like Beckham;* and also spent a few months coaching at Southampton, appointed by Sir Clive Woodward during his time at the club as Performance Director. But best of all, he actually ended up buying his own football club by acquiring non-league side Garforth Town – and then proceeded to bag stacks of publicity for the Yorkshire-based side by utilising his contacts in the Brazilian football world to bring various legends out of retirement to play for them. Most famously, Socrates made an appearance for Garforth at the age of 50.

All in all, I found Simon a fascinating bloke, and it was great that someone who clearly had a lot going on in his life had taken time to get in touch simply because he was keen to support a fundraising campaign for a statue of someone who he'd admired since he was a kid. By the end of that Sunday evening I was in no fit state to drive home to Nottingham - without hesitation though, despite the fact that he'd only known me for a few hours, my new friend offered me use of the spare room at his house in Leeds.

As well as being passionate about sport Simon is also a huge *Star Wars* fan, and consequently I woke up the next day to the rather surreal sight of a lifesize model of Chewbacca towering over me! I drove back to Nottingham that morning feeling rather worse for wear – and traffic on the M1 was so bad that it resulted in me having to go straight to work, where I turned up late and in a somewhat dishevelled state, given that I was still wearing the previous day's clothes. Still, the most important thing was that I'd returned from Leeds with a promise from Simon that he'd make a substantial personal donation to the fund, and also send us a load of signed memorabilia to auction on eBay. He was a good as his word – with the signed stuff including a football autographed by Pele.

Over the course of our fundraising campaign, myself and the others on the statue fund committee also organised a series of events to raise money. The first of these was an 'Audience with…'-style evening, where fans were able to put questions to a panel of former Forest players. As mentioned in an earlier chapter, I took on the responsibility of phoning up Nigel Jemson to ask if he'd be willing to take part, and inadvertently woke him up!

By far our biggest event though was a formal dinner held in May 2016 – which came about after Nottingham City Council offered us the opportunity to have full use of the Council House ballroom for one night at no cost. Sarah took on the majority of the responsibility for organising the dinner, and it's fair to say that she played an absolute blinder. After fixing a date, we made 200 tickets available at £40 a pop – and with Forest's owner Nigel Doughty having agreed to sponsor the event, basically footing the bill for most of the costs such as catering and decorations, pretty much every penny we made from ticket sales went straight to the fund.

It was a great night, with several members of Brian Clough's family attending - including his wife Barbara. Also present were various legends from the Forest team of the late 70s such as John Robertson and John McGovern, who both shared some brilliant Cloughie stories during the evening.

The biggest star of the night though was Duncan McKenzie, who we'd decided to book as the main after-dinner speaker – and who brought the house down with some hilarious anecdotes about his years as a footballer. McKenzie had of course played for Forest in the mid-70s – and while his time at the City Ground was pre-Brian Clough, he did cross paths with Cloughie during his career after the great man signed him from the Reds during his time as manager of Leeds in 1974.

Alas, the two of them would only have a brief working relationship – because as everyone knows, Cloughie was sacked by Leeds after only 44 days. However, McKenzie still had a wealth of fantastic stories about Cloughie – not least a tale about the build-up to his debut for Leeds in the Charity Shield at Wembley, when he asked the great man whether he'd be able to have a couple of complimentary tickets so his parents could come and watch him play. Alas, this request was immediately met with a classic Cloughie one-liner: "If your mother and father won't pay to see you play, how can you expect anyone else to?"

Along with money generated from people buying tickets to attend the dinner, further cash was made on the night through a raffle and an auction – and by the end of the evening we'd raised a total of £9,000.

I do think we missed a trick though with the dinner. Back in his Forest days, Duncan McKenzie had been renowned for his party trick of being able to jump over a Mini - so I think we should have borrowed a Mini, parked it outside the Council House on the evening of the event, and challenged him to see if he could still do it! Still, the night was a great success, and took us a massive step closer to our goal of raising £60,000 for the statue – and as 2006 rumbled on, it began to look more and more likely that we'd achieve our goal before the year was out. In the end, it was actually another event that pretty much got us over the line – a live music night just before Christmas that we billed 'Clough Aid'.

Clough Aid came about because a lad called Dave Marmion had got in touch, who was both a massive Forest fan and singer in a local band called the Fakers. At the time the Fakers were playing regular gigs in pubs around Nottingham – and having heard about the statue fund, Dave decided it'd be a great idea to put on a night of live music to raise some money for the cause. Myself and the rest of the statue fund committee were more than happy for him to get on with this, and along with he other guys in the Fakers he did a superb job in making the event happen. They persuaded various other bands to play, and also blagged free use for the night of the Rescue Rooms - one of Nottingham's foremost gig venues.

As a renowned Sinatra fan, I'm not quite sure what Brian Clough would've thought of the music on the night – which was pretty much a solid barrage of indie rock. The great man did get to put his stamp on the evening's entertainment though – my mate Mat McCallum had kindly agreed to DJ at the event between the various bands, and whilst working his magic on the wheels of steel he mixed a load of samples of classic Clough quotes into the tunes he was playing. Naturally this was very well received by the 350 or so people who'd paid a fiver to come along on the night.

All in all then it was another successful evening for the statue fund – and one moment that I always remember came towards the end of the evening, when one of the door staff at the Rescue Rooms ushered me into the backstage area of the venue.

As I was led down a dingy corridor and into a dimly lit office it felt a bit like I was in some sort of dodgy gangster film. But happily, once inside the office the manager of the venue opened a massive safe and casually handed me a huge wad of notes that turned out to be just shy of two grand - which was how much money the gig had generated in door takings.

A short while later I remember feeling slightly paranoid carrying such a large amount of money on my person as I wandered round Nottingham city centre in the early hours of the morning in search of a taxi. But once the cash had been safely banked, we were pretty much there in terms of achieving our fundraising target – as we'd had an agreement in place for some time that if we got close to hitting £60,000, Forest and Nottingham City Council would get us over the line by chucking in £5,000 a piece.

A few days later then, we were able to go public with the fact that it was 'job done' - something that gained a lot of coverage in the local media. As part of this, arrangements were made for myself and the rest of the statue fund committee to pose for a 'team photo' for the *Nottingham Post* – and the other guys looked great in this snap when it appeared in the paper. Regrettably though, the photographer had decided to position me slightly behind everyone else when arranging us for the pic - so I ended up looking like a random tramp who'd decided to 'photobomb' the rest of the group!

There was also an official presentation on the pitch at half-time at Forest's next home game, where folk from the club and the city council each handed over 'big cheques' to myself and the rest of the committee to represent the £5,000 donations they'd each made to the fund. Once again though I ended up looking ridiculous in the photos of this event. Granted it was a cold afternoon, but to this day I still wonder why I decided it was a good idea to wear a ridiculous furry hat that made me look like some sort of Siberian border guard!

Still, dodgy photos aside, I was incredibly proud of what we'd achieved in just 18 months. However, there was still the small matter of agreeing a location for the statue and finding the right sculptor.

It was obviously important to get these two things right – particularly the latter. We've all seen examples of terrible statues - and after all our efforts in raising the money, we were keen to ensure ours didn't fall under that category. And let's face it, Brian Clough deserved nothing less than something fantastic.

After much debate, it was eventually agreed that the perfect place for the statue would be the bottom of the 'V' of King and Queen Street, just up from

Market Square. And of the dozens of sculptors who tendered for the job of recreating Cloughie in bronze, it was Hampshire-based Les Johnson who was eventually chosen, following a lengthy consultation process involving both the public and the Clough family.

Les duly spent much of 2008 working on the statue, and other members of the statue fund committee travelled down to his studio see the work in progress. At this stage though I'd decided to take a step back from my involvement in the project, as I was busy with other commitments. As such, the first time I actually got to see the statue was when the 'big reveal' finally happened on Thursday 6 November 2008.

The logistics of the official public unveiling event were largely organised by Nottingham City Council – and it's fair to say they did a great job. I'd arrived early to find the statue hidden beneath a silk tarpaulin in 'Clough green' – and as crowds began to build, there was a definite buzz of anticipation.

Having been part of the statue fund committee, I was afforded the privilege of a pass to stand in a designated 'VIP area' directly adjacent to the statue. This area was a veritable Forest 'who's who' – with numerous former players from the Cloughie's all-conquering team of the late 70s and early 80s, along with the current Reds squad and various members of the Clough family. It was pretty crowded - at one point I found myself in the bizarre situation of being sandwiched uncomfortably in a crush of people between Nigel Doughty and Colin Calderwood, who at the time were the Reds' owner and manager respectively.

The city council had hired the sports broadcaster Gary Newbon to perform the role of Master of Ceremonies on the day – which was an appropriate choice really, as he was someone who had interviewed Cloughie on TV numerous times over the years, and been made to look like a complete tool by the great man on more than one instance. On this particular occasion though Newbon managed to make himself look a complete tool all by himself - by accidentally referring to Nottingham as 'Birmingham' when addressing the crowd!

Still, it gave everyone a laugh, and by time of the big reveal at 1pm an estimated 5,000 people were crowded around – with folk even leaning out of upper floor windows of some of the buildings on King and Queen Street to get a better view. It was an amazing turn-out for a weekday – and it really hammered home just how excited people were about finally being able to see the statue.

However, for myself and the rest of the statue fund committee, the excitement was mixed with a certain amount of nerves when the time finally came for Barbara Clough to pull a cord to remove the green tarpaulin and unveil the fruits of everyone's hard work. Needless to say though, it was an amazing and incredibly emotional moment to finally get to see my hero immortalized in bronze.

To be honest I found it hard to take it all in – but the immediate and spontaneous outbreak of applause from the crowds told us everything we needed to know about what the public thought of Les Johnson's stunning creation.

Following the big reveal there were numerous formal group photos taken with the statue – it felt a bit like being at a wedding. Eventually the crowds started to disperse, and at that point my brother Al and I jumped aboard one of a number of buses laid on by the city council to ferry people to an official post-unveiling reception event that was being held in one of the hospitality suites at the City Ground.

Bizarrely, we found ourselves sat on the bus with Forest legends Viv Anderson and Tony Woodcock! Over the course of the short journey we discovered that Viv Anderson has such a bone-crunching handshake that we actually considered asking the driver to take a detour via the QMC just so we could pop in for a quick precautionary X-ray; while with his flowing locks, my abiding memory of Tony Woodcock is that he looked like he was on his way to audition to become singer in a Led Zeppelin tribute band! Alas though, I was so caught up in the excitement of seeing the Cloughie statue for the first time that I never thought to take the opportunity to ask Viv how on earth he ended up teaming up with Trevor Francis back in the early 80s to record that strange duet of 'You'll Never Walk Alone' as mentioned in an earlier chapter - so I'm afraid that will just have to remain a mystery for now.

A few months after the big reveal, myself and the rest of the statue fund committee were invited to have dinner with the Clough family – an occasion initiated by the family, who were keen to thank us for all our efforts in making the statue a reality. Sadly Nigel Clough was unable to attend as he'd not long become Derby manager and was away on official club duties, but it was lovely to spend the evening with Barbara Clough and Nigel's siblings Simon and Elizabeth. It was particularly heartening to hear Barbara speak about how much she liked the statue, and how she felt it really captured her late husband. This was probably the highest piece of praise we could possibly have asked for – after all, Barbara knew the great man better than anyone else.

Over the years I've remained in touch with the other guys from the statue fund committee, and each year we try and get together for a bite to eat and to reminisce about those crazy few years when all the fundraising activity took over our lives. Following the unveiling, Marcus actually wrote a book titled *Young Man, You've Made My Day* - which offers a far more definitive account of the statue campaign than I've managed here. Sadly over time we've lost a number of key people associated with the statue – including Colin Tarrant who passed away in 2012, Barbara Clough in 2013, and Mick Mellors in 2016.

The statue itself however has become an established landmark in Nottingham – although life is of course a broad church of opinion and you always get the odd naysayer. To this day, I still hear the occasional gripe that the statue should've been paid for by Forest or the city council – an opinion I always struggle to get my head around. After all, as well as the fact that Les Johnson did a brilliant job of capturing Cloughie, I think one of the things that makes the statue special is the fact that it was paid for by the public. It gives people ownership – if you bought a badge during the fundraising campaign, you can justifiably claim that you personally paid for one of Cloughie's eyelashes.

There have also been a few critics saying that the statue should've been a statue not just of Brian Clough, but Brian Clough and Peter Taylor. My answer to that though is always "Fair enough – if you feel that strongly, why don't you get off your backside and raise £60,000 for a statue of Peter Taylor to stand next to Cloughie?"

But as myself and the others on the statue fund committee know only too well, it's far more difficult to raise sixty grand than people might think. When we first launched the fund I remember quite a few people suggesting we had an easy task. After all, with Forest having a regular fanbase of approximately 20,000, surely all we had to do was get each of them to chuck in three quid - and hey presto, we'd have the money?

In actual fact, raising the cash took 18 months of hard graft. And I think raising £60,000 would be even harder these days. We may now have social media , which makes it a lot easier to raise awareness of anything that you happen to be doing. However, with Britain having been in the grip of government austerity measures for several years, people tend to be a bit less free and easy when it comes to sticking their hand in their pocket.

Indeed, since the Cloughie statue was unveiled there have been a number of attempts in Nottingham to raise money for statues of other local icons that have barely got out of the starting blocks – one for a statue of the writer Alan Sillitoe, another for a statue of the ice skaters Jayne Torvill and Christopher Dean, and another for the bare knuckle boxing champion William 'Bendigo' Thompson. It's a shame, as the people in question are all bona fide Nottingham legends who each in their own way deserve to be celebrated just as much as Cloughie. But getting people to part with their hard-earned cash really isn't that easy.

Myself and the rest of the Brian Clough Statue Fund committee managed it though – and I'm proud of the fact that our efforts enabled the creation of what has become a much-loved Nottingham landmark. Whenever I'm in the city centre I always make a point of taking a walk down King Street - and regardless of whether it's day or night, more often than not you tend to find someone taking a photo of the statue or just stopping for a look.

Even Jose Mourinho, who has spoken many times over the years about his admiration for Brian Clough, revealed in 2015 that he'd travelled up to Nottingham incognito just to come and see it. I even once met a fellow Forest fan who's had a picture of the statue tattooed onto his arm.

Here's hoping Cloughie will remain a focal point in Nottingham city centre for many decades to come - and that the statue will help future generations learn about a brilliant man and everything he did to help put Nottingham on the map.

20. The Dragon

"Amusingly, the fact that Status Quo had come up in conversation led to McGovern going off on a massive rant about the veteran rockers…"

While I'm too young to have experienced Forest's glory days of the late 70s and early 80s under Brian Clough and Peter Taylor, I've been lucky enough to have met pretty much all of the players from that era.

There are some encounters that I've already mentioned in previous chapters - such as the time I spent an hour with Frank Clark in 1993, shortly after he returned to the City Ground as the Reds' new manager and he agreed to let me interview him for *Forest Forever*.

In addition, the explosion of 'Audience with' evenings in Nottingham has made the Reds legends of the past fairly accessible in recent years. I'm a big fan of these sorts of events, although less probably said the better about the time I went to one and met Peter Shilton – and emboldened by several bottles of red wine, decided to ask him when questions were thrown open to the audience about the infamous incident back in his days at the City Ground when got caught with his trousers down and ended up crashing his car.

I honestly thought he was going to hit me!

As well as Shilts, 'Audience with' evenings have enabled me to meet numerous other Forest legends, from John Robertson to Trevor Francis to Garry Birtles – and also some of the players who often get overlooked when people talk about the Reds' achievements of the late 70s and early 80s. One such player was Colin Barrett, who I found to be an absolutely lovely bloke when I got to have a quick chat with him. It's well documented that the former full-back has earned an honest living since he finished playing football by working as a painter and decorator – and I've often had idle thoughts about trying to hire him to do some jobs round at my house.

After all, how cool would it be to be able to tell people that you had your hallway painted by a man who once scored a goal for Forest against Liverpool in the European Cup?

Of all the Forest legends though from that golden era, there's one man who I have a particular soft spot for - and that's probably because there have been no less than three occasions over the years when I've been fortunate enough to spend quite a bit of time in his company.

And that man is one John Prescott McGovern.

Of course, it's no secret that the former Reds skipper is very amiable and approachable. Indeed, for quite a few years during the early part of the new millennium, he could often be found drinking after Forest home games in the pub on London Road that was, at that time, called the Globe – and he'd always be happy to share a drink with fans and chat about however the Reds had got on.

For me though, my dealings with John started via BBC Radio Nottingham. For much of the 'noughties' I regularly wrote bits and bobs for the Radio Nottingham website – and during that time I also played five-a-side football for a while with a load of the guys who worked there.

As well as being a fine commentator and a nice bloke, I can confirm that Radio Nottingham's Forest correspondent Colin Fray has an absolute hammer of a left foot. It's also quite disconcerting playing on the same team as him, when you suddenly hear him shouting at you for the ball with *that* voice that you've spent many an hour listening to on the radio.

But where does John McGovern come into all of this?

Well the period when I played footy with the Radio Nottingham guys saw me take part in a couple of tournaments where we competed against other BBC teams from around the country. These were always highly enjoyable occasions, although there was one time when tempers became a little frayed during a match against the cast of the BBC drama series *Doctors*. Despite being a rubbish programme, the *Doctors* guys were all strutting around like they were Hollywood A-listers – and the game nearly descended into a mass brawl after one of the delicate petals took exception to a hard-but-fair tackle from one of our lot!

Generally though the tournaments were very good natured – and my favourite one was a knock-out competition hosted by BBC Radio Shropshire during the summer of 2006.

The tournament was taking place on a Sunday down in Shrewsbury, and arrangements had been made for our team to depart early from Nottingham in a convoy of three cars. With my brother Al having also been roped into playing, he'd agreed to be one of the drivers – so it made sense for me to get a lift with him. And brilliantly, a few days beforehand, we discovered that one of Al's other passengers would be none other than John McGovern!

Yes, at the time John was doing quite a lot of work for Radio Nottingham as a co-commentator on their live coverage of Forest games – so the guys at the station had persuaded him to travel with us to the tournament to be our manager. Come the day then, Al and I went and picked him up bright and early from outside the Radio Nottingham building – and duly spent the next couple of hours enjoying what was essentially a private audience with the captain of Forest's greatest ever team as we made the journey down to Shropshire.

It was a surreal but amazing experience. Most Forest fans will have heard John talk endlessly about football, but as he held court from the back seat of Al's car we actually covered all sorts of other things - everything from family holidays to the time after he finished playing when he decided to go and live on a narrowboat.

John also shared a great story about the rock band AC/DC, who he's a massive fan of. He told us about how he'd got to know the band's singer Brian Johnson very well over the years – and how through their friendship, he usually gets full VIP treatment whenever AC/DC play live. On one occasion the band were playing a huge outdoor show in Germany with the Rolling Stones - and having decided to go along, John ended up hanging out backstage with Mick Jagger and co!

Eventually we arrived in Shrewsbury – and though we didn't win the tournament, I think we represented Radio Nottingham pretty well on the whole, qualifying from the initial group stages and getting all the way to the quarter-finals in the knock-out stage. Not only that, I also personally covered myself in glory by scoring a cheeky lob from the halfway line in our match against BBC Radio Cornwall, after I spotted their keeper off his line. My heroics however led to a classic piece of Brian Clough-style man management from John. Naturally, I was strutting around the pitch all smug because I'd bagged a spectacular goal – though John clearly thought I needed bringing down a peg or two, because he promptly went and subbed me.

Bastard!

Still, it was a great day. My favourite moment though actually came during the drive home, when we were all chatting away again – only for us to be suddenly interrupted by the sound of John's mobile ringing.

"Excuse me lads," he said as he fished his phone out of his pocket and saw who was calling. "I've got to take this call – it's The Dragon…"

Needless to say, discovering that the man who captained Forest in their back-to-back European Cup triumphs affectionately refers to his wife as The Dragon was a highly amusing revelation for Al and I. What's more, we couldn't help but get the gist of what John and The Dragon were talking about, with us all sat together in a fairly confined space - and their exchange offered a fascinating insight into domestic life at Chez McGovern.

That said, when John eventually bade farewell to his wife, we discovered that he wasn't massively impressed with the culinary delights that she'd been lovingly preparing ready for when he got home.

"So then lads," he told us, his voice rising in mock outrage. "It's been a long day today - we've travelled all this way and given our all in this tournament… and do you know what I've got to look forward to when I get home? Bangers and bloody mash!"

Priceless!

Of course, it can shatter your illusions a bit when people you admire drop their guard and show that they're just an ordinary person underneath it all. For instance, the sense of mystique that David Bowie has held for most of my life would probably have been destroyed forever if I'd ever ended up in a situation where I got to overhear him talking to his wife about what they were going to have for tea.

But with John, it just felt really refreshing. In this day and age even a lot of bang average footballers seem to have massive egos and swan around like they're superstars – so it was great to find that a man who won more honours than most modern players was just 'one of us'.

A great day then, and I was quite sad when we arrived back in Nottingham and the time came for Al to drop John back at the Radio Nottingham building. Brilliantly though, despite the fact that he was the one who'd done us a big favour by giving up a day to help us out, John actually insisted on giving Al a crisp £20 note to go towards his petrol costs. A true gent.

That trip to Shrewsbury actually led to another encounter with John only a few months later.

As documented in the previous chapter, I was part of the small group of Forest fans who raised the money for Nottingham's Brian Clough statue – and being someone who loves music as well as football, one of my favourite moments from the entire fundraising campaign was a gig that we held called Clough Aid.

During the process of organising Clough Aid, it had occurred to us that we needed someone to come along on the night and be compere. But who?

Suddenly though, I had a flash of inspiration – what about John McGovern? After all, as well as being the one player people most associate with Brian Clough - having played under the great man not only at Forest, but also at Hartlepool, Derby and Leeds - I knew from all the chat we'd had in Al's car a few months previously that he was a massive music fan.

I duly got a message to John via one of the guys at Radio Nottingham, to ask if he'd be up for the job of compere at Clough Aid. Pleasingly, word quickly came back that he was definitely interested... and could I ring him on his mobile to discuss the whole thing further? I'm not ashamed to admit that it took me about three days to pluck up the courage to do this – after all, while it was only a few months since I'd spent the whole day with him and found out that he referred to his wife as The Dragon, it was still the man who had lifted two European Cups!

Typically, when I finally took the plunge and made the call, I ended up just getting John's voicemail. Later that day though, I was sat at work when my mobile started ringing – and when I picked it up, my heart did several somersaults when I saw the screen flashing with 'John McGovern mobile'!

After taking a deep breath, I took the call... and it turned out John was more than happy to give up a Friday night to come and host the gig for us.

When the evening arrived, I had the job of going on stage at the start of the gig and introducing John to the crowd. Just as the two of us were waiting in the wings I remember turning to him and suggesting that he'd find his task as our host for the evening an absolute walk in the park, with him having worked as an after-dinner speaker for many years. John's reply was classic. "To be honest I was more comfortable playing in front of 100,000 people at Wembley," he said, "after all, at least I knew what I was doing then!"

Happily Clough Aid was a great night and John was a brilliant host, introducing all the various bands who played, telling loads of great Cloughie stories, and mingling with the hundreds of people who showed up on the night. As a thank you for his services, I got his face Photoshopped onto the body of Keith Richards from the Rolling Stones - and then had it printed onto a canvas, which I presented to him at the end of the gig.

I like to think he has it hanging in pride of place in his downstairs bog!

My third and most recent encounter with John meanwhile took place during the summer of 2015. At the time, Nottingham had just been named Sport England's first ever 'City of Football' – a title that brought significant funding to help nurture the beautiful game locally at grass roots level. Through work I'd had some minor involvement in Nottingham's successful bid for the title - and this led to me being invited to go and interview John for the independent Nottingham culture magazine *Left Lion*.

By this time John was working for Forest as a club ambassador, so I met him one afternoon down at the City Ground – and as well as Nottingham's new status as City of Football, we also covered a whole host of topics. At the time of the interview Forest had just completed the signing of Jamie Ward from Derby, which was a somewhat controversial acquisition given that the player had been at the heart of most of the on-field handbags that had taken place during Forest-Derby games over the previous couple of seasons. With John having also been a player who had had to work hard to win over the fans when he arrived at Forest following a long association with Derby, I decided to ask him if he had any advice for Jamie Ward – and his suggestion was short and to-the-point.

"Win your first tackle in your first game that you play," he said. "Clatter somebody! That'll get you accepted by the Forest fans straight away."

John and I also spoke a fair bit about Forest's past. The majority of Forest fans will have heard most of John's Cloughie stories over the years, but I'm pleased to say that I managed to tease out a brilliant tale that I'd never heard before - about a time when he got into trouble with the gaffer for, of all things, playing an imaginary musical instrument.

"I was playing for Derby County at the time," John recalled, "and I was out on the pitch an hour before kick-off, just checking the surface so I could see what studs to use... when a Status Quo song came on over the loudspeakers.

"I started air guitaring away in the centre of the pitch, but all of a sudden I realised that Brian Clough was stood looking rather sternly at me. As I walked past him, he said to me 'You'd better play well today'! Fortunately I did, and we won the match."

Amusingly, the fact that Status Quo had come up in conversation led to John going off on a massive rant about the veteran rockers. The previous year the band had taken a radical departure from their usual brand of raucous boogie rock and released an acoustic album – something John was clearly not very happy about, making it known in no uncertain terms that he felt they should "stick to what they know".

All in all then, just like that trip to Shrewsbury and the evening at a sweaty gig in Nottingham, it was a pleasure that afternoon to once again spend some time with John. The guy is simply a top bloke – and incredibly down-to-earth for a man who has lifted the biggest prize in European football not once but twice.

Of course, there's always been a sense that the Forest team of late 70s and early 80s never got the credit they deserved for their achievements from the wider footballing community, so I was delighted when a bit of recognition finally arrived later in 2015 with their induction into the National Football Museum's Hall of Fame.

I was really pleased for all of them – but particularly for John.

Though I still haven't quite forgiven him for subbing me after my wonder goal against BBC Radio Cornwall!

21. Everywhere we go…

"I decided it was a golden opportunity to try and make Forest the biggest football team in Mongolia.."

As I've got older, travel has joined Forest and music as one of my big passions in life. And to be fair, the mighty Reds can probably take some responsibility for this – as it was almost certainly my early experiences of going to away games as a teenager that gave me the bug for adventure and visiting new places.

Over the years, there have been numerous times when Forest have actually played second fiddle to my wanderlust.

Like most football fans, much of my life has been carefully organised over the years around the Reds' fixture list. However in 2007 I actually missed half a season, having decided to take time out to go on a round-the-world backpacking trip - a five-month adventure that saw me fly out to Australia and then slowly work my way home via eleven other countries ranging from Vietnam to Nepal.

To be fair, Forest were enduring their second season in the doldrums at the time, after the humiliation of relegation to League One in 2005. And while the Reds' first season down in English football's third tier had had a certain novelty value, the appeal of playing teams like Cheltenham and Leyton Orient – not to mention competing in Johnstone's Paint Trophy and having to start in the first round of the FA Cup - had begun to wear pretty thin.

As such, if I was ever going to spend half a football season on the other side of the world, then the first half of 2007 was probably the best time to do it.

The trip proved to be an amazing experience – with all sorts of highlights from swimming with wild dolphins in Australia to climbing mountains in New Zealand to hiking through a jungle in Malaysia.

But for all the amazing places that I was visiting during my travels, I never completely forgot about the beautiful game. With my Grandad having been born in India during colonial times, I even made contact with the Indian FA while I was passing through Asia to try and bag a trial for the Indian national team – although they never even gave the courtesy of a reply. Their loss!

And of course, I always kept tabs on how Forest were getting on wherever I happened to be. Early on in my trip, I had the surreal experience of watching live TV coverage of a Chelsea v Forest FA Cup tie in the small hours of the morning in a sports bar in Melbourne – probably the strangest situation in which I've ever watched a Reds game. Meanwhile, most weekends I would usually find myself seeking internet cafes at strange times of day and night in order to check on scores.

One particularly cruel moment during my time travelling was the debacle of Forest's infamous play-off defeat against Yeovil, which happened towards the end of my trip.

The first leg had been the tough away one at Huish Park. By this point I was in China, where I was about to embark on the first part of my journey home via the Trans-Siberian railway. The match was due to finish at approximately 5.30am Beijing time - and as such, I'd set myself an early alarm so I could give my brother Al a call immediately after full-time, to find out how Forest had got on. Naturally, I was chuffed when he answered my call and told me that the Reds had cruised to a comfortable 2-0 win.

At this point I immediately started making plans to ensure I'd be back home in time for Forest's first ever visit to the new Wembley. By the time of the second leg against Yeovil I was part of the way through my Trans-Siberian adventure, and enjoying a stop-off for a few days in the Russian city of Irkutsk. The match at the City Ground had been due to finish around 4.30am local time – but I was so relaxed about the whole thing that I didn't bother setting an alarm. Instead I enjoyed a lie-in, only taking the short walk down the road to the local internet café a good few hours after full-time.

And there it was, in stark text.

Nottingham Forest 2, Yeovil Town 5.

At first, the scoreline seemed so ridiculous I honestly thought I'd been victim of an elaborate practical joke. I genuinely had suspicions that my brother Al had finally executed the ultimate revenge for a Riccy Scimeca-based prank that I'd played on him a few years earlier - by using his IT nous to hack into the Forest website in order to make me think the Reds had fluffed their chance of promotion in the most spectacular fashion.

But no – visits to several other sport websites revealed that it really was true.

I remember spending the rest of the day wandering around Irkutsk in a daze. Still, at least I was in the Siberian wilderness, where no-one really gave a monkey's about the League One play-offs. It was the other 20,000 Forest fans who I felt truly sorry for - those who had to go into work or school or college the next day and face the derision of their colleagues.

And for me I guess there was a silver lining in the dark cloud – as with dreams of Wembley having been cruelly dashed I was suddenly no longer in such a hurry to get home to the UK, and thus able to spend a few extra days in Russia.

Oh, and if you're wondering what the Riccy Scimeca-based prank was – well, sometime in the early part of the new millennium, Al and I went through a phase when we the two of us kept playing practical jokes on one another. This was all inspired in the first place by a friend of ours called Russ, who played a hilarious prank on Al by paying to have an advert placed in *Loot* magazine with the immortal words 'Dog-sized hamsters for sale' – accompanied by Al's mobile number.

Brilliantly, Al was actually inundated with calls!

Somehow Russ never suffered any retribution for his actions; however, his moment of comedy genius very much captured mine and Al's imaginations, and the two of us began a bit of a phase where we started orchestrating all sorts of japes at the other's expense.

And it was mostly pretty innocuous stuff.

However one day I decided to up the stakes, by submitting an application to the UK Deed Poll service to have Al's name changed to Ricardo Scimeca - what with the Reds midfielder being a player who the two of us treated as something of a scapegoat figure at that time.

Amusingly, this led to my esteemed sibling getting a call from a lady at the Deed Poll office, asking for his credit card details so she could complete his application – and she wasn't particularly happy when it became apparent that he'd been victim of a practical joke!

Going back though to that backpacking adventure in 2007 – the trip was something I'd decided to do simply because I'd reached my late 20s and it had suddenly dawned on me that I hadn't really seen much of the world.

I thought spending a few months travelling might scratch an itch, and that would be that. In actual fact though it had the opposite effect, and only increased my passion for travel and experiencing new places. Over the years since I've spread my wings even further and visited all sorts of destinations from South Africa to Peru. And whenever I go off on a foreign jaunt I always make a point of taking a Forest shirt with me - simply because football can be a great icebreaker when you're a long way from home.

One time on a road trip around Italy, I actually took the 'taking a Forest shirt on holiday' thing one step further...

Yes, I decided in the run-up to that trip that it'd be a good laugh to pay tribute to one of Forest's most underwhelming signings - and acquired (via eBay) a replica Forest shirt from the mid-90s, which I then went and had 'Silenzi' and a number 15 printed on the back!

Despite having been a massive flop at Forest, it became clear during my holiday that Andrea Silenzi was still remembered in Italy – with numerous locals commenting on my 'Silenzi shirt' as I travelled around the great man's native land. There was one particularly surreal incident when I was accosted by a bloke whilst at the top of Mount Vesuvius – a chap who turned out to be a massive fan of Napoli, one of the clubs who Silenzi had played for in Italy prior to his move to Forest. Chatting to him, I discovered that Silenzi had apparently been known as 'The Paintbrush' during his time in Naples.

'The Bog Brush' would've been a more appropriate nickname for his time at the City Ground!

By far and away the greatest lengths I've ever gone to though to share my passion for Forest with the world came in the summer of 2008 – when I joined forces with my mate Ed, who I'd met at uni, to drive all the way from London to Mongolia in a knackered Peugeot 106.

The reason for this ridiculous caper was because we'd decided to sign up to take part in the Mongol Rally – an annual charity event which basically involves intrepid idiots attempting to drive 8,000 miles across all manner of terrain in completely inappropriate vehicles. And as if what we'd signed up to do wasn't silly enough already, I decided it was a golden opportunity to try and make Forest the biggest football team in Mongolia!

As well as being an excuse to go on an amazing adventure, the Mongol Rally is all about supporting worthy causes in Mongolia – which is one of the poorest countries on earth. Ed and I had decided to use our trip to raise money for an orphanage in Ulaanbaatar, the country's capital – and having discovered that we'd get the opportunity to visit this orphanage when we reached Mongolia, I decided it was only right and proper that we should take a load of Forest shirts to give out to the children.

Though not a Forest fan, Ed was happy to go along with this idea – and we launched a media appeal, asking people to donate us their old Forest shirts.

Brilliantly, this actually led to a phone call from Forest's very own Terry Farndale – or Terry the Kitman, as he was better known to Reds fans. Good egg that he is, Terry sorted us out with a load of old Forest shirts, and also some training tops – which I gratefully popped down to the City Ground to collect.

All in all, by the time the day came for us to set off on our adventure, Ed and I had about 100 Forest shirts crammed into our car – and they joined us on an eventful odyssey that saw us banned from Germany's Nurburgring racing circuit, attacked by wild dogs in the Ukraine, making friends with a gold-toothed mafia boss in Kazakhstan, and having to bribe the police in Russia to avoid being slung in a Siberian gulag!

As well as all the Forest shirts, we also set off with a solitary Derby shirt - which someone had given us as a joke after we'd launched our media appeal. Naturally we subjected this Derby shirt to all sorts of indignities as our trip unfolded. As our wreck of a car struggled its way across Europe we'd regularly find ourselves having to tinker under the bonnet – so what better to use to wipe up any oil?

Our abuse of the Derby shirt became all the more entertaining after we made friends with another couple of guys also doing the rally called Mark and Chris - and we discovered that Chris was a massive Derby fan!

Not that he was particularly keen to shout about this at the time, with Derby having just broken the record for the lowest ever number of points gained in a Premier League season!

As it turned out, the Derby shirt ended up falling victim to a ceremonial burning one night, after we'd decided to camp in the middle of a forest in Transylvania and built a campfire to keep warm. And with all the oil that was smeared all over it by this point, it made an impressive fireball.

Fair play though to Chris, he took all of our baiting in good humour, and we've remained friends to this day. Top fella that he is, he even came on my stag do a few years later, knowing that he'd be the sole Derby fan among a group consisting largely of Forest fans – and only a few days after Forest had tanked Derby 5-2 at the City Ground!

Living in London as he does, Chris also kindly let me kip over at his gaff when I came down to the capital in 2013 to watch Nottingham's world champion boxer Carl Froch fight at the O2 arena. I had to leave early the next morning – although before I left, it seemed only right to thank a still-snoozing Chris for his hospitality by decorating his entire flat in Forest posters that I'd smuggled down to use for that very purpose!

Anyway, some three-and-a-half weeks after we set off on our Mongol Rally adventure, Ed and I did eventually make it to Mongolia – although not all of the Forest shirts did. Yes, at one point during the trip whilst driving through Romania, we stopped at a scrap yard to try and find a new spare wheel for our car – and the guys who ran the place were all big football fans and insisted on us paying them in Forest shirts rather than cash!

But the Forest shirts that did make it were very well received by the Mongolian children that we gave them out to.

In fact, I can't help but wonder whether our gift may have kickstarted a minor footballing revolution in Mongolia – as the following year, the Mongolian national football team rocketed up the FIFA rankings from 192 to an all-time high of 171!

Which is not bad at all really for a country that barely even has any grass.

Sadly though, the 'Forest factor' clearly wore off after a while – as the Mongolians have since slipped back down the rankings are now (at the time of writing) languishing in 203rd place.

 That said, it remains a great source of amusement to me that there are probably still young people who can be seen wandering around Ulaanbaatar wearing Forest shirts with 'Bennett 29', 'Clingan 16' and various other long-forgotten names printed on the back!

22. COME ON YOU FOREST MEN!

"Carl became something of a cult figure on one of the main Forest internet forums - with many users gleefully adopting his catchphrase of 'COME ON YOU FOREST MEN'!"

It's fair to say that the first decade of the 21st Century is not one that many Forest fans will look back on with much fondness.

In fact, there were quite a lot of occasions when we could've done with having some sort of Samaritans-style helpline to give us an avenue to share our inner turmoil.

Alas, nobody ever provided any such service – but thanks to BBC Radio Nottingham, there were a few years when we had probably the next best thing.

And it was called the Matchline.

The Matchline was basically an answerphone – and for a couple of years from around 2009, Radio Nottingham would encourage Forest, Notts County and Mansfield Town fans to call it every Saturday at ten-to-five and leave messages giving their knee-jerk thoughts on how their team had got on that afternoon. The station would then play a selection of the messages as part of their post-match coverage.

It all probably sounds fairly innocuous – however, the Matchline led to the creation of a mythical character who remains something of a cult figure among many Forest fans.

A character called Carl from Carlton...

To date, the true identity of Carl from Carlton has only been known by a select few people.

Nearly a decade on though, I've decided that the time is now right to let the cat out of the bag.

The birth of Carl all came about during a particularly dull Forest home game midway through the 2008-09 season – a campaign in which the Reds found themselves mired in the turgid grind of yet another relegation battle. I can't recall who the opponents were that afternoon, but I was sat in my usual seat in the upper Bridgford End – and as such was in the company of my brother Al, our friend Graham, and also another chap called Jeff who sat on our row who the three of us had all become quite pally with.

With little of excitement going on on the pitch, Al, Graham, Jeff and I spent most of the game amusing ourselves with idle chat – and at some point during the 90 minutes, the subject of the Matchline had come up. All of us were regular listeners of Radio Nottingham's post-match football coverage, and it turned out we'd all been finding it increasingly amusing due to some of the absolute lunatics who would invariably phone the Matchline each week. Some of the comments that made it onto the airwaves were utterly deranged - and to add to the general sense of unhinged madness, it was quite common for callers to throw in a rousing rally cry of "COME ON YOU REDS!" or something similar at some point during their monologue.

"Dave from Top Valley here," a typical message would go, "just on my way home from the City Ground. Great three points – we need to start doing this week in and week out though. COME ON YOU REDS!"

But as the discussion unfolded between Al, Graham, Jeff and I, there was unanimous agreement that our very favourite callers were those who rang the Matchline despite the fact that they hadn't even been to whatever game they'd called up to talk about. Quite why anyone would feel compelled to phone up a radio station to share their views on a match they'd not even seen is something I've never been able to fathom – but nevertheless, many did…

"Pete from Sandicare here," they'd cry, "Couldn't get down today – I really don't know though what Billy Davies is playing at with his team selections. He needs to have Earnshaw on the pitch from the start if he wants us to score goals. But anyway, COME ON YOU REDS!"

The discussion between Al, Graham, Jeff and I went on for much of the game. And at some point, the suggestion was made that all four of us should call up the Matchline ourselves during our respective journeys home, as a little competition to see if any of us could make it onto the airwaves. But rather than offering any sort of carefully considered insight, it was agreed we should all unleash ridiculous torrents of absolute nonsense - as a parody of the kind of drivel we'd all started to know and love each week.

We also agreed that we should all do this under fake names – and after much deliberation, the four of us chose pseudonyms for ourselves based on where we were all living at the time. Al would be Ged from Gedling… Graham would be Arnie from Arnold… Jeff would be Grant from Grantham… while I would be Carl from Carlton!

Out of the four of us, I don't recall who came up with this idea for having aliases. It's likely though that it was inspired by Graham, who had entertained us on numerous occasions over the years with tales of an old friend of his - who used to regularly amuse himself by wandering down to a phone box near from his house in order to call up local radio stations, and talk absolute nonsense on air under the non de plume of 'Lance from Radford'!

Of course though, many words are said in jest – and after we all filed out of the City Ground following the full-time whistle, it turned out only one of the four of us actually went through with our little plan. Yes, feeling a bit self-conscious and not wanting to be overheard, I'd legged it to a quiet spot at the far side of the car-park at the back of the Brian Clough Stand, pulled my phone out of my pocket and dialled the Matchline number…

Following a brief recorded message enunciated by the dulcet tones of Radio Nottingham's Robin Chipperfield, there was a beep – which was my cue to put on a dorky voice and share Carl from Carlton's very first message to the world…

Unfortunately, the thrust of what Carl actually had to say has long been lost in the mists of time – but his opening gambit consisted of nine words that would come to define him.

"Carl from Carlton here – COME ON YOU FOREST MEN!"

I'm not entirely sure where the idea for "COME ON YOU FOREST MEN!" had come from, but it just seemed a suitably ridiculous rally cry – like something Reds fans might have shouted in the 1890s. Clearly not too ridiculous though for the Matchline – because Carl's ramblings actually made the cut only 20 or so minutes later. I was still driving home at the time, and nearly crashed the car on the Colwick Loop Road when I heard my new alterego's first appearance on the airwaves!

Naturally the maiden voyage of Carl was a source of great hilarity to Al, Graham and Jeff – and my three matchday companions all demanded a repeat performance after the following home game.

A star had been born – and over the remainder of that season, slipping into character as Carl from Carlton to make a quick call to the Matchline became an established part of my matchday routine. I even quickly developed a pretty solid five-part formula:

1. "Carl from Carlton here.
2. "COME ON YOU FOREST MEN!
3. "Couldn't get down today.
4. "But (insert some sort of banal opinion about how Forest played).
5. "COME ON YOU FOREST MEN!"

As with my first call to the Matchline, each attempt to get Carl onto the airwaves would start with me leaving the ground at full-time and quickly finding a quiet spot on the far side of the car-park at the back of the Brian Clough Stand. I basically needed to be away from any large body of fans – not only because I felt a bit self-conscious about beung Carl, but also because my alterego's trademark claim of 'couldn't get down today' would've been rapidly undermined if it was obvious that he was calling up from the middle of a crowd.

There were odd times when Carl's ramblings were presumably deemed too ludicrous even for the Matchline, and left on the cutting room floor. Generally though, his thoughts were regarded as perfectly acceptable fodder for Radio Nottingham's listeners. And while only a few of us were in on the joke, I'm reliably informed Carl became something of a cult figure on one of the main Forest internet forums - with many users gleefully adopting his catchphrase of 'COME ON YOU FOREST MEN'!

In fact, we knew that Carl had gone down in local legend when one week Radio Nottingham played their usual montage of calls made to the Matchline – and someone else had called in and shouted "COME ON YOU FOREST MEN" as part of their message!

All in all I think I managed to get Carl from Carlton onto the radio a good ten or 12 times. For much of this period Forest were fighting a relegation battle, and the football wasn't much to write home about – so for Al, Graham, Jeff and I, Carl's few seconds in the spotlight were often the highlight of an afternoon at the City Ground.

The amusement generated by our little in-joke was such that we even started to build a picture of what Carl would be like if he was actually a real person. We decided he was a slightly overweight lad in his 40s, who still lived with his mum and dad and wore NHS-issue specs. He had a slightly sweaty top lip and was a bit lax when it came to personal hygiene – and getting to address the world via the Matchline was pretty much the only thing he lived for.

Sadly though, all good things come to an end – and sometime around late 2011, the Matchline was axed by Radio Nottingham for reasons never specified. Suddenly then, Carl had no means of being able to share his wisdom with his many fans. It was all quite sad really – if the Matchline had continued I'm quietly confident that Carl would've ended up securing his place alongside David Brent and Borat as one of the all-time great satirical characters.

Perhaps though Carl could be resurrected? After all, Radio Nottingham still to this day has regular live phone-in programmes where fans of the local teams are able to go on the airwaves and share their views – and I've been dared on more than one occasion by some the very few that are 'in the know' to call up and do Carl from Carlton 'live'!

I honestly don't think I'd ever be able to do this though without descending into a massive fit of the giggles.

But to a select few, the name of Carl from Carlton will always live on. Indeed, if you go on Twitter and type "COME ON YOU FOREST MEN" into the search box, you'll find literally dozens of instances where Reds fans have used the phrase in a slightly tongue-in-cheek fashion – with some of the examples from a good few years after Carl last graced the airwaves.

I'm just sad that I never thought to capture Carl's various radio appearances for posterity. I only have one recording, a message that Carl left in early 2010, following a game where Forest had bounced back from a defeat away at Derby by beating Sheffield Wednesday 2-0 – with both of the Reds' goals scored by big striker Dexter Blackstock.

"Carl from Carlton here… COME ON YOU FOREST MEN! Couldn't get down today, but it's good to get back to winning ways after last week against the sheep. Wasn't the most sparkling football from what it sounded like on the radio – but Dexter Anthony Titus Blackstock, you are the man! COME ON YOU FOREST MEN!"

All in all, I only hope I haven't ruined any illusions for any of my fellow Forest fans by revealing that Carl from Carlton was actually a made-up character rather than a real person.

COME ON YOU FOREST MEN!

23. A simple game that's complicated by idiots

"We even had that rarest of commodities in the world of primary school football – a goalkeeper who could actually clear the halfway line with a goal kick!"

As a football fan, it's always satisfying when you get an opportunity to indulge your love of the beautiful game in the name of work – and this is something I've managed to do on numerous occasions over the years.

One instance of this was in my first proper job after I graduated from university, when I found employment with a company that produced news packages that were sent out by satellite to cruise ships - enabling both passengers and crews to stay up-to-date with what was happening in the world while they were out at sea.

My role as an editor with this company was to put these news packages together, and when doing the UK sport bulletins I always tried to get away with sticking the latest goings on at City Ground among the top stories - despite the fact that the Reds didn't really warrant being included at all.

Throughout my working life though, there's one job I've had that was greater than any other in terms of the sheer amount of opportunities it provided for my love of both Forest and football in general to take centre stage. And that was during my late-20s, when I decided to embark on a change of career and become a primary school teacher.

Now the idea of going into teaching is something that had lurked at the back of my mind for quite a few years - ever since my student days up in Liverpool.

Throughout my first two years up on Merseyside, I was in a relationship with a girl mentioned in several previous chapters. She was a few years older than me and as such had completed her studies - and throughout the time that we were an item, she was working as a teacher at a primary school in Birkenhead, a stone's throw from Tranmere Rovers' ground.

Like most students, I had a fair amount of free time – so she'd often twist my arm into going into the school to help out.

And it was really good fun.

Before this point in my life I'd never once thought about the idea of becoming a teacher. However, the time I spent in my girlfriend's classroom in Birkenhead got me thinking about what a brilliant and rewarding job it must be.

As it was though, I was already well on my way down a completely different career path - so I just put the idea to the back of my mind. And eventually, after a couple of years, myself and Miss went our separate ways.

But a seed had definitely been planted - and over the next few years I was further inspired by my great friend Andy Best.

You may also recall Andy from an earlier chapter – he's the friend who I met in serendipitous circumstances during my time at uni, and formed a firm friendship with largely based on our shared love of Forest.

Well after we graduated from uni, Andy eventually decided he wanted to go into teaching – so committed himself to a further year of study in order to get qualified.

Now I must admit, I did initially find the idea of Andy being in such a position of responsibility absolutely hilarious, having been privy to some of his ridiculous drunken behavior over the years. Fair play to him though, he's absolutely brilliant at his job – and I was enormously proud of him when he succeeded in becoming a head teacher at the age of just 33. This means he now gets to give regular assemblies to his whole school – in which he often takes the opportunity to indulge his passion for Forest by talking about the mighty Reds to an audience of several hundred confused Sussex children!

After a few years then of following Andy's career with great interest, I eventually decided to take the plunge myself in 2007.

In some ways it was a bit of a gamble. By this point I'd acquired some of the trappings of adult life such as a mortgage. As such, the only way I could afford to go back to full-time education to do my teacher training was to move out of my house and rent it out, and go back to live with my Mum and Dad.

But sometimes in life you just have to take these risks.

The training programme I did was a one-year one, where you get thrown into a school from pretty much day one and learn how to be a teacher 'on the job'. It was an enormous learning curve, and not just in terms of the actual craft of teaching. Yes, very early in the course after an ill-advised decision to go out and get wrecked on a 'school night', I found out the hard way that a massive hangover and a class of 34 rowdy children is the worst possible combination!

After an intense year though, I was very proud in the summer of 2008 when I received confirmation that I'd achieved Qualified Teacher Status. What's more, the school in inner city Nottingham where I'd done most of my training were so impressed with me that they offered me a job – and as September 2008 approached, I found myself both excited and slightly terrified by the prospect of having responsibility for my first ever class. Each class in the school had a number - and when I found out mine would be Class 11, I immediately went out and bought a brand new Forest shirt and had my surname and the number 11 printed on the back. If nothing else, I would at least look the part on 'P.E. days'.

Over the next few months I quickly got to know the kids in my class, and it turned out that one of them was actually related to Julian Bennett - who was probably my favourite Forest player at the time. Sadly my attempts to utilise this connection to get 'Benno' to come into the school and do a coaching session were unsuccessful – although in some ways that was probably just as well, as he would've probably ended up injuring one of the kids with one of his trademark two-footed lunges!

I'd discovered by this point that being a teacher is incredibly hard work - but the job was amazing, and just as rewarding as I hoped it would be. I quickly learned that one of the most important parts of the role is building rapport with the kids – and I discovered that football offers you a great 'in' on that score, particularly with boys.

Some children I worked with reminded me so much of myself when I was a kid – and never more so when I was required to grab my Acme Thunderer whistle and head outside to do playground duty. Every day you'd find huddles of kids swapping 'Match Attax' cards – the new generation's equivalent of the Panini stickers of my own youth – and you'd usually find a game of football going on too.

The urge to join in with the footballing action on the playground was always massive. Generally I'd try to maintain a professional distance – although from time to time the temptation would simply prove too great. There was one particular occasion when I spotted a loose ball heading in my direction – and when it arrived, I casually flicked it up before it hit the ground with my left foot, and then volleyed it into the top corner of the goal with my right. This probably gained me more respect from some of the boys than anything I'd ever done with them in lessons!

That said, I did manage to find excuses on numerous occasions to bring the subject of football into the classroom. This might sound self-indulgent - and I won't deny to some degree that it was.

However, the kids did also benefit. It's well-known in the education world that it can be hard to get boys excited about writing – and this was very much the case with a lot of the lads at the school where I worked. With most of them being massively into football though, I would try whenever I could to give them opportunities to write about the beautiful game – and it was amazing what a difference this made in terms of their enthusiasm levels.

There was also an occasion when I managed to find what I felt was a perfectly justifiable excuse to show my class a DVD with highlights of Forest's famous victory against Hamburg in the 1980 European Cup final!

This event occurred on an afternoon when we were supposed to go outside and do P.E. Alas though it was chucking it down with rain - so the DVD was basically my back-up plan.

Of course, none of the kids in my class had been alive when Forest were last even in the Premier League, let alone conquering Europe – so to most of them, the idea of the Reds being in the final of what they knew as the Champions League was probably absurd.

But as well as offering an insight into Forest's glorious history, my decision to put the DVD on had actually been rooted in a desire to educate my class in one of the most important aspects of football in general. At seven and eight, all kids really care about when out on the playground or down the park is scoring goals. By showing them how Forest grittily put 11 men behind the ball though in Madrid to hold on to the slenderest of leads, I wanted to illustrate that defending as a team is actually just as important a factor when it comes to winning games.

Happily, the kids were soon engrossed in the DVD – and all started jumping around and cheering when we got to the final whistle and Forest were confirmed as champions of Europe!

That said, you probably won't be surprised to learn that a lot of kids who I worked with during my time in teaching supported the big Premier League teams rather than Forest or Notts County. As is only right, I would give them quite a lot of grief about this – and I tried hard to show them a more righteous path. During each of the first four years of my time as a teacher, I actually managed to get a different Forest legend to write a message to my class. In 2008 it was Martin O'Neill, who I collared at an event held in Nottingham to celebrate the success of the Brian Clough statue campaign; while Trevor Francis, Garry Birtles and John Robertson each did the honours in 2009, 2010 and 2011 respectively when I met them at different 'Audience with..' events.

"To class 7," Birtles wrote, "listen to Sir – you'll learn a lot. Yours, Garry Birtles."

Through little touches like this I was successful in converting a fair few children towards the Forest cause. In fact, there was one lad who got the bug to such a degree during his time in my class that he'd always grab any opportunity, no matter how tenuous, to crowbar the mighty Reds into his schoolwork. There was one time in a literacy lesson when I was getting the kids to practice starting sentences with an adverb – and later on when I was marking this particular boy's book, every single sentence he'd written was something to do with Forest.

"Amazingly, Raddy Majewski hit the ball into the West Brom net."

"Impressively, Chris Cohen won the ball in midfield."

"Hilariously, Derby County lost again…"

Bless him, the lad in question was far from being the brightest kid in the class – it always amused me though that while he struggled in spelling test every week, he was always spot on when it came to writing the name of Forest's mecurial Polish midfielder.

In some ways it probably wasn't a bad thing that most of the kids that I worked with supported teams other than Forest. During my first year in teaching there was one time at a Forest home game when I happened to turn round just before kick-off – and realised to my horror that I had a child from my own class sat with his Dad just a few rows behind me!

Now I like to think I'm largely capable of keeping control of my emotions whilst watching my team– but let's face it, most of us have our moments when we lose it and vent our rage at the referee or whoever. And though I was 'off duty', the fact that I had one of my own class sat just feet away caused me to spend that whole game worrying that I might betray my responsibility of being a positive role model at any moment.

Fortunately I managed to make it all the way to full-time without disgracing myself. Sadly the same can't be said for Forest, who slumped to an insipid defeat to Wolves.

All in all, my favourite memories from my time as a primary school teacher are largely related to an extra responsibility I was entrusted with after I'd been doing the job for a couple of years – and a responsibility that was probably always destined to come my way sooner rather than later. When you're a male teacher in a primary school you tend to be in a massive minority – and regardless of whether or not you actually have any knowledge of football, it's pretty much a given that you'll end up running the school team at some point!

Now when us football fans talk about our all-time heroes from all the years we've spent supporting our teams, the names we trot out will usually be pretty much a 50/50 split between players and managers who have served with distinction. As I've already stated in a previous chapter, the two people who I hold in highest regard are Stuart Pearce and Brian Clough - so for me, the scales actually tip more towards managers than players, with Psycho having obviously performed both roles at the City Ground.

When you think about it then, it's quite strange that, while we all fantasise when we're kids about making it as a player, few of us ever have similar dreams about becoming a manager.

Brian Clough, as he often did, probably hit the nail on the head. His achievements as a manager were obviously peerless – yet I always remember him talking during an interview about how none of it came even remotely close to the buzz he used to get during his playing days from being out on the pitch and scoring goals.

Much as I'd never really had any aspirations of becoming a manager though, I quickly discovered when I started doing it that I really enjoyed it. The school team played in a league with various other schools from around Nottingham, so most weeks there'd be a day when I'd be straight off with the players and a massive sack of footballs, bibs and cones as soon as my day of teaching had finished - for either a training session or a match.

To be honest, my role was quite easy – but then I'm a big believer in the famous quote from legendary former Liverpool manager Bill Shankly about football being a simple game that's complicated by idiots. Let's face it, we've all seen the joy sucked out of kids' football by overbearing adults on the touchline thinking that they're Jose Mourinho - and I didn't really want to be part of that sort of nonsense.

All I ever really did then was pick the team and reel off a few classic Cloughisms by way of instruction - such as not worrying about the opposition, showing respect to referees, and of course the great man's famous quote about how God would've built pitches up in the sky if he'd wanted football to be played in the clouds. Sometimes I'd even wear a green sweatshirt just to hammer home the point.

It soon became apparent too that that Cloughie bloke must have known what he was talking about – because bless 'em, after I'd finished dispensing my second-hand pearls of wisdom, the lads would generally go out and thrash whoever we happened to be playing. Indeed, we won the league title in both of the two years that I was in charge of the team – each time without losing a single game.

In fairness though, I think this impressive record was far more down to being lucky enough to have a really good group of players who gelled brilliantly as a team. We even had that rarest of commodities in the world of primary school football – a goalkeeper who could actually clear the halfway line with a goal kick! The lads were a real credit to themselves and the school, both in the way they played and the way they conducted themselves. Some of them already played for teams outside of school, in the local under-11 and under-12 leagues. But there were also quite a few who had never really played competitive football before – and it was particularly satisfying to watch those players flourish.

And while my default 'management' style was very much a case of letting the lads get on with playing without getting on their cases too much, there were the odd few occasions when I made a point of offering the lads more specific instructions. There was one particular game when we were playing against another school who had a team of really big lads, and who were renowned for being quite physical. I swear one of their players was actually about 15 – he was a gigantic surly youth, who looked more like he was about to skulk off for a crafty fag than play a game of football.

As my players were limbering up ready for the match – or rather just taking it in turns to leather shots as hard as they could at our keeper, which was about as sophisticated as our warm-ups ever got - they seemed a bit subdued and intimidated. Just before kick-off then, I decided to call them in for a quick chat, where I tried my best to give them a bit of reassurance. Most importantly though, I also took our centre half to one side for a quiet word, instructing him to go in hard at the earliest opportunity on the big lad from the other team!

Now some might take a dim view of steering ten and eleven year-olds towards the uglier side of the game - and I must admit, I did feel a bit like the nasty dojo master in *The Karate Kid*. But like it or not football *is* a competitive sport – and you do sometimes have to play people at their own game. And happily my centre half did me proud, absolutely flattening the big lad within about 30 seconds of kick-off – winning the ball too in the process. An important psychological battle had been won from the off, and our lads went on to win the game comfortably.

Far more though than any technical input, I found man management to be by far the biggest part of my job of managing the school team. Some of the kids needed a bit of encouragement, while others were sometimes a bit over-confident and needed bringing down or peg or two.

Of course, dealing with all the different characters and temperaments was nothing different to what I'd be doing in the classroom on a daily basis as part of the day job anyway.

One piece of man management I think I got spot on was my choice of captain. The lad in question was often in trouble in class, so my decision initially raised a few eyebrows among some of my teaching colleagues. But he was a natural leader on the pitch, who took enormous pride in being given the armband – and over time I think the responsibility helped bring an improvement to his behaviour in the classroom. Indeed, not long after I made him captain he'd been caught by a dinner lady vandalising the school bogs – which, for a member of a primary school footy term, is probably equivalent to a professional footballer being spotted falling out of a nightclub the night before a big game. As a punishment for his behaviour he received a one-match ban – something he was absolutely gutted about. However, a harsh lesson had been learned, and from that point on he tried hard to be a bit more mature and stay out of trouble.

As well as the league, the school team also competed in a number of cup competitions, including a big tournament that took place every year over the course of a single afternoon – with the players and I all excused from our respective lessons in order to go and take part.

The first time I got to take a team to this tournament was at a time when I was teaching a year group best described as 'challenging'. As such, I'm not sure who was most excited about the prospect of escaping from the classroom for half a day– me or the players!

Each year at the tournament, a member of the Forest team would usually come down to present medals. On this particular year it was Wes Morgan - and though we got knocked out in the semi-finals, the lads still got to have a team photo with the Reds stalwart.

Now many modern footballers have delicate egos, and I can only hope Big Wes isn't one of them – because as the lads were assembling for the photo, our centre forward turned to him and casually asked "So who are you then?"

A priceless moment – made all the funnier in hindsight by the fact Wes Morgan would end up being a Premier League-winning captain just a few years later.

And big Wes Morgan wasn't the only well-known footballer who the lads got to rub shoulders with. During my time involved in running the team the school had a brand new astroturf pitch installed, and arrangements were made for Jermaine Jenas and Tom Huddlestone to come along and cut a ribbon to declare the new facility officially open.

With Jenas and Huddlestone both having grown up in Nottingham, it was great for the lads to meet two real life examples of how kids just like them could go on and make the grade at the highest level if they worked hard enough – indeed, at the time both players were playing for Tottenham, and had both been capped by England. Happily Jenas was brilliant – he was all smiles and made a real effort to chat to the kids. Huddlestone on the other hand was miserable as sin, and gave the impression that he'd rather be anywhere else.

Still, he ended up getting sold to Derby a few years later. Karma!

Another major highlight of my time involved in the school team meanwhile was when we got to the semi-finals of one of the cup competitions – a fixture that the lads got to play on the pitch at Meadow Lane during the half-time interval at a Notts County home game.

I can't remember who Notts were playing that afternoon, but we were given a load of tickets so myself and the lads and their families and some of the other teachers could all go and watch the match. We were sat quite near the away fans - and there was a highly amusing moment when our goalkeeper started chanting "'Oo are yer?" at them. In my role as a teacher I should've probably had a word – in the end though I just turned a blind eye.

When the time came for the team to take to the pitch it was a pretty quick match, with the half-time interval only lasting 15 minutes. The lads weren't overawed at all by playing in front of such a big crowd – well, a big crowd for them at any rate – and I think it's fair to say that they laid on far more entertainment in 15 minutes than Notts managed in 90. Not only that, a dramatic late goal was enough to see us go away with a 1-0 win. I managed to capture the winning strike on video, so on the Monday morning there was a playback in assembly in front of the entire school. The team were given a standing ovation and felt like absolute rock stars.

Apart from those odd occasions where myself and the lads would get special permission to sneak out of lessons to go and play in tournaments, the hours that I spent running the school team were entirely my own time, which I was giving up voluntarily. And not only that, my responsibilities sometimes stretched far beyond those of my contemporaries like Steve Bruce and Arsene Wenger. I'd often end up washing the kit or pumping up footballs; while trips to away games would involve enduring lengthy periods stuck in Nottingham's rush-hour traffic on a minibus that absolutely reeked of Lynx deodorant – which the lads were inexplicably obsessed with dousing themselves with.

What's more, on returning to the school having secured another three points I'd often be stood waiting for ages in the freezing cold with some of the lads outside the school entrance, due to parents being too disorganised to come and collect them on time.

There was also one time when I ended up refereeing a match, when the bloke who usually reffed for us had to cry off at the last minute. Needless to say, having one of the competing teams' managers acting as the man in the middle is a slight conflict of interest to say the least – not that it ever stopped Alex Ferguson trying during his years as Manchester United manager. I did try to be as fair as I could, but to be honest I'm not sure I succeeded judging by some of the absolute dog's abuse that I got over some of my decisions from parents of the kids on the other team. The whole experience certainly made me realise that referees have a far harder job than most of us ever give them credit for.

For all its trials and tribulations though, my extra-curricular role never felt like a burden. When I look back on my own childhood, playing for the school football team is definitely among my favourite things I ever did at primary school – so it felt great that I was enabling a new generation to create similar memories. Some of the lads weren't the most gifted academically, so it felt very satisfying being able to help them achieve something they could feel truly proud of – in some cases, possibly for the first time in their lives.

And for some of the lads, their footballing exploits could have gone much further than playing for the school team – as during my time in charge a couple of them caught the attention of a scout from Forest, and were invited to take part in some training sessions down at the club's academy. One of those lads in particular was a great player – a powerful defender who, despite only being ten years old, put me on my backside on more than one occasion during training.

The interest from Forest was naturally pretty exciting, although from a selfish point of view I did have some mixed feelings – as when young lads get signed up by a professional club's academy, it's often stipulated that they're not allowed to play for their school team any more. Suddenly then, I was in danger of losing a couple of my best players.

I'm not entirely sure what the reasons are for club's academies trying to restrict kids from playing any other competitive football. Presumably it's to avoid them getting injured, or picking up bad habits from people like myself who don't have their FA coaching badges? It always seemed a bit daft to me, and a far cry from an era not so long ago when Forest players like John Robertson would play against Liverpool or Arsenal on a Saturday and then - according to legend - join in with a kickabout down the local park the following morning, purely for the sheer love of the game.

As it was, the two lads from my team went down to the Forest academy quite a few times, although sadly it never led to anything. Still, they got closer to properly living the dream than most of us ever have.

All in all then, my short stint as a manager was a memorable and rewarding experience – but it came to an end when I decided to leave teaching altogether at the end of 2012 after five years in the profession.

It was a difficult decision, because on many levels I loved the job. Sadly however, everything you read about teaching and the intense workload is true. You end up putting in so many hours that it's hard to have much of a life outside of work for 39 weeks of the year – although I did give it a real good go. During my first couple of years in the profession I was going through a phase where I was going to watch the England football team a lot as well as Forest - and in 2009, I actually managed to squeeze in a trip to see Fabio Capello's men play a World Cup qualifier away at Kazakhstan in the middle of term-time!

Looking back, it was a bit ridiculous really. The match was on a Saturday evening, and as soon as I'd dismissed my class at 3pm on the Friday I was straight in the car and down to Stansted to fly to the Kazakh city of Almaty, where the match was taking place. Due to the seven-hour flight time and time difference, I arrived at midday on the Saturday – and then spent an enjoyable afternoon in Almaty before heading to the stadium to watch a comfortable 4-0 win for England. It was then straight back to the airport to fly home – and I was back in my local pub for Sunday lunch, and back in my classroom on the Monday morning.

After five years though of burning the candle at both ends I was feeling completely worn out - and having had a career already that was frankly much less demanding than teaching, it simply became too tempting to not just go back to it.

Still, I have no regrets about any of it. My time in teaching enabled me to develop numerous invaluable skills, many which have remained useful since I walked away. And while it's a good few years now since I left the profession, I still get treated like a minor celebrity whenever I happen to wander through the area of Nottingham where I used to work - which is always lovely. Forget the end-of-year attainment levels that are treated as the be-all and end-all in the education world these days, you know you must have done something right when kids who were once in your class or their parents stop you in the street and make a fuss of you.

Best of all though, my time in teaching gave me some fantastic memories – and strangely enough, a lot of the best ones are football-related.

24. Living the dream # 2

"A few minutes into the second half Kenny Burns decided the Boots team needed some fresh legs, and told me to get myself warmed up..."

I guess we're all guilty sometimes of being a bit greedy.

In a previous chapter, I talked about the time in 2004 when I got to fulfil a lifelong ambition by playing a match on the hallowed turf of the City Ground.

And you'd have thought I'd have been content with that.

In 2010 though, I got to live the dream once again in a different way, by playing alongside some of my childhood Forest heroes... including a man who played a major part in one of the most famous goals of all time.

This opportunity came about after I got the chance to take part in a charity match organised for Children in Need.

It all started with my brother Al, who was working at the time for Boots at their head office in Nottingham. Boots have always supported Children in Need in a big way - and in 2010, Al decided to throw himself into the company's fundraising efforts by getting a staff football team together – and with the two of us having come to know quite a lot of people over the years who work at BBC Radio Nottingham, my esteemed sibling decided to challenge them to a game.

Happily the BBC guys accepted - and a suitable venue was secured when Carlton Town FC kindly agreed to give up their ground facilities for an evening.

Now Boots' head office is a pretty big place – and I think it's fair to say that Al could've probably filled several teams of 11 players with the amount of colleagues who were keen to play in the match. Bless him though, despite the fact that I didn't actually work at Boots, he still held a place for me as a 'ringer'. In view of this, I was more than happy to settle for being one of the subs – and I immediately began looking forward to what would no doubt be an entertaining evening and also a great opportunity to help raise some cash for a good cause.

And as it turned out, things started getting even more exciting as match night drew closer...

Due to the nature of their work, the Radio Nottingham guys are pretty well connected within the local footballing world. And in the process of assembling their team for the Children in Need match, our friends at the station began taking great delight in letting us know how they'd been raiding their contacts books and enhancing the quality of their squad by securing the services of various ex-pros.

As you can probably imagine, there were all sorts of protests about this from our side – although fair play to the BBC boys, they agreed in the end that the various ex-pros who'd agreed to play would be split equally across the two teams.

Now I can't remember exactly how it was decided which team would have which ex-pros. However, assuming it was sorted out in time-honoured playground fashion, then I can only assume that we must have had first pick – because it was announced in the run-up to the game that we'd managed to bag none other than Steve Hodge!

'Harry' had long since retired from playing by this point in time – and at 48, we all knew he wouldn't be quite the same player he was during his peak at the City Ground back in the 80s. Nevertheless, it was exciting knowing we'd be getting to play alongside a bona fide Forest legend, and the man whose sliced clearance while playing for England in the 1986 World Cup led to Maradona's infamous 'hand of God' goal.

Hell, it was as though you'd been doing karaoke in pubs your whole life, but then suddenly getting the chance to sing alongside Stevie Wonder for one evening.

Joining 'Harry' on our team was Lawrie Dudfield - a former Notts County striker who had retired from playing a few years previously, but was still a relative spring chicken at the age of 30. Meanwhile, the Radio Nottingham team would also be calling upon a former Forest player in the shape of Nigel Jemson, along with Des Coleman – better known as Des The Weatherman off BBC East Midlands Today.

In addition, both the two teams would also have an ex-pro as a manager for the night, each of them also City Ground legends – with Kenny Burns entrusted with the responsibility of inspiring greatness from the Boots team, and Steve Sutton doing the honours for Radio Nottingham.

All in all, I like to think it was the most eagerly anticipated football fixture Nottingham had seen in many a year – and come the big night, a crowd of several hundred were in attendance as the great and good of Boots kicked off against the might of Radio Nottingham.

Being on the bench, I spent the first half standing in the technical area alongside Kenny Burns - which was an entertaining experience in itself. I was already reasonably familiar with Kenny's company, as around this time the Navigation pub on Meadow Lane was my usual pre-match watering hole when Forest were playing at home - and the man who Brian Clough had insisted on addressing as Kenneth would often be in there too on a matchday. As such I'd exchanged pleasantries with him on numerous occasions – in fact, he even nicked a handful of my chips once!

Obviously Kenny didn't actually know most of his players, but nevertheless he threw himself with great enthusiasm into his task of shouting advice and encouragement from the touchline. My abiding memory is of him constantly yelling at a rather diminutive member of our team and calling him 'Stuart Little'!

Watching from the sidelines, it quickly became apparent that some of the ex-pros had definitely still 'got it'. Though not as mobile as perhaps he once was, Steve Hodge rolled back the years in our midfield with some exquisite touches. However, it was Nigel Jemson on the Radio Nottingham team who had the most immediate impact on the game. After about 15 minutes Jemmo received a pass with his back to goal about 25 yards out – and with seemingly effortless ease, he swivelled and volleyed the ball into the top-left hand corner of the net to put his side a goal up.

We were suddenly chasing the game then – although we quickly had the opportunity to bring the scores level when Steve Hodge took a blatant dive in the box and the ref immediately pointed to the spot. As our captain, Al was entrusted with the responsibility of taking the penalty - alas though, facing Robin Chipperfield who was in goal for Radio Nottingham, he proceeded to spanner his kick against the bar.

At half-time then we were in need of some inspirational words from Kenny, and early in the second half, our esteemed manager decided the Boots team needed some fresh legs. I was duly told to go and get myself warmed up - and a few minutes later, I got the nod…

"Right then lad, you're on!", Kenny barked at me.

"Okay Kenny – but where am playing?"

"You're a big lad – so centre half!"

What Kenny didn't know was that I'd never really played centre half in my life - what's more, I was pretty useless at heading the ball. Perhaps not the wisest of tactical substitutions then, given that I'd be going straight into the heart of a back four that was having to deal with a lively strike partnership of Nigel Jemson and Des The Weatherman!

I was particularly concerned about Jemmo. Al had been marking the former Forest striker in the first half, and had found him to be a bit physical to put it mildly – including a sly elbow when the two of them were challenging for a header. It was an interesting insight into the 'win at all costs' mentality that many professional footballers will probably never be able to shake off. Unlike most of us involved in the game, who were treating it as a bit of a laugh more than anything else, Jemmo was clearly taking it very seriously indeed.

In fact, when he'd signed up to play, Jemmo had initially said he'd just play the first half – but he must have been enjoying himself because he threw a bit of a strop when he was told at half-time that he'd be making way for another player. Not wanting to cause a scene, the Radio Nottingham guys decided to let him stay on for however long he wanted.

Of course, Kenny Burns was renowned during his playing days for his 'robust' style of defending – so had I consulted him before I went out onto the pitch, he would've no doubt advised me to put Jemmo in his place by clattering him as soon as I got a chance. As it was, pretty much my first involvement in the game was a clumsy challenge – but rather than on Jemmo it was on Des the Weatherman, who I left lying in a crumpled heap after a horrendously mistimed lunge.

I was working as a primary school teacher at the time, and the first thing I saw as I picked myself up off the floor was a kid from my class in the crowd, looking mildly horrified that I'd just flattened a minor local TV celebrity. Not my greatest moment then really, especially given that I'd taught a PE lesson only days earlier where I'd been preaching the virtues of fair play.

Des the Weatherman got his own back though a few minutes later - burying his studs into my ankle - and making a point of coming over immediately afterwards and giving as sarcastic an apology as you could ever wish to hear. Perhaps sensibly he and I gave each other a wide berth for the rest of the game, leaving me to concentrate on Jemmo – and I'm happy to say that I managed to keep him pretty quiet for a good 20 minutes. There was one point when the BBC team launched a counter attack, and Jemmo and I found ourselves in a one-on-one race in pursuit of a clearance that had been hoofed up towards one of the corner flags. I just managed to get there first to whack the ball out for a throw-in – although having just sprinted a good 40 yards, the two of us both ended up bent over one of the advertising boards and gasping for breath!

At the other end of the pitch meanwhile I made a rare foray forward when the Boots team won a corner, and actually ended up setting up a goal for Lawrie Dudfield – chesting down the ball to the former Notts man, who duly lashed it into the corner of the net.

The match then descended into farce thanks to some shocking cheating from the Radio Nottingham team – with Steve Sutton persistently sneaking extra players onto the pitch. At one point I think it was something like 17 against 11. But it was all good fun, and provided the crowd with a bit of a laugh.

By the time the full-time whistle went we'd played out an entertaining 5-5 draw. It had been a brilliant experience, although after only 40 minutes or so of running around a football pitch I was gasping for breath - and I immediately came to the sad realisation that, at the mere age of 31, my days of being able to hack playing 11-a-side were probably over.

Still, I'd just played in the same team as Steve Hodge, one of my childhood heroes. So much like Zinedine Zidane finishing his playing career in 2006 by appearing in a World Cup final, I was bowing out at probably the highest point I would ever reach.

I even went one better than Zidane by actually managing to stay on the pitch – although Des the Weatherman might question whether I deserved to

25. We all live in a world of Brian Rice

"The fact that I had a direct hotline to Brian Rice was a source of much amusement, although I feared it was only a matter of time before the poor guy ended up getting a late night phone call from a load of drunken Reds fans wanting to serenade him with a rendition of The Brian Rice Song..."

I've talked a fair bit in previous sections of this book about my Forest heroes.

From my own years as a Reds fan, Brian Clough and Stuart Pearce are without question the two who I hold in the highest of regard. And while his days as a Forest player were before my time, John McGovern is also someone who I have enormous respect for – both for his achievements during his playing days at the City Ground, and also due to some very enjoyable personal dealings that I've had with him.

I think it's fair to say though that there are different categories of hero when you're football fan.

The Cloughs, Pearces and McGoverns of this world are your unquestionable, all-time legend type heroes.

But there are also other types of heroes.

There's the players who wouldn't get anywhere near your all-time greatest Forest eleven – but who nevertheless stood head and shoulders above most of their team-mates during the time when they played for us. In my time as a fan, I'm thinking the likes of Brian Laws, Colin Cooper, Andy Reid and Robert Earnshaw.

There's also the unsung heroes – the sorts of players who just get on quietly with their job, allowing others to steal the headlines. The likes of Steve Sutton, Steve Chettle, David Phillips and Wes Morgan.

And then there are the cult heroes. Those players who don't really fit any of the above categories, but who still manage to gain enormous levels of affection among the fans. Examples of such players who have played for Forest over the last few decades include the likes of Jason Lee and Julian Bennett.

But without doubt, the biggest City Ground cult hero of all is a man who arrived at the club from Scotland in the summer of 1985, signed by Brian Clough from Hibernian for the princely sum of £175,000.

Now given the ridiculous amounts that footballers change hands for these days, £175,000 might not sound like a huge amount of money. But it was a decent sum back in the mid-80s - not much less in fact than what Forest paid that same summer for Neil Webb (£250,000 from Portsmouth) and Stuart Pearce (£210,000 from Coventry). Indeed, as a young player who'd shown increasing promise up in Scotland at Hibs, big things were expected of Brian Rice when he arrived at the City Ground. There were even whisperings of him being 'The next Kenny Dalglish'.

In reality though, the young Scottish midfielder never quite lived up to that potential. In fact, far from the Liverpool legend to whom he was fleetingly compared, Brian Rice was the sort of guy who didn't even remotely resemble a professional footballer. He was a tall, ginger bloke, with a slightly awkward gait, and frankly looked like he couldn't tackle his way out of a paper bag.

However he did have his moments during his occasional appearances in a red shirt, usually on the left wing. There was a goal against Liverpool at the City Ground in front of the Trent End, and also a dramatic last-minute effort fired into the very same net to earn the Reds a 2-1 win against West Ham.

But despite it having secured three points for Forest, Brian Rice's winner against the Hammers has been largely forgotten. Instead, everyone remembers the Reds' opening strike that night - a 40-yard thunderbolt free-kick by Dutch midfield maestro Johnny Metgod, which is still regarded as one of the finest goals ever seen at the City Ground.

There was one moment though of Brian Rice's career at Forest that has never suffered the fate of being overshadowed. I refer of course to his winning goal for the Reds away at Arsenal in the quarter final of the FA Cup in 1988 - a moment of audacious greatness that instantly earned him legendary status among an entire generation of Forest fans.

There's no need for me to describe the goal – as most of you reading this will have seen the clip hundreds of times. Some of you may even have been there.

And those of you aren't familiar with the goal – well, just stop what you're doing right now and go and find it on YouTube…

It wasn't just the fact that our hero kept his head and scored in such a 'heart in mouth' moment. It was the manner in which he did it.

In such a massive game, having beaten Arsenal's infamous offside trap and found themselves clean through on goal, most footballers would've gone for the safe option and drilled the ball low - or maybe even tried to go round the advancing keeper.

No-one in their right mind would go for the cheeky chip, would they?

It could've gone horribly wrong and probably should've done. But no – despite the fact the ball seemed to hang in the air for an agonising period of time, it eventually dropped gloriously into the back of the Arsenal net. And 10,000 Forest fans crammed behind the goal on Highbury's old Clock End terrace went absolutely barmy.

The goal proved enough to send the Reds through to the FA Cup semi-final - and with just one deft flick of his left peg, Brian Rice had secured his status as an eternal Forest hero.

There really should be a blue plaque unveiled on the former site of Highbury – which now consists of fancy apartments following Arsenal's move to their swanky new Emirates Stadium. I actually discovered recently that there's a website where you can get very authentic looking blue plaques made, featuring whatever wording you like. I may have to get one knocked up, and then go down to north London in the dead of night and stick it up somewhere.

For me personally though, the funny thing about Brian Rice's greatest moment is that it actually came slightly before my time as a supporter. But much like the Reds' glory days of the late 70s and early 80s, it's something I've grown up hearing fellow fans talk about in hushed tones – and by the time I started getting into Forest, the cult of Brian Rice was very much in full swing. The *Brian* fanzine even launched its own Brian Rice Appreciation Society – although the most notable form of homage, and something that lives on to this day, was the Trent End launching 'The Brian Rice Song'.

Sung to the tune of 'Yellow Submarine' by the Beatles, The Brian Rice Song is a song that's probably endured over the decades because of its glorious simplicity as much as anything. Over the years I've heard some particularly epic renditions that went through all the entire Forest team's squad numbers and then continued into the club's backroom staff – going even as far as the kitman and the tea lady being Brian Rice.

Sadly of course, Brian Rice never again reached the heights of that winning goal at Highbury. But to be fair, who could have? Over the next couple of years following that afternoon at Highbury he drifted in and out of the Forest team… although briefly, in 1990, he did grace the same line-up as one David Currie.

Yes, Currie and Rice!

That comedy moment though was pretty much Brian Rice's last hurrah - he left Forest later in 1990 to go back to his native Scotland, having clocked up barely more than 100 appearances for the Reds in five years at the club. He went on to spend the rest of his playing career turning out for a string of Scottish clubs, eventually hanging up his boots to go into coaching - and during the early part of the new millennium he became assistant manager of Falkirk.

Now around this time I happened to be writing for the Reds fanzine *Blooming Forest*. I felt it was time to furnish my fellow Reds fans with a proper update on what Brian Rice was doing with himself – so I duly made contact with Falkirk and put in a request for an interview. The next thing I knew, I found myself sat on my sofa one evening, dialling the great man's mobile number…

I'm pleased to say that Brian Rice seemed like a really nice guy during our 30-minute chat – and unsurprisingly, after getting the initial pleasantries out of the way, it wasn't long before we started talking about *that* goal…

"I'll always remember it," he said. "Nigel picked the ball up and played a great pass through to me, and I wasn't the quickest player but I got myself clear. I knew how much time I had, and one thing I never did was panic. I knew exactly what I was doing. In the dressing room afterwards, Mr Clough actually came up to me and said 'If there was one person I would've wanted to go through one on one with the keeper, it was you.'"

It was apparent as we spoke that Brian Rice looked back on his time at Forest with great fondness. He was also commendably honest when reflecting on why he never achieved the sort of impact at the City Ground that people thought he might have done when he first arrived.

"I'd be the first to admit that I wasn't the greatest of players," he said. "I feel I was an honest player – I worked hard in training and I'd go out every game and give my best. I think the problem I had though was with self-confidence. After I came down from Hibernian I was suddenly rubbing shoulders with all these great players like Nigel Clough and Stuart Pearce, and I spent a long time feeling like I wasn't really worthy of playing alongside them. Self-confidence is if course so important when you're a footballer – and I have no doubt that it did hinder my career at Forest."

But while Brian Rice perhaps didn't do his own abilities justice for much of his time at the City Ground, he did hint during our chat at having played a key role in something that no-one has ever really given him any recognition for – namely, the development of Stuart Pearce in the late 80s into one of the best players in the country.

"I'd always played in the middle of the park," he told me, "but Brian Clough got me to play on the left. He actually gave me some credit for helping Stuart make his mark at Forest, as it was often me who was covering him when he made his runs forward, or playing balls through to him."

Probably the most startling revelation of our conversation though was when Brian Rice revealed the reason why he left Forest. For years I'd always thought he'd moved on simply because he was no longer in Brian Clough's first team plans. Chatting to him though, I discovered that he had actually experienced an incredibly distressing time towards the end of his stay at the City Ground – with one of his daughters becoming seriously ill with meningitis at just 18 months old.

Happily she did make a full recovery. Nevertheless, it was a difficult time for the Rices – and as a young couple living in Nottingham with no other family at close hand, it made them decide that it was time to move back up to Scotland and their roots.

That sad note aside, it was great to chat to the ginger ninja – and naturally, I kept his phone number stored in my mobile for some time afterwards. I did end up deleting it though after a while – as while the fact that I had a direct hotline to Brian Rice was a source of much amusement to some of my Forest-supporting friends, I feared it was only a matter of time before the poor guy ended up getting a late night phone call from a load of drunken Reds fans wanting to serenade him with a rendition of The Brian Rice Song!

Indeed, I'd already seen the dangers of having the phone number of a footballing legend stored on your mobile phone. Back in 1999 when I was doing my journalism degree, I did a long-term work placement at a regional newspaper up in the north-west of England – and at that time, a certain former England footballer had landed his first managerial job with one of the local non-league teams. This team was covered by one of the sports reporters at the paper – who was duly entrusted with the ex-England man's mobile number, so he could call him for comments and suchlike.

Initially this wasn't a problem. However, the reporter in question must have bragged to a few people about having the number – because one fateful evening, one of his mates 'borrowed' his mobile and sent the former player a text. And it was a text roughly along the lines of: "I don't know how to tell you this, but over the course of all the conversations we've had, I've started developing feelings for you…"

A brilliant prank, only a costly one for the reporter – the former England player was quite put out, and refused to speak to him again after that.

But though I no longer had Brian Rice on speed dial, I like to think that I've definitely done my bit over the last few decades to keep his name alive at the City Ground - including coming up with an idea sometime around 2006 that led to a large group of Forest fans joining together to create a unique tribute to the ginger ninja.

You may well have gathered from the preceding chapters of this book that I'm the sort of person who is prone to whimsical ideas. Well for years I'd been saying it'd be funny to take The Brian Rice Song one step further by getting a group of 11 Reds fans to get Forest shirts with 'Rice' printed on the back and the numbers one to 11. At some point my brother Al shared this idea on one of the online Forest forums – and lots of the other forum members were immediately very enthused by the suggestion.

Before I knew it, everyone was allocated a number – and the 'gathering of the Rices' then took place in the Trent Bridge Inn prior to a Forest home game. Having thought of the idea, I got to be number one – and even bought myself a Forest goalkeeper top to get the name and number printed onto. I can't remember now exactly how far the numbers went up, but it was way beyond 11 – and to this day when on matchdays at the City Ground, I still occasionally spot people in Forest shirts with 'Rice' and a random number on the back.

But what about the other clubs Brian Rice played for – how is he remembered by *their* fans?

Well other than Forest, the highest profile team he ever played for was probably Hibernian – and in 2008, I actually ended up chatting with quite a well-known Hibs fan about the ginger ninja: namely, the author Irvine Welsh.

Best known for being the man who wrote the cult novel *Trainspotting*, Welsh was doing a book reading in Nottingham to promote a new book that he'd written called *Crime*. Being a fan of the man's work, I'd gone along - and when the audience were asked if they had any questions, I immediately seized the opportunity.

As it was, Welsh's recollections of Brian Rice were of him having been one of the better players in a struggling Hibs team. And not only that, he also said he wouldn't rule out the possibility of him cropping up in one of his future novels!

Alas, this still hasn't happened. But in 2015 I did have a second encounter with Brian Rice to follow on my interview back in 2003 – and this time, it was completely unexpected.

It all came about through BBC Radio Nottingham. At the time, the station was running a regular series of features on Forest players of the past. And for one particular feature, the station's Forest correspondent Colin Fray was sent up to Scotland to meet the ginger ninja – who at the time had just been appointed as assistant manager of Inverness Caledonian Thistle.

The whole thing made for a great piece. The one thing that really made it though was the fact that Colin Fray asked Brian Rice if he'd be up for going out on Inverness Caledonian Thistle's pitch and having a go at replicating his famous goal at Arsenal. To his credit, the great man was well up for this – and the resulting video went down an absolute storm with Forest fans when Radio Nottingham posted it on their Facebook page.

But that's not all.

No, the night Radio Nottingham shared the video I wrote a comment on their Facebook post, tagging my brother and also a Forest-supporting mate of ours called Jonny Heald. This led to a flurry of comments between the three of us - just general eulogies about Brian Rice, and how great it was that Radio Nottingham had persuaded him to replicate the goal.

What happened next though amazed me.

Looking at my laptop where I had Facebook open on a web browser, the little red '1' digit popped up to show that I'd got a new notification.

Nothing earth-shattering there – however, when I clicked on the notification, I couldn't quite believe what I was reading.

Yes, "Brian Rice also commented on BBC Nottingham Sport's post"!

My first suspicion was that someone must have set up a fake Brian Rice Facebook profile. A few clicks revealed though what looked like the real deal – and the notification revealed that he'd left a comment saying how the interview with Colin Fray had brought back some happy memories of his time at Forest.

Of course, the modern age has opened up all sorts of possibilities in terms of being able to enjoy direct lines of communication with the great and good from the footballing world – and having dabbled a fair bit myself with social media, this was not the first time I'd digitally rubbed shoulders with one of my red-shirted heroes. In 2013 I'd also been quite excited when I got 'retweeted' on Twitter by French midfielder Guy Moussi, who was also very much a cult figure at the time among Forest fans.

But Brian Rice popping up on Facebook was taking things to a whole new level.

I instantly added another comment of my own in reply to Brian Rice's comment: "So here we are, talking on Facebook about Brian Rice, and the ACTUAL BRIAN RICE only turns up and joins in. This is instantly one of my favourite ever moments in nearly 30 years as a Forest fan!"

And amazingly, within about two minutes, Brian Rice spoke once more!: "I always look out for the results," he wrote, "and hope one day Forest are back where I know they belong. Fantastic to have this opportunity to talk to you all. Cheers lads!"

Naturally, myself, Al and Jonny were all buzzing. And so was half of Nottingham to be fair – Radio Nottingham's video of Brian Rice recreating his famous goal was shared hundreds of times on social media, and got quite a lot of people excited.

Even Radio Nottingham seemed taken aback by the reaction to the video – so much so that, a few days later, the station decided to have Brian Rice as the main topic of discussion on their breakfast show.

As mentioned in a previous chapter, Radio Nottingham often contact me if they want someone to talk on one of their programmes about Forest-related matters - and on this occasion, they called me to ask me if I could go on the show to try and explain the cult of Brian Rice to their listeners.

Unfortunately I had to decline this invitation as I had other commitments – and as it turned out, this meant missing out on the once-in-a-lifetime opportunity to sing a live duet on the radio with Brian Rice!

Not being available myself, I'd suggested to Radio Nottingham that another Forest fan who they could call upon instead might be my friend Max Newton – brother of my old college mate John Newton mentioned in an earlier chapter, and someone who is well accustomed to talking on the radio through the line of work that he's in.

I duly got in touch with Max to ask him if he'd mind his number being passed on, although to be honest it's quite surprising he was even talking to me at this point in time – because back in 2010, I'd stitched him up in spectacular style when he announced that he was going to do the Great North Run to raise money for charity. As a gimmick to help with his efforts to get sponsors Max had decided he was going to run in fancy dress, but let his sponsors choose his outfit – with each person who stumped up some cash getting one vote. I couldn't resist sabotaging this – by getting loads of people to sponsor him and vote that he do the run dressed as Robbie Savage, who was Derby County's captain at time!

Graciously, Max accepted his fate of having to run 13 miles dressed in full Derby kit and a long blond wig. What's more, we also ensured Robbie Savage himself got to hear about the whole caper. A few weeks before the Great North Run football's favourite panto villain had just had his autobiography published, and was doing a series of book signings to promote it – so Max and I decided to go along to Waterstones in Leicester to ambush him!

Whilst embarking on this mission the two of us made no attempt whatsoever to hide our allegiance to Forest. In fact, I actually wore a T-shirt that day featuring a photo of Nathan Tyson's famous celebration after Forest had beaten Derby the previous year, when the Reds striker had grabbed one of the corner flags and waved it at the Derby fans – an incident that led to a massive brawl among the two sets of players, with Savage right in the thick of the action.

For all his reputation though, Savage actually proved to be a lovely bloke – happily posing for photos with us, and also helping Max get a few more sponsors by sharing details of what he was doing via his social media accounts. He also wrote "Best wishes Red dog!" when I decided to buy a copy of his book and got him to sign it.

All in all, it was a nice reminder of how things should be as far as I'm concerned when it comes to football rivalry. Though most of us Forest fans will profess to 'hate' Derby, when all the fighting talk's done I firmly believe that we should be able to have a bit of a laugh and joke with our friends from the other end of the A52.

But anyway, back to Brian Rice…

As it turned out, Max was well up for appearing on Radio Nottingham to talk about the ginger ninja – and brilliantly, after he'd unleashed a dramatic description of the infamous goal away at Arsenal, presenter Andy Whittaker surprised him by revealing that he actually had Brian Rice on the line!

As you'd expect, Max was slightly flustered – and even more so when he was then asked if he could serenade Radio Nottingham's listeners with a rendition of The Brian Rice Song… as a duet with the man himself! Granted, this is unlikely to go down in history alongside 'Under Pressure' or 'Islands in the Stream' as one of the all-time great duets – but it did make for a great piece of radio.

As it turned out, Brian Rice was already familiar with The Brian Rice Song – and I can actually take some of the credit for that.

This all goes back to 2008, and an appearance I made on Sky Sports' Saturday morning TV show *Soccer AM,* when I was part of a group of Forest fans who were on the show as 'Fans of the Week'.

Over the years I've actually appeared on *Soccer AM* three times as part of a group of Forest fans – in 1997, as mentioned in an earlier chapter, and also in both 2005 and 2008. And it was on the second of those three appearances when I decided there was a golden opportunity to pay tribute to the ginger ninja on national TV, by choosing The Brian Rice Song when we got our cue to introduce ourselves at the beginning of the show by launching into a Forest terrace anthem.

Alas, my plaintive appeals to the rest of the group were outvoted in favour of "We all agree, Nottingham Forest are magic!" – which did sound great to be fair, with us successfully pulling off the "… are magic… are magic… are magic…" echo effect.

In 2008 though, I once again stated a case for The Brian Rice Song – and this time, the others finally caved in and agreed.

Now I gather austerity measures have since kicked in - but back in those days, Sky Sports used to pay for their 'Fans of the Week' to travel down to London the night before the show, and stay in a fancy hotel close to the studios. Needless to say we milked this opportunity for all it was worth on each occasion by ringing room service and ordering shedloads of beer on Sky's tab. Fuelled then by free booze, it seemed only right the night before our 2008 appearance to embark on a lengthy and raucous rehearsal of The Brian Rice Song – something which didn't go down well with fellow residents, and led to threats from the hotel to sling us out into the street.

Practice made perfect though – as despite some colossal hangovers among the group, The Brian Rice Song sounded glorious on the show the next morning. We'd decided beforehand we were going to see how long we could keep the song going – although the *Soccer AM* producers quickly cottoned on to its potentially endless nature, and we only got as far as "Number seven is Brian Rice!" before they cut us off…

A clip of this moment of TV history was subsequently uploaded to YouTube – and amusingly, it's since been viewed over 30,000 times at the time of writing. There's a few comments on the video too, with most folk generally seeming to appreciate our efforts with the song. You can never please everyone though – and there's also one person with the YouTube username of 'Kegrams' who has simply commented: "Rent boys"!

But what I didn't realise until seven years after our appearance on *Soccer AM* was that it was our rendition of The Brian Rice Song that day that led to Brian Rice himself learning of the song's existence. Yes, in the same interview in 2015 when he replicated his famous goal against Arsenal, the great man revealed to Radio Nottingham that he'd been out playing golf that morning, when suddenly his mobile rang. It was one of his mates. "Hey Brian, you won't believe this," he said, "but I'm watching Sky Sports and there's a group of Forest fans on singing a song about you!"

So there you have it.

Scarily, it's actually now more than a quarter of a century since Brian Rice last graced the City Ground turf - although despite the passing of time, it feels like the cult of the great man is only growing. A few years ago the Forest club shop had a Brian Rice T-shirt on sale for a while, showing a football team line-up with all 11 playing positions filled with Brian Rice; and I've also noticed quite a few Reds fans starting to declare 12 March each year to be Brian Rice Day, with the date in question being the anniversary of that goal at Arsenal. Indeed, it's no coincidence that this book just so happened to be published on 12 March 2018 – exactly 30 years to the day that the ginger ninja executed his greatest ever moment in a Forest shirt.

Who knows where it will all end? 'Audience with...'-type events featuring former Forest players have become popular in Nottingham in recent years - and I'm hoping the folk who organise them will eventually get Brian Rice to come down from Scotland to do one. It would be a great night. You could even throw in a game of Brian Rice bingo where, instead of all the traditional catchphrases like legs eleven and two little ducks, every number called out could be Brian Rice.

When it occurred to me that I probably ought to ask someone to write a foreword to this book, Brian Rice just seemed like the right person – and it was a massive honour when I got in touch with him and he immediately agreed. He duly sent me a few hundred words via email - and brilliantly, in the course of our correspondence, I couldn't help but notice that his choice of Googlemail address actually appears to make a subtle reference to his legendary goal away at Arsenal!

Of course, Brian Rice is unlikely to end up with a statue like Cloughie has.

Nevertheless, I have done my bit to ensure that he has a permanent tribute at the City Ground.

In 2015 Forest announced that they were to build a special commemorative wall at the back of the Trent End as part of the club's 150th anniversary celebrations – and offered fans the chance to buy bricks in the wall and have them inscribed with a message of their choice.

Inevitably, as with pretty much anything that the club decides to do, there were a fair few naysayers among the City Ground faithful. Some fans talked about how it was sadly symbolic of how disenfranchised fans are these days that they were being offered the opportunity to simply be, in the immortal words of Pink Floyd, 'another brick in the wall'. Others muttered darkly about how it was appropriate for the club to build a wall because of how often us fans have felt like banging our heads against one.

Personally I thought it was a good idea – and when it came to deciding what I'd have written on my brick, it was a no brainer.

Yes, as a nod to both our hero and also the Forest fanzine that I published for six years back in the 90s, I chose to have my brick inscribed with:

Rich Fisher
Forest Forever
"Number one is Brian Rice!"

Who knows how long that wall will last, or indeed, how long Forest will remain at the City Ground – but I like the idea that in generations to come, kids might stop to read all the hundreds of messages and find themselves thinking 'Who's Brian Rice'?

With smartphones invariably close to hand these days, all they'll need to do is to tap the name into Google – and suddenly the world of Brian Rice will have officially been passed down to the next generation…

26. Drifting away # 2

"Looking back, it makes me smile to think that the final act of Steve Cotterill's forgettable reign at the City Ground consisted of him basically getting heckled by a load of pirates!"

I've already talked in earlier chapters about how I drifted away from Forest in the late 90s - but then got sucked back in.

Well the year 2015 saw me drift away once again – giving up my season ticket and my seat in the upper Bridgford End after 15 years.

Now a lot of people who know me might think that this decision was all down to certain developments in my life. By the time I reached my late 20s, my back story in terms of my lovelife wasn't untypical for a bloke of my age - with a couple of failed long-term relationships under my belt, and also a fair few casual flings.

Around Christmas 2008 though, I met a girl called Emma - and I quickly realised she was somebody very special....

She was kind.

She was funny.

She was talented.

She was beautiful.

Oh, and as well as her many personal attributes, she also happened to live in a flat with a parking space only a few hundred metres from the City Ground.

She was literally my dream woman!

There was an alarming moment though very early after Emma and I met, when we spent an evening exchanging text messages – and in the course of our communications, she happened to mention that she used to live in Derby. At that moment, my heart flipped. I was already falling for her in a big way – and I was sent into a tailspin of panic as I mentally dreamt up a nightmare scenario in which she was from Derby and from a family of hardcore Derby fans.

Surely this would prove an irreconcilable difference?

Fortunately, it turned out that Emma was Nottingham born and bred – and had only crossed the border into the badlands of Derby for work. In fact, while she wasn't in the same league as me in terms of her passion for Forest, Emma very much regarded herself as a Reds fan – and had been to numerous matches with her Dad as a kid.

Thinking about it, all of the women that I've been in serious relationships with over my life have had more than a passing interest in football - which is interesting, as I don't think it's a characteristic I've ever consciously looked for in a potential partner. Perhaps it's only those who have sympathies with the beautiful game who are able to put up with idiots like me who plan their lives around a fixture list?

Indeed, only a few weeks after Emma and I met, there was one fateful evening when Forest were beaten at home by Derby in a midweek FA Cup replay, despite having been 2-0 up at one stage during the game. And to rub salt into the wound for us Reds fans, the winning goal had been scored by Kris Commons – a player who'd controversially left Forest the previous summer in order to sign for Derby.

As you'd expect, I wasn't a happy bunny as I left the City Ground after the full-time whistle, and duly texted Emma to grumble about what a frustrating evening it had been. She immediately replied and invited me to come over to hers to drown my sorrows in a bottle of wine – something that definitely helped take the edge off the huge sense of disappointment I was feeling.

While the Reds had let me down badly then that night, the redhead certainly hadn't – and mine and Emma's relationship continued to go from strength to strength over the next few months. There was even a period of time not long after we met when she was able to offer me an unparalleled insight into life in the inner sanctum of the Forest dressing room - after her and one of her friends went on a night out in Nottingham and ended up meeting a member of the Reds' first team squad in a bar.

In the interests of protecting the innocent I sadly can't divulge the name of the player in question – however, the encounter led to Emma's friend and the big striker beginning a relationship that went on for a number of months. This provided a regular source of fascinating gossip - with my favourite nugget of information being the amusingly mundane revelation that the silver-tongued target man always ironed his club tracksuit in the morning before heading out to training!

Over the years Emma has actually joined me on a fair few occasions on trips to watch Forest, including a memorable trip to West Brom on a Friday night in January 2010 - where the Reds pulled off a brilliant 3-1 win. That night was possibly the coldest I can ever remember feeling at a football match, though this was largely because Emma had inexplicably neglected to bring a coat despite the sub-arctic conditions – so I ended up giving her mine.

On Valentine's Day in 2010 meanwhile, I actually decided to eschew the usual clichés of chocolates and flowers - and instead presented Emma with a ticket to join me at a Forest game against Sheffield United that was taking place a few days later.

Contrary to what you might think, she was actually really chuffed!

In fact, around the Easter of 2010, Emma and I went on a weekend away together down to Somerset – and by sheer coincidence, it just so happened that Forest were playing away just down the road at Bristol City on the Saturday. I imagine a lot of womenfolk of the world would be deeply unimpressed at a romantic break being interrupted by the football – however, not only was Emma more than happy for me to go to the match, she actually insisted on coming with me. We were rewarded by a pretty forgettable 1-1 draw and me then getting a speeding fine afterwards on our way back down to Somerset.

Still, I guess at least *someone* managed to get three points!

With her working as a physiotherapist for a living, Emma would actually offer some interesting perspectives on Forest's pre-match warm-up routines when she came along with me to matches. Her expertise within her profession is more centred around getting stroke and brain injury patients walking again – nevertheless, she knew enough about the general principles of physio to be able to state with authority that a lot of the stretches the players were doing were simply inadequate as a means of getting prepared for 90 minutes of high-level sport. It's no wonder really that Forest have often seemed to have half their squad out injured for much of the last few decades.

All in all, you probably won't be surprised to learn that Emma and I were married within two-and-a-half years of the day we first met.

Our wedding took place in 2011 – and naturally, there were a few little Forest related touches on the day. Not least the order of service for our marriage ceremony, which I designed myself – having somehow managed to persuade my bride-to-be that it'd be a great idea to do it as a spoof matchday programme, complete with lines-up for 'team groom' and 'team bride'!

In the run-up to the wedding, Emma had also surreptitiously sent off letters to numerous celebrities, asking them to write messages to us wishing us good luck as we embarked upon married life. She then attached all the replies she received back to a big noticeboard – and arranged to have this put on display at the venue where we got married as a surprise for me on the big day.

Less said the better in hindsight about the message sent to us by Rolf Harris – however, the other replies that Emma managed to get included congratulatory words from a certain William Macintosh Davies, who was Forest's manager at the time.

Sadly 'King Billy' refrained from the strange tendency he often showed when giving media interviews of referring to himself in the third person. Nor did he slip in any of his classic catchphrases such as 'unfinished business', 'it is what it is' or 'stellar signings'.

Nevertheless, his message contained some lovely sentiments.

"It gives me great pleasure to offer my congratulations to Rich and Emma on their big day," he wrote.

"I hope you have a long and happy life together. I just hope that Rich will still be able to find the time to follow our fortunes now that he has tied the knot!"

Whatever anyone says about Billy Davies, I will always have a soft spot for him for those kind words alone.

After getting married, Emma and I decided to start a family, and we now have two beautiful boys - with Arlo born in 2014, and Jude following in 2016.

When throwing around ideas for names after we first learned we were going to be parents, I'd actually lobbied pretty hard for Francis as a possible boy's name. I can honestly say that this was mainly because I really liked it – but I can't deny that there was also significant appeal in the idea of our first born sharing his name with the man who'd scored the winning goal in the 1979 European Cup final.

Alas though, Emma quickly vetoed Francis as soon as she got wind of my motives – and for all her sympathies with the beautiful game, made it clear that any Forest-related names were strictly off-limits!.

Of course, you hear about a lot of blokes who stop going to the football after they get married and have kids, because their wives give them grief about clearing off to the match every other Saturday. Fortunately though for me, Emma has never tried to stop me from going to watch Forest in the time that I've known her.

So if it wasn't settling into family life that made give up my Forest season ticket, what was it?

Well it's quite simple really – by 2015, I'd simply become completely disillusioned with what my beloved team had become.

Throughout this book, I've already alluded to the fact that us Forest fans have had to put up with a lot of dross over the last few decades – and there had been number of occasions over the previous five or six years when I'd seriously considered giving up my season ticket. Certainly, if I'd felt as disenchanted about any other relationship in my life as I had done at those points about my relationship with Forest, there's no way I would've allowed things to just drift on.

But as we all know, football is somehow different – and for all my threats of not renewing, I'd always end up caving in and committing myself to another season down at the City Ground.

Looking back, one of the most depressing seasons for me of my entire time as a Forest fan – even worse than those years in the doldrums in League One - was the 2011-12 campaign.

This was the year when the Reds started off with Steve McClaren as manager – an appointment that quickly proved to be a dreadful one.

Though he'd inherited a Forest team that had made the Championship play-offs the previous season, it became quickly apparent that the Wally with the Brolly was incapable of getting them to perform. After ten matches the Reds were plummeting towards the bottom of the table - and pretty much the one good thing McClaren did during the few months he was in charge was decide it would be in everyone's best interests if he resigned.

Initially, it was a huge relief to hear that McClaren had gone – but his resignation turned out to be the start of a chain of events that would have a huge impact on the club.

Forest by this point were owned by Nigel Doughty – a self-made multi-millionaire who'd taken control in 1999.

Born and bred in Nottinghamshire, Doughty was a lifelong Reds fan, and a philanthropist who quietly used his wealth to try and make the world a better place – making huge donations to charities, as well as pumping tens of millions into his beloved football team.

For all his investment though, Doughty never managed to get Forest back to the Premier League – and sadly, this led to him facing increasing abuse from some fans.

The failure of McClaren was the straw that broke the camel's back. The decision to appoint the Wally with the Brolly had been Doughty's and Doughty's alone – and as such, within minutes of the news that McClaren had resigned, Doughty announced that he would be stepping away from Forest too.

In one fell swoop then, the club had found itself in a position where it not only needed a new manager, but also new owners.

Unsurprisingly it was a new manager that arrived first – with Steve Cotterill appointed.

Sadly though things didn't improve a great deal on the pitch. With Nigel Doughty no longer on board to balance the books out of his own pocket, Forest were suddenly in a position where they were having to sell key players to keep the club afloat.

The financial constraints certainly made Cotterill's job a tough one. However, he didn't do himself any favours either, quickly moulding a dour Forest team that served up some of the most excruciatingly dull football I've ever experienced.

At the time I was actually experiencing a fairly serious health problem for the first time in my life, having been diagnosed with a rare eye condition that was causing my vision to deteriorate. It took quite a while for me to access the right treatment to make the problem manageable – and as such, I spent a good few months attending matches where I couldn't really tell what was going on at the far end of the pitch. The way Forest were playing though, this probably wasn't a bad thing!

Sometimes in life you find yourself in a situation where you have little choice but to try and make your own fun - and Forest under Cotterill were so abysmal that I actually started a new pre-match ritual before home games of going to the Ladbrokes kiosk inside the ground and sticking a quid on last scorer. This was purely because it gave me a little bit of hope to cling onto right to the very end, even during the dreariest of performances from the Reds.

Usually when deciding which Forest player to bet on to bag the game's final goal I'd choose one of the defenders, as the odds for them to score obviously tend to be much higher – meaning I'd win big if my bet actually won. Naturally then, I'd find myself shouting "SHOOT!" whenever my player had the ball anywhere vaguely near the opposition goal, despite the fact that the likes of Luke Chambers and Chris Gunter weren't exactly renowned for bursting the back of the net from 40 yards.

On most occasions it invariably ended up being a quid down the drain – but there was one game in March 2012 against Brighton when I was quids in after deciding to back Joel Lynch at 40-1. By injury time that afternoon Forest were losing 1-0, and as a last throw of the dice the big centre-half was pushed up front in a desperate bid to try and salvage a point – and brilliantly, he actually managed to poke the ball into the back of the Trent End net. A great moment – decisive last-minute goals are always fantastic anyway, but even more so when they make you £40 richer! Sadly Lynch moved on to pastures new a few months later – however, in the unlikely event that you're reading this Joel, I'll gladly buy you a pint if you're ever in Nottingham.

For all my success though with my little flutter on that particular afternoon, I would probably have been better off on most occasions backing an opposition player to grab the game's final goal – as Steve Cotterill's time at the City Ground included a run spanning three months and six matches where Forest failed to score a single goal at home. It was an excruciating period – and not only was the football utterly turgid, us fans were also subjected to increasingly bizarre post-match interviews from the hapless manager on BBC Radio Nottingham. With his west country burr, it was like listening to Worzel Gummidge on crack.

Don't get me wrong, I have nothing personal against Steve Cotterill – and I'm sure he's a lovely bloke and everything. Just an absolutely terrible Forest manager.

That said, there were the odd few glimmers during the Cotterill era - most memorably a 7-3 win away at Leeds. It was one of those bizarre evenings that happen every now and again where seemingly every shot goes flying into the back of the net – like the professional football equivalent of one of those games of five-a-side that finish up with a scoreline of 23-19.

But happy times were few and far between – and the worst day of all came one Saturday afternoon in February when news broke that Nigel Doughty had been found dead at his home just months after his decision to quit as Chairman.

He was just 54.

All in all, it was a miserable time to be a Forest fan – one of those seasons that we were only too happy to confine to the dustbin of history as soon as the final ball had been kicked. In fact, some of my brother Al's Forest mates were so glad to get it over and done with that they actually organised a post-match party on the day of Forest's final home game of the 2011-12 campaign – to celebrate the fact that it was finally over.

This party was held on board one of the pleasure boats that can often be seen cruising up and down the River Trent - so naturally it was decided to make it a pirate-themed fancy dress event. This meant that I enjoyed the surreal experience of going to watch Forest play Portsmouth as part of a group of about 30 people all dressed to the nines in buccaneering apparel!

All of us in the group had decided to give up our normal season ticket seats for the day so we could sit together and get the celebrations started. A block booking of around 30 tickets in the lower tier of the Brian Clough Stand was duly arranged - and we watched Forest pull off a rare 2-0 win against Pompey.

Despite the fact that it had been a dire season in which Forest finished only three places above the relegation zone, Steve Cotterill had insisted that the players still do a lap of honour after the full-time whistle. It was all quite embarrassing – although when players and coaching staff reached the part of the ground where we were sitting, myself and the rest of our group decided to try and lighten the slightly awkward atmosphere by getting into the full pirate spirit and serenading 'Cotters' with a rousing chorus of "What shall we do with the carrot cruncher?" – to the tune of 'What Shall We Do With the Drunken Sailor'!

We didn't know it at the time, but that stroll around the pitch with his beleaguered team would prove to be Steve Cotterill's last public appearance as Forest manager. Looking back, it makes me smile to think that the final act of his forgettable reign at the City Ground consisted of him basically getting heckled by a load of pirates!

But terrible as the 2011-12 season was, I still went down to the City Ground and renewed my season ticket during the summer of 2012. In fact, once us fans had had a few weeks to recover from the misery of the previous nine months, a wave of optimism for the new campaign began to spread in earnest – with news that the club was finally being taken over by new owners.

Of course, most top English football clubs are run by foreign owners these days – in many cases, very successfully. And on their arrival at the City Ground, the Al Hasawi family certainly said all the right things. Sacking Steve Cotterill within minutes of confirming their takeover was always going to go a long way to get me on side – and on a childish note, the fact that Forest were owned by a fridge magnate was also quite amusing.

The sense of positivity generated by the arrival of the Al Hasawis quickly evaporated though over the course of the 2012-13 season, when it became apparent that the family's figurehead Fawaz was on a doomed ego trip - and running Forest in the manner of a rich kid with a lavish Subbuteo set.

Unsurprisingly, his constant chopping and changing of managers got Forest nowhere in that first season.

Or the season after that.

What's more, Fawaz had turned the club into a circus - with his embarrassing antics on Twitter, his inability to do basic things like ensuring bills were paid on time, and his apparent obliviousness to the fact that he was blindly steering the club towards the iceberg otherwise known as a transfer embargo.

Probably the one thing that riled me more than anything though about the way the club was being run during Fawaz's time as owner was when I renewed my season ticket again during the summer of 2013 - only to find out a few weeks later that there were plans to boot me and loads of other fans out of our seats so the upper Bridgford End could be given to away fans.

Had we all been given plenty of notice that we were being 'evicted', and perhaps been offered first dibs on all the other vacant seats available, then I might have grudgingly accepted the decision. However, to take our money and then only tell us weeks later that we'd have to relocate to a different part of the ground seemed a very shabby way to treat loyal fans.

As it was, many of those affected made their feelings known about the proposal in pretty blunt terms, myself included – and in the end the whole idea was shelved.

Fans 1, Fawaz 0.

Unfortunately though, occasions when Forest's owner actually saw sense were generally few and far between – and as the 'Fawaz era' rumbled on, it started to feel more and more like all off-the-field goings on at the club were overshadowing what was happening on the pitch.

Some weeks, this was probably no bad thing!

But I was becoming increasingly hacked off with it all. Forest had basically turned into all the things I utterly despise about modern football - and I was becoming so disgruntled that I was starting to resent giving up my precious time and hard-earned money to go to matches.

The sacking of Stuart Pearce in early 2015 – who, at the time, was the sixth manager to have departed under Fawaz's reign in less than three years - was the point where I decided enough was enough.

The fact that Psycho would eventually return to Forest as manager at some point had always felt inevitable – although when it finally happened in the summer of 2014, many of us fans questioned whether his appointment was actually that good an idea.

Nevertheless, his first game in charge saw him get a hero's welcome when he walked out of the tunnel at a packed City Ground – and things got off to a great start, with the Reds top of the Championship table by the end of August after winning four of their opening five games.

Psycho was also saying all the right things. Around this time I attended a Q&A event with the new manager organised by the club – and he spoke with great passion about wanting to bring back some unity to the club after the fractious reign of Billy Davies. We also learned that Psycho's howitzer of a left foot was still occasionally put to use – as he revealed that he sometimes took the free kicks during training sessions when his team were practising defending set pieces.

"What do the players make of that?" someone asked - and Psycho's immediate reply was absolutely priceless.

"They shit themselves!"

Sadly though, the honeymoon period didn't last – with those of us who'd had reservations about Psycho returning as manager being proven horribly right. By Christmas the wins had dried up, and Forest were sliding towards the relegation zone. It was horrible to watch a man who was a hero at the City Ground floundering in the dugout, and we all hoped beyond hope that he'd somehow manage to turns things around. Emma and I even showed a bit of solidarity with Psycho around this time by trying out a recipe that he'd contributed to a new cookbook that had just been published in Nottingham, featuring ideas for dishes from various local celebrities. Though it sounded grim, Stuart Pearce's corned beef pie was actually quite nice – an old recipe that he apparently learned off his mum!

But for all of Psycho's surprise culinary abilities, I think even the most die-hard fans of the great man were starting to admit that, for whatever reason, it simply wasn't working. And while a memorable win away at Derby bought him a little bit more time, I think we all knew what was coming.

However, the manner in which Psycho was sacked – with the club ditching him and then announcing his successor just an hour later - was utterly lacking in class, and no way to treat a man who will always be a legend at the City Ground.

With having a season ticket I continued going to matches for the remainder of the season – but it just felt like I was doing no more than fulfilling a contractual obligation.

There was of course a brief resurgence in performances under Psycho's successor – as is often the way when a new manager is appointed.

And Dougie Freedman's arrival also inspired one of the greatest songs to be sung at the City Ground in recent memory – a little ditty to the tune of 'Blame It On The Boogie' by the Jacksons that would be belted out with gusto whenever Forest were winning.

"Sunshine… moonlight… good times… Dougie!"

Nevertheless, my mind was made up – I definitely wouldn't be renewing my seat for the following season.

And it wasn't just me.

Yes, my brother Al was also feeling just as disillusioned about Forest as I was, to a point where he'd sometimes not even bother going to games any more - despite the fact he had a season ticket.

In the end, the decision we both made to relinquish our season tickets became one of those "I will if you will" situations.

The worst thing for Al and I was telling our great friend Graham, who by this point had been our matchday companion for 14 years. To be fair, one of Graham's daughters had got a season ticket with us by this point in time too, so it wasn't like we were leaving him to sit on his own. But even so, breaking the news to him honestly felt worse than dumping someone.

Mine and Al's final game as season ticket holders then was Forest's final home game of the 2014-15 season, against Cardiff – and it felt quite strange arriving at the ground knowing that what I regarded as 'my' seat would no longer be mine by the end of the 90 minutes.

Indeed, no-one else had ever really sat in my seat for well over a decade - and I guess I'd become quite attached to it.

One of the very few occasions when my seat was occupied by someone else was when Forest played Leicester at home in a League Cup game back in 2007, and the club decided that away fans could have both the upper and lower tiers of the Bridgford End. As a result I was forced to relocate to the Brian Clough Stand for one night, and I recall feeling slightly violated at the thought of my seat having some Leicester fan's sweaty backside perched on it for 90 minutes.

And this wasn't anything personal against Leicester – like most Forest fans, I've never really had any beef with them. I just didn't like the idea of someone else encroaching on my territory – particularly someone supporting another team. I even made a point of bringing a pack of Dettol wipes to the next home game so I could give it a good clean before sitting down! A bit childish I know, but it had to be done.

It's fair to say then that the afternoon of Saturday 2 May 2015 was a pretty notable landmark in my history as a Forest fan – though to say it was such a significant occasion, I'm sad to say that I can't remember a single thing about the game. You'd have thought the Reds would've at least made me have a few second thoughts about giving up my season ticket by pulling a vintage performance out of the bag – but no, the 90 minutes consisted of the usual diet of forgettable mediocrity that we'd become increasingly accustomed to under the Fawaz era. It's only through the wonders of Google that I even know it finished in a 2-1 defeat for Forest - with Dexter Blackstock bagging a late consolation goal for the Reds after Cardiff had raced into a 2-0 lead.

Perhaps the saddest thing of all though about giving up my Forest season ticket is that I never heard anything from the club as the renewal deadline came and went – not that it would have made a jot of difference.

Of course, I wasn't actually surprised at this. After all, given that Forest seemed incapable during the Fawaz era of even organising themselves to pay bills on time, it's hard to imagine they would've had any kind of system in place to keep track of whether individual fans were renewing their season tickets or not.

But in any other industry, if a loyal customer suddenly walked away from your business after having spent hundreds of pounds every year for umpteen years, you'd surely bust a gut to try and win them back round?

Ultimately, I guess the radio silence from Forest was just a stark reminder of the harsh reality that the financial contribution us fans make is increasingly insignificant these days.

My early days of going to watch Forest back in the 90s were before all the big money TV deals – and when Dad stumped up hundreds of pounds each summer to pay for our season tickets, it genuinely felt like he was making a significant investment into the club. Like we were buying shares.

Since then though, football has become awash with money. As a fan, you can still fork out a whole month's disposable income on a season ticket – but players now command such obscene wages that your 'investment' will probably go little further than covering an hour's pay for some mediocrity on 30-odd grand a week. And let's face it, Forest have had more than their fair share of those in recent years.

For all my disillusionment though with both the Reds and football in general, I did worry as the 2015-16 season approached that I'd find it difficult to get used no longer going to matches.

Of course, I'd done it before – however, that was when I was an 18-year-old and had a whole new life at university in a different city to throw myself into.

Surely it would be harder at 35, and without those distractions?

There was only one way to find out…

27. Full circle

"I started thinking that Fawaz should just go the whole hog and do what they sometimes do with guest presenters on Have I Got News For You, *and just have a different guest manager every game..."*

Having given up my Forest season ticket in the summer of 2015, it certainly felt strange when the 2015-16 season got underway and I was no longer going to matches.

As it turned out though, I actually found it far easier than I thought getting used to my new status as an armchair fan.

Over time, it actually started to feel quite liberating no longer having my life governed by the Forest fixture list. And while my little family weren't the reason for taking a step back from the Reds, I quickly began to appreciate the extra hours at the weekend that I was suddenly able to spend with them.

Of course, when I'd made the decision to give up my season ticket, I always assumed I'd still get myself down to the City Ground for the odd few games. However, now I was no longer committed to going to every match, I soon found that I felt very little desire to go and watch Forest at all.

I did go to a game in early October 2015 – but only because it was my mate John's stag do, and he'd decided he fancied a trip to the footy.

The day as a whole was entertaining – and it almost certainly goes down in history as the only time that a group of 15 men have descended on the City Ground all wearing matching Julian Clary masks. But the actual match was totally uninspiring – with the Reds losing 1-0 to Hull, and doing nothing to make me regret the decision to give up my season ticket.

The antipathy I was feeling towards Forest was also hammered home by the release around the same time of *I Believe In Miracles*, Jonny Owen's movie about the all-conquering Reds team of the late 70s and early 80s. The film was brilliant – but great as it was, I couldn't help but feel a tinge of sadness as I sat and watched it. It all just felt like a stark reminder of what a soulless shadow

Forest had become of their former selves.

Such a soulless shadow in fact that I didn't bother going to another game for the entire remainder of that 2015-16 season.

And I certainly wasn't the only Forest fan feeling completely disengaged with the club - with crowds for home games starting to dip well below 20,000 as the season rumbled on. The levels of disillusionment weren't helped either two-thirds of the way through the campaign, when the Reds found themselves at the wrong end of the table and Fawaz al Hasawi decided it was time to sack yet another manager.

Having been in charge for just over a year, Dougie Freedman had actually been one of the longest-serving lieutenants under the Fawaz era. And when the news broke that he'd got the bullet, speculation immediately kicked off as to who would be the next poor sod to be appointed. The media began bandying about the usual out-of-work chumps like Glenn Hoddle and Steve Kean - basically the managerial equivalents of the random tat you get in the middle aisle in Lidl.

Usually, as a fan, your club's search for a new manager is something you tend to follow very closely. But in this instance, I remember feeling largely indifferent.

"Who cares who ends up getting the job?" I found myself thinking. "Whoever it is, they'll only get sacked after six months."

Indeed, I started thinking that Fawaz should just go the whole hog and do what they sometimes do with guest presenters on *Have I Got News For You*, and just have a different guest manager every game…

Despite my disaffection though, I still listened to pretty much every Forest game on the radio – and would also watch the occasional Reds matches that were televised live on Sky Sports. On some occasions I'd even go as far as embracing modern technology and searching online for a live stream to watch certain games.

It's all quite funny really, because when I was a snotty teenager, I used to look down my nose at those fans who didn't actually bother going to games. But my views have shifted quite drastically since those days. Over the years I've gradually started to understand that the passion you have as a fan for your team isn't something than can be measured by how many games you go to.

In fact, I've come to realise that being a football fan is a bit like being a music fan – and I'd reached a point with Forest that I sometimes reach with certain bands.

Take veteran indie rock combo the Charlatans for instance. I fell in love with their music as a 17-year-old when I first heard their classic debut album *Tellin' Stories* – and for many years they were one of those bands where, if they released a new album, I'd make a point of going out to buy it the day it came out.

After a decade or so though the Charlatans sort of lost their way a bit – and much like giving up my Forest season ticket, there came a point where I stopped buying their albums.

But just like I'll always be a Forest fan, I'll always be a Charlatans fan. What's more, I'd never rule out the possibility of the Charlatans regaining their mojo at some point and pulling another classic album out of the bag. And as the 2016-17 football season got underway – the second season of my self-imposed exile – I still maintained faint flickers of hope that Forest might pull themselves out of their malaise and do something special to lure me back into the fold.

But it wasn't to be. The 2016-17 season was the fifth season of Fawaz's tenure as Forest's owner. During each of the previous four campaigns the club's final positions in the league table had been getting progressively worse – from 8th to 11th to 14th to 16th. So it was no surprise really when the 2016-17 campaign saw the Reds continue this worrying trajectory by ending up in the middle of a proper relegation battle.

And strangely, I actually had the surreal experience during this time of spending an afternoon with half the Forest first team squad.

Now over the course of my career there have been numerous occasions when I've had cause to rub shoulders with our local football stars in the name of work. Back in 2013 I ended up organising a photoshoot with half the Notts County squad as part of a project I was involved in – and amusingly one of the Notts players who took part was a certain Dean Leacock, who a few years previously had been playing for Derby and had been at the centre of some serious handbags after Forest had beaten Derby 3-2 in a bad-tempered game at the City Ground. As it happened, Leacock actually turned out to be a really nice bloke and was a pleasure to deal with.

Three years on meanwhile I was doing some work for the NHS organisation that runs the two main hospitals in Nottingham – and one day in the run-up to Christmas 2016, arrangements were made for a group of Forest players to visit the children's wards at the QMC to give out presents for poorly kids.

As we all know, these sorts of visits are all about PR as much as anything else – and in my role, I was required to try and squeeze as much positive media coverage out of the visit for the QMC as I could. As such, I ended up accompanying the Reds players as they made their way around the wards, along with a gaggle of local journalists who I'd arranged to come in.

Now once upon a time I would've been quite excited at the prospect of getting to hang out with a load of Forest players. On this occasion though I felt more inclined to give them a piece of my mind – as a few days previously I'd tuned into Sky Sports and watched the very same individuals give one of the most gutless footballing performances I'd seen in a long time in a 3-0 defeat away at Derby. Of course, I had a duty to try and remain professional – but as we made our way through the hospital, I felt like pointing out all the doctors and nurses and other healthcare professionals running around, and asking them how it felt to see people doing proper jobs.

It quickly became apparent though that most of the Forest players who had come along were actually really nice blokes. Gradually then my attitude softened, and over the course of the afternoon I had really nice chats with most of them. Britt Assombalonga spoke about having recently become a dad, and how he was familiar with the QMC from his own injury problems; Eric Lichaj told me about his upbringing in America and how he tries to go back to visit his family every summer; while Danny Fox and David Vaughan talked about their own children, and were clearly moved by the plight of some of the poorly kids we met as we made our way around the children's wards.

Also present along with the players was Philipe Montanier, who was Forest's manager at the time. I remember being quite mesmerised by just how much he looked like Alexander Armstrong, host of the TV quiz show *Pointless* - which seemed amusingly appropriate, given how the Reds were going through a period of form where they couldn't even buy a point!

Montanier turned out to be a lovely fella though - we somehow ended up talking about the cheese shop that his parents used to run back in his native France; and he also laughed when I made a joke about Henri Lansbury's hair.

All in all, the visit was really positive, and the kids loved meeting the players. In fact, the only real negative from the whole afternoon was hearing some of the players bickering about young defender Joe Worrall, who'd recently broken into the Forest first team and had given a blunt post-match interview to BBC Radio Nottingham questioning the commitment of some of the more senior members of the Reds' squad. Of course, such comments are always likely to ruffle a few feathers – however, it seemed a bit unprofessional of the likes of Matt Mills to be openly bitching about the issue in a public place.

For all my initial cynicism then it had in the end been quite an exciting afternoon – and as soon as I'd waved off Philipe Montanier and his players as they departed on their minibus, the first thing I did was get my mobile out so I could text all my Forest-supporting friends and brag about what I'd been up to. I guess it had served as a reminder of the fact that, although I hadn't been down to the City Ground for a while, it didn't mean I cared any less about the mighty Reds.

In fact, I actually started going to a few games again towards the end of the 2016-17 season - my first in early March 2017, when I decided to go and watch Forest play at home against Brighton.

By this point I hadn't been to a Reds match in nearly 18 months – and with relations between the fans and Fawaz having reached breaking point amid rumours that he was attempting to sell the club, I'd vowed not to go again until the hapless Kuwaiti had cleared off.

But then my great friend Andy Best announced that he was travelling up to Nottingham for the Brighton game – and asked if I fancied coming to watch the match with him.

Given that I hadn't seen Andy for a while, it would have felt petty declining his invitation just for the sake of continuing my childish one-man protest against Fawaz. As such, after racking my brains to try and remember what my client reference number was, I popped down to the City Ground to buy us a couple of tickets.

For old time's sake I'd bought tickets for Andy and I in my old stomping ground of block U1 in the upper Bridgford – although nearest I could get to my old seat on row A was a spot a couple of rows behind on row C.

It certainly felt strange seeing someone else sitting in what had been my seat for 15 seasons.

And there were a few other subtle changes as well. The burger seller on Trent Bridge who had amused my brother Al and I for years due to his uncanny resemblance to one of Al's mates was no longer there. And it seemed the City Ground had taken a giant leap towards the 21st Century since my last visit – with the turnstile operators now using an electronic gadget to scan tickets, as opposed to just ripping off the stub like in days of old.

By and large though the whole matchday experience was one of just like pulling on a favourite old jacket that you haven't worn in a while - and after a year-and-a-half away, I liked the fact that I was able to go back to the City Ground and find everything pretty much exactly how I'd left it.

Even some of the things that have always driven me mad during my years as a fan had a strangely comforting familiarity – such as Forest's long tradition of being useless at taking corners, or the Reds' opponents that afternoon opting to wear their away kit even though they could have worn their traditional colours without any risk of a clash.

But above anything else, one of the most enjoyable things of all about the whole afternoon was picking up where I'd left off with my old mate Graham – who to this day still sits in the same seat in on row A of block U1. Though after all these years, I'm sad to say he no longer looks so much like Gordon Ramsay – which I guess is a consequence of us all having got older, while at the same time the sweary TV chef has had more and more cosmetic surgery!

So what of the actual game then?

Well perhaps inevitably, it wasn't that great to be honest.

However, there was one moment of magic around an hour or so in, when a string of patient passes from midfield led to Forest winger Jamie Ward finding some space on the right-hand side of the Brighton penalty area.

Ward duly squared a great ball across the box to Clough – who stroked the ball into the back of the Trent End net.

Yes, Clough.

It felt like my whole life as a Forest fan had gone full circle.

Of course, Zach Clough isn't any relation to the great Clough dynasty that will always be a big part of Forest's history. Nevertheless, the fact that he of all players had scored the first goal I'd seen for nearly two years felt strangely poetic.

The goal also served as a reminder of the simple joy of being a football fan.

At the time of that game against Brighton, I was actually going through a particularly stressful point in my life. I was dealing with the grief of the tragic death of a close family member, as well as some significant financial worries having recently found myself unemployed.

Over the course of those few seconds though as the ball hit the back of the net and the City Ground erupted, all my troubles were completely forgotten – I was just lost in the exhilaration of seeing my team score a great goal. Not even the irritation of the execrable 'goal music' that's sadly become a feature of Forest home games in the last few decades could rain on my parade.

For all its frustrations, it's fair to say that being a football fan offers you occasional snatches of unparalleled nirvana – and an unrivalled form of escapism.

Maybe that's ultimately the thing that keeps us coming back…

28. Reflections

"Maybe it's just like that theory about monkeys and typewriters and the works of Shakespeare – and if you give Forest an infinite number of attempts, they will eventually strike gold and get back to the Premier League?"

And so here we are at the end.

But of course, it's not really the end.

After all, as a man in my late 30s as I write these words, I like to think I'll have at least another three or four decades of following Forest to look forward to.

Lord help me!

I must say though, it's been fun looking back on my years as a Reds fan to date in the process of writing this book.

One of the things I've most enjoyed has been reliving a lot of the old matches from 'back in the day' – something that's pretty easy to do nowadays, with YouTube only ever a few clicks away.

Indeed, there have been numerous occasions when I've gone online with the intention of just finding a clip of one particular game – only to end up disappearing for several hours down a Forest wormhole, reliving all sorts of memories.

There's the obvious moments like Stuart Pearce's thunderbolt free-kick at Old Trafford in 1990, or Bryan Roy's sublime winner against Malmo in the UEFA Cup in 1995.

However, the true joy of wallowing in nostalgia via YouTube is some of the more obscure delights you end up unearthing that you'd completely forgotten about. A good example is Forest's game away at Millwall in 1994 - where highlights range from a home fan running on the pitch to try and deck Stan

Collymore, to the Reds conceding a goal seemingly scored by Jeremy Beadle.

Okay, so it was actually a bloke who played for Millwall back then called Dave Mitchell who bore an uncanny resemblance to the late TV prankster – though let's not let that get in the way of a good story.

But fun as it's been taking a stroll down memory lane, what was it that made me decide to put pen to paper?

Well over the years, there have been numerous occasions where I've had people tell me "You should write a book about all the stuff that you've done." And with quite a lot of the 'stuff that I've done' in my life having been in some way related to Forest, it was always likely that the mighty Reds would end up being the central theme if I was ever to accept the challenge.

For a long time though, I was quite dismissive of the idea. I'd always thought it seemed a bit vain and self-important when people decided to write a memoir.

And in many ways, I suppose it is.

I did however ponder for a while whether there might be mileage in a book focusing on the ups and downs of Forest in the 90s. After all, it was a hugely eventful decade at the City Ground – and what's more, it was also a seismic time of change for English football in general.

Unlike the 60s, 70s and 80s though, it was an era of the Reds' history that hadn't yet been properly documented in book form.

But ultimately, I think I was largely put off by the sheer amount of Forest-related books that have been published in recent years. Such was the sheer volume, I wasn't sure the world really needed another one.

My attitude started to shift though in early 2015, after I spent a couple of months doing some work with a friend of mine called Alex Walker – a fellow Forest fan, and founder of the unofficial Reds website LTLF.co.uk. At this time Alex was running a business ghostwriting autobiographies for people who felt they had a life story worth recording for posterity – and one thing I learned from working with him on some of these books is that most people have a story worth telling if you scratch below the surface.

Not that this book is an autobiography. However it does touch upon most of the important events that have happened in my life both good and bad, simply because Forest have usually been there - either in a starring role, or just lurking somewhere in the background. In fact, there are certain landmarks in my life where I can only remember what year they happened because I can relate them to what the Reds happened to be doing at the time!

The process of writing the book has certainly been an interesting one – and one that began in earnest, ironically enough, during a period of my life when I'd actually decided to have a bit of a break from going down to the City Ground. In hindsight, I think putting a bit of distance between myself and Forest was probably necessary for me to make any kind of sense of my relationship with them.

I began work on the book by writing lists of key memories and then worked from there – although in the end I had to be fairly selective in terms of what to include, or else the final word count would've been in danger of rivaling that of *War and Peace*! Indeed, after completing a first draft I went back through everything I'd written and ended up putting a red pen through literally thousands of words. There were some good stories too among the material that didn't make the cut – but ultimately, they were all tales that I felt didn't really add much to the overall narrative.

I do think the book is all the better for my brutality in the editing process, although there are a few tales I omitted that I sort of wish I'd kept in. Everything from a childhood friend getting his whole street closed off by the bomb squad after an ill-advised attempt to make home-made explosives; to the times during my secondary education when my *Forest Forever* partner in crime Sanjay would invite half the school to cadge a lift home in his Mum's car, resulting in her Volkswagen Polo wheezing its way up the hill towards where we all lived with as many as eight people crammed inside!

There was also an entire chapter that I decided to leave out – a section focusing on a difficult time in my life when, as a 20-year-old, my world was turned upside down by not one but two tragic deaths. Those experiences have undoubtedly played a significant part in shaping who I am as a person, and I found writing about them hugely cathartic. However, there came a point when it dawned on me that neither of those bereavements directly impacted on my life as a Forest fan – and so once again, the red pen prevailed.

Still, getting those still raw emotions down on paper has probably saved me a fortune in therapy bills if nothing else.

It was certainly hard to get to a point with the book where I felt I was able to take a step back from the thousands of words I'd written and feel happy that it was definitely finished. I must say, I have a lot more sympathy now with those individuals from the music world like Axl Rose from Guns N Roses, who spend years in the studio labouring over making an album and driving themselves insane in the elusive search for perfection!

In fact, there were some dark days when I seriously asked myself whether what I was writing was just a load of drivel that should never be allowed to see light of day.

Even now, I'm still not entirely sure!

Ultimately, I guess I was putting myself under quite a lot of pressure to do justice to Forest and the not inconsiderable part that they've played in my life. There have been times during my years as a fan when the Reds' fixture list has been pretty much the only structure I've had in my little world - and apart from immediate family such as my parents and my brother, my relationship with Forest is by far the longest-standing relationship I've ever had.

As is invariably the case with any long-term relationship, the Reds and I have certainly had our ups and downs.

There have been some periods where I haven't been sure whether I even like them any more – and where I've felt like I'd love to be able to just wash my hands of them.

But for better or worse, I've come to realise over the years that being a Forest fan is a huge part of who I am.

And on the whole, I have absolutely no regrets.

Yes, I've spent thousands of pounds following Forest over the years – and based on an average of attending roughly 25 games per season for more than 25 years, I've worked out that I've spent over 1,000 hours at Reds matches. That's equivalent of well over a whole month of my life.

When you add to that the amount of time I've spent travelling to those matches, queuing for tickets, or simply sitting at home swearing at the radio –

well, I shudder to think....

I do feel though that I've got quite a bit to show for all this time I've invested in Forest – not least some brilliant memories. And in the process of trawling through my memory banks whilst working on this book, the one thing that really stands out is some of the ridiculous lengths that I've gone to over the years in the name of supporting the mighty Reds.

There was one time way back in 2001 when Forest were playing away at Hartlepool in the first round of the League Cup – and for some reason, the game was being shown live on Sky Sports.

There was a slight problem for me however in that I didn't have Sky Sports - and living in Liverpool as I did at the time, it seemed unlikely that any of my local pubs would be showing the game.

Naturally then, I did the only thing that seemed sensible. Yes, I got the train from Liverpool all the way to Leeds just to go and watch the match round my mate Jon's house - because he *did* have Sky Sports!

Happily, I was rewarded with a 2-0 Forest win.

There was also another time after I'd moved back to Nottingham when the Reds were playing away, and I was about to listen to the game live on the radio – only to discover shortly before kick-off that the one radio I had in the house had decided to stop working. I ended up spending the whole afternoon sat out in the freezing cold, listening to the match in the car!

There are of course many other examples that I've already mentioned in previous chapters of silly lengths that I've gone to over the years for Forest – everything from queuing overnight to secure tickets to certain matches, to spending days on end on a smelly bus in order to watch the Reds away in Europe.

Another episode I haven't already mentioned previously though involved going to extreme lengths just to get home from a Forest match – specifically, a midweek FA Cup tie at the City Ground against Tottenham back in 1996, which famously had to be abandoned due to a sudden deluge of snow.

I'd been planning to walk into town after the game and get the bus home from there – but the snow had come down so thick and fast that buses were no longer running. I therefore had little choice but to attempt to walk the full five miles home – however, the conditions were so extreme that I only made it so far before admitting defeat and deciding to head to the house of some family friends who lived a short distance outside Nottingham city centre.

These were the days before mobile phones, so I'd turned up at John and Andrea's unannounced. When they got a knock on the door at around 10pm they'd wondered who on earth it was – and for years afterwards, they laughed about how they'd found a sorry figure resembling the abominable snowman stood shivering on their doorstep. Happily they let me straight inside and helped me defrost with some hot soup before letting me kip over in their spare room. I finally completed my journey home the next morning, a full 12-hours after the match was abandoned!

At the time of that cup tie against Spurs though, going to such daft extremes in the name of supporting Forest never really felt all that ludicrous – probably because the Reds just so happened to have a really good team at the time. And something that I've increasingly realised over the years is that I was incredibly lucky to spend my first few years as a fan - those years when your team probably matters to you more than at any other point in your life - watching Forest in the late 80s and early-to-mid 90s.

Of course, it wasn't quite the late 70s and early 80s in terms of the levels of success achieved. But even so, I was lucky enough to enjoy not one but two brilliant Forest teams - the last great Cloughie team of the late 80s and early 90s, and also Frank Clark's side of the mid-90s.

Looking back I think I was massively guilty of taking this for granted – I think we all were. During my first few years as a Forest fan we'd talk about 'the annual trip to Wembley' – while there were certain 'squad players' where you'd groan when you heard their name as the teams were being read out over the tannoy on a Saturday afternoon. Terry Wilson and Phil Starbuck spring to mind - below average players at the time compared to others in the Reds' squad, but both of them would have walked into most of the Forest teams of the last 20 years.

Indeed, it makes me sad when I think about younger Reds fans and the slim pickings that they've grown up with – and it breaks my heart a bit when I hear them talking about David Johnson as their all-time favourite player.

Okay, he had one good season.

But with all due respect, is he really anywhere near to being one of Forest's best ever players?

Along with all my memories, I've also amassed quite a few Forest-related mementoes over the years.

You won't be surprised to know that I still have the signed football that I received as a birthday present off Cloughie when I was a kid, as documented in an earlier chapter.

And though it no longer fits me, I still have my first ever Forest shirt - the one with 'Shipstone's Fine Ales' printed on the front.

I also have copies of pretty much every Forest fanzine ever published… part of an old wooden sign from above the old Trent End terrace turnstiles… and a copy of the popular kids' book 'Dogger' signed by Stan Collymore!

More than any memories and trinkets though, the one thing that I value more than anything else from all my years as a Forest fan is the fact that it's been a key part of so many important relationships in my life. As a kid it gave me some wonderful shared experiences with my Dad - and while Dad stopped going to matches regularly back in the mid-90s he's always kept tabs on how Forest are getting on, and the Reds are still usually one of the first things we talk about whenever we see each other. It might just be 11 men kicking a bag of wind about, but it's part of the tie that binds us.

And as for my brother Al, it's only in the last few years that I've started to realise what a big part Forest have played in our relationship. With there being less than two years between us, Al and I have always been close. We did everything together growing up - and through going to watch the Reds together, we continued to spend a lot of time together into adulthood.

It's fair to say though that we've drifted apart a bit since we both decided in 2015 to give up our Forest season tickets. For years, we'd see each other every other week simply because of the Reds' fixture list. But now, we actually have to make an effort if we want to spend time together – and with both of us having busy lives, that doesn't seem to happen as often as it probably should.

Beyond my own family meanwhile, Forest have played a huge part in many enduring friendships over the years. Of all the stories I've shared in this book about the friends in question – everyone from Rach and Andy to Graham the Gordon Ramsey lookalike - I only hope they remember everything in the same way that I do…

Of course, the million dollar question in terms of my relationship with Forest is whether I'll ever get sucked back in to a point where I become a season ticket holder again. And you'll note there my deliberate use of the term 'season ticket' – like one of those old codgers who still calls a right winger an outside right, I refuse to even acknowledge this new trend of the last few years of calling them 'season cards'!

But joking aside, committing myself once again to going to every home game isn't really on my agenda just at the moment.

 That said, I wouldn't rule out the possibility that it might happen again at some point in the future. After all, I've already managed to get myself lured back into the world of Forest once before after a time when I'd drifted away.

These days I tend to go and watch the Reds approximately once a month. Realistically though, I imagine whether I ever jump in with both feet again will probably come down to my children.

I must say, I do love the idea that one day I'll end up being one of those Dads who takes his kids to the match. In fact, as I write these words I'm actually pretty much the same age that my Dad was when he first started taking me to go and watch Forest – which feels a bit strange when I think about it.

At the time of writing though my boys are aged just one and three – so they're both far too young really to be getting into football properly. But it'll certainly be interesting to see how things pan out over the next few years. I'm intrigued and slightly nervous to know whether they'll get the Forest bug - or decide instead to support Chelsea or Manchester United like a lot of kids seem to do these days.

Or maybe they simply won't be bothered about supporting a football team?

In some ways, I don't it'd be a bad thing if they weren't.

I certainly don't feel like I'm under any pressure to ensure some sort of torch is passed down to the next generation. After all, as I've mentioned in the earlier sections of this book, my Dad was never exactly a massive Forest fan when I was a growing up – it was more a case of him starting to take me to matches because of me pestering him to do so, rather than the other way round.

I like to think that I won't try and force my children to become Forest fans – but to be honest, I don't think us parents are ever fully capable of holding ourselves back when it comes to inflicting our passions on our kids. In fact, my eldest, Arlo, was only a few hours old when attempts were first made to steer him towards the righteous path of the mighty Reds - when my Dad scored himself some serious brownie points on his first day as a Grandad by turning up on the maternity ward at Nottingham's City Hospital and presenting him with a baby-sized Forest shirt!

I also had Arlo kicking a ball pretty much from the moment he was walking, having bought him one of those lightweight plastic ones that were known when I was a kid as a '99p flyaway' – though thanks to the wonders of inflation, they cost about three quid these days! From the age of two I also started taking him to a weekly Saturday morning session for kids that runs in Nottingham called Socatots – and with his ginger locks and sweet left foot, I'm hoping he may end being the next Brian Rice.

Usually the Socatots classes start with the coaches getting everyone warmed up by singing a nursery rhyme and doing all the accompanying actions. Whenever it's 'Heads Shoulders, Knees and Toes', I have to fight the urge to change the words to a certain retro Trent End ditty to the same tune – particularly given that one of the coaches is, controversially, a Derby fan!

There's a circus in the town, in the town, Robert Maxwell is the clown, is the clown…

In many ways I'm actually enthused far more by the idea of my kids getting into playing football than watching it. Back when I was a kid, a lot of footballers genuinely seemed like really good role models. Not only were the likes of Stuart Pearce and Steve Hodge brilliantly talented players, they also epitomised all sorts of positive attributes in the way they went about their business – honesty, determination, bravery, passion, selflessness, respect and humility to name just a few. In particular, I remember being massively inspired by Psycho and the fact that he'd still been playing amateur football until he was well into his 20s - yet through sheer guile and determination, ended up playing at the highest level and captaining his country.

Aside from a few notable exceptions though, I'm not sure today's players are necessarily such a positive influence on young impressionable minds…

However, for all the many unpleasant aspects of the modern game, I still think that playing football (or indeed any sport) is a great way for young people to learn important life lessons – everything from being a team player to being a gracious loser.

But maybe I'm being unrealistic though in sort of hoping that my kids inherit my love of playing the game but decide they're not that bothered about actually supporting a team? After all, I know from my own experience that the two things feed each other to a large degree.

As things stand, Arlo does show a certain level of interest whenever we're at home and I happen to be watching football on TV. To be honest, I don't think there's any imminent danger of it eclipsing dinosaurs as his main passion in life - however, he learned from a very early age to shout "Goalll!" whenever he saw the ball fly into the back of the net, and he's also starting to show a basic understanding of the rules of the beautiful game.

That said, one of my lowest ever points as a parent was when Arlo saw the hapless former Forest manager Steve Cotterill on TV, by now in charge of Bristol City, and immediately pointed at him and shouted "Daddy!"

Arlo has already made his first trip to the City Ground to watch a match – although rather than a proper Forest match, it was a charity game where a team of Reds fans were taking on a team of Derby fans.

I'd decided to go along to this game because a friend of mine was playing in the Forest team. Arlo was just over 12 months old at the time, and it seemed a good opportunity to introduce him to the world of the mighty Reds safe in the knowledge that all 11 players would actually be showing a bit of pride in the shirt - something that's sadly been far from a given for much of the last few decades.

Encouragingly, the little man seemed to enjoy his first ever matchday experience – and with it being a relatively low-key occasion, he even got to have a run around on the pitch at half-time and have sit in the home team dugout. Even at the tender age of just one, I think it's fair to say that he probably had a better grasp of football than some of the chumps who have sat in the same spot!

That afternoon also saw Arlo end up getting his hands on the European Cup, which was on display in one of the hospitality areas. However, rather than treating it with the sort of reverence of most fans who were present, he was more interested in using one of the handles as a giant teething ring!

Meanwhile, Arlo's little brother Jude has also started showing great enthusiasm for kicking a ball about at any opportunity. What's more, there's been encouraging signs too that he's unlikely to be intimidated out on the field of play. Yes, in the summer of 2017 I took him along with me to an event where we met Forest legend Kenny Burns, who kindly agreed to pose for a photo with us. And the resulting snap is priceless – it shows Jude taking the opportunity to unnerve one of the hardest players in the history of the game by fixing him with the sort of unwavering death stare that only a 12-month old can muster!

But as I said, both of my kids are still far too young at this point in time to be getting the bug.

And that's no bad thing really. After all, it buys Forest a few years to build a decent team!

For let's face it, whether my kids get properly sucked into the world of Forest will probably come down ultimately to whether or not the mighty Reds become properly good again. If they continue to languish in English football's wilderness as they have done now for the best part of two decades, I can't say I'd feel massively motivated if I was a young person to get myself down to the City Ground.

As I write these words, it's quite depressing how long it's now been since Forest were last in the Premier League. It's scary, but when I was a kid I spent a fair amount of time watching videos of Brian Clough and Peter Taylor's all conquering team of the late 70s and early 80s – and while it was exciting to learn about the Reds' glorious history, I did feel quite far removed from it. It felt like what I was watching may as well have happened hundreds of years ago – no different really to black and white clips of the Beatles playing at the Cavern Club, or old footage from World War Two.

At the time though, Forest's European triumphs had only taken place a decade or so earlier. It's a sobering thought then that for the nine and ten year old Reds fans of today, just Forest being in the Premier League – let alone actually winning stuff - is much further back in time than those European Cups were for me.

With each passing year, the idea of the Reds rejoining the elite of English football feels more and more of an unattainable goal. The end of the 2016-17 season saw Forest complete their 17th season outside the top flight – and during the summer of 2017, I sat down and worked out how many different teams had won promotion to the top flight during those 17 seasons in which the Reds had failed to do so. I was staggered to discover that the total was no less than 33 clubs – with perennial yo-yo teams Hull, Burnley and West Brom managing it no less than four times each.

In fact, of all the other teams who competed alongside Forest in the Championship during the 2016-17 season, the only other clubs who hadn't actually achieved promotion to the Premier League at some point during the previous 17 seasons were MK Dons, Rotherham, Burton Albion, Bristol City, Leeds, Preston, Brentford, and Sheffield Wednesday. And with all due respect, it's probably only Wednesday and Leeds out of all of those teams that have ever really had serious pretensions of wanting to make it up to English football's highest level.

Incredible really.

Maybe it's just like that theory about monkeys and typewriters and the works of Shakespeare – and if you give Forest an infinite number of attempts, they will eventually strike gold?

That said, when I think about it, I do have hugely mixed feelings about the idea of the Reds making it back to the top flight.

I do think the way the Premier League is talked about so much as English football's equivalent of the promised land can sometimes blind us to the reality of how difficult it actually is for newly promoted teams to survive up there these days. I don't think the standard of football in English football's highest echelon has necessarily improved all that much in the last few decades – however, I do think there's been a massive increase in the gulf in class between the first and second tier. You only have to look at how Forest have generally been played off the park on most of the occasions in recent history when they've drawn a Premier League team in one of the cups.

In some instances in fact, it's been a case of them being played off the park by the opposition's *reserve* team.

There have of course been a few exceptions – one of the most memorable such occasions back in 2009, when the Reds pulled off an unlikely 3-0 win away at Manchester City in the FA Cup.

Though typically, they then went and got knocked out by a bunch of no-marks in the next round.

The contrary bunch of sods.

All in all then, given how Forest almost seem to have gone out on a limb in recent years to find new and inventive ways to embarrass us fans – be it relegation to League One, losing to Accrington Stanley in the cup, or ballsing up play-off semi-finals in spectacular fashion – my biggest fear if they were to go up to the Premier League is far greater than the thought of them merely going straight back down. No, I'd be genuinely worried that they might also 'beat' Derby's proud record of the lowest ever points total while they were at it!

Which all begs the question: do I ever actually want the Reds to go up?

Well 2016 saw the launch of an excellent new Forest fanzine called *Bandy and Shinty* – and in their sixth edition, one of their writers, Phil Juggins, pretty much hit the nail on the head as far as I'm concerned.

"Do you want your expectations and your excitement to be so utterly reconfigured, as to be celebrating the occasional draw against City or Arsenal as the highlight of a season?," he wrote. "Is it right that a snatched and spawny win against Chelsea or United – teams we've beaten for fun, even in my lifetime – would now assume a kind of 'I was there', open-topped bus gravitas?"

Not to mention the chilling thought of the street peddlers outside the ground flogging those awful 'half and half' scarves at any of those 'big games'. Or Sir Paul McCartney's threat to come to the City Ground and sing 'Mull of Kintyre' live if Forest ever get back to the top flight – an event that would be so teeth-grindingly cheesy that I almost hope the Reds stay in the Championship forever just to ensure it never happens.

Or at least not until the day comes where Sir Paul is finally reunited with his old mate John.

But joking aside, as we all know there have been teams that have made it up to the top flight and survived - and some who have established themselves. What's more, some have even done it without actually spending silly money. Most impressively, Leicester City managed the unthinkable in the 2015-16 season, just two years after getting promotion from the Championship. Their success was truly exceptional though, and I don't think anyone other than the criminally insane would expect Forest do the same if the Reds went up.

That said, there are a number of other teams who have hit the sort of heights in recent years I think Forest could realistically aspire to - including the likes of Southampton and Swansea. But as far as I can tell, those clubs have achieved what they have due to having a long-term plan in place – and that sort of vision is something Forest have been distinctly lacking for much of their recent history.

The club may finally be moving in the right direction though on that score – as the summer of 2017 saw the Fawaz Al Hasawi era finally draw to a close after five long years. And it was an ignominious finale for the hapless Kuwaiti too - with the malaise at the City Ground under his regime having reached such desperate levels that the Reds only narrowly escaped relegation down to League One in the final game of his tenure as the club's owner.

I don't think those of us who were there at the City Ground that afternoon to watch Forest take on Ipswich will ever forget the tense rollercoaster of emotions we all experienced over the 90 minutes – in particular, a good 40-minute chunk of the game when the Reds were mathematically doomed based on how all the results around the country were stacking up.

Thankfully it all worked out okay in the end - although the sight of fans running on the pitch after the final whistle to celebrate Forest clinging on to their status as a Championship club on goal difference was, in some ways, one of the most depressing things I've ever witnessed in all my years as a Reds supporter.

That said, the sense of relief at avoiding relegation *was* enormous.

Back in 2005 when Forest last dropped down to League One, I don't think anyone doubted that they'd bounce back eventually.

But as the Reds headed into the final few games of the 2016-17 season, with the threat of relegation very real, it all felt very different.

By this point in proceedings it was widely known that Fawaz had been trying for months to wash his hands of Forest - with it having finally dawned even on him that his ego trip of buying an English football club had massively backfired.

However, there was the huge worry that no-one would've wanted to buy the club if the Reds were to slide into League One. And it simply didn't bear thinking about being plunged into English football's third tier whilst stuck with an increasingly disinterested owner who'd succeeded only in achieving year-on-year decline during his five years at the City Ground.

All in all, you couldn't help but fear a genuine danger of Forest plummeting into oblivion in the same way that teams like Coventry and Portsmouth have done in recent years.

The plight of Coventry actually makes me feel really sad, given all the epic tussles that Forest had with them during my early years as a Reds fan. In particular I'll always remember the two-legged League Cup semi-final back in the 1989-90 season, largely became Forest ended up getting to Wembley after winning 2-1 on aggregate.

But there was also another titanic battle between the two sides in the same competition the following season, that was unlike any game I've known since. On the night at Highfield Road, Coventry raced into a 4-0 lead with only half an hour or so on the clock – only for Forest to pull the score back to 4-4. A fifth goal for the Reds would've capped an incredible comeback – however it was the home side who had the final say in the end, scoring late on to secure a 5-4 win.

Looking back, that remarkable victory probably represented some sort of peak for that successful Coventry team of the late 80s and early 90s. The Sky Blues spent the rest of the 90s seemingly finishing 17th in the top flight every year, like one of those stubborn turds that won't flush away. They finally succumbed to relegation in 2001 – and have been in free fall pretty much ever since, even losing the right to play at their own ground at one point and suffering the indignity of having to squat with Northampton Town some 30 miles away.

Thankfully of course, Forest managed on that tense afternoon in May 2017 to do something they've so often failed to do in recent decades – and that was to pull a big performance out of the bag on an occasion when it *really* mattered.

But though the 3-0 win against Ipswich was enough for the Reds to narrowly escape the slippery slope, it was uncomfortably close - and by the end of Fawaz's five years as owner, I think it's fair to say that most of us fans were so sick of him that we would've been happy to see him flog the club to pretty much anyone, just for the sake of getting him out of the door.

As it turned out, the new owners ended up being a consortium headed up by the Greek shipping tycoon Evangelos Marinakis. And while it was a huge relief to see the back of Fawaz, at first you couldn't help but fear that we were about to go straight out of the frying pan and into the fire – as there were all sorts of reports in the media about the way Marinakis has allegedly conducted some of his business in Greek football.

To be fair though, after the whole sorry saga with Fawaz, I imagine us Forest fans will probably have 'trust issues' for quite some time with whoever owns the club. Personally, I'm trying to keep an open mind about the new Greek overlords – and while it's still early days at the time of writing, it was impressive to see them move so quickly in getting a chairman and a chief executive appointed to take care of the day-to-day running of the club only a matter of days after completing the takeover.

This represented more structure being put in place in the space of a few weeks than Fawaz had managed in half a decade.

That said, Marinakis and company have already sacked a manager barely six months after assuming control – with Mark Warburton handed his cards on New Year's Eve 2017, after a string of indifferent results had left the Reds nudging towards the bottom half of the Championship table.

Maybe some things never change.

In fact, part of me thinks us Forest fans might find life easier if we just accept that the Reds are stuck in the Championship because that is ultimately what we are – a bog average team in English football's second tier. That's certainly what we were until a certain Mr Clough arrived in Nottingham in 1975.

Naturally, now that I've gone and written these closing words – in early 2018, midway through the 2017-18 season - Forest will probably go on a remarkable late burst and squeak into one of the promotion spots just to prove me wrong.

The bastards!

But joking aside of course - if they did manage this, then no one would be happier than me.

Yes, I still have mixed feelings about the idea of the Reds getting back into the Premier League.

However, it's easy to say that when the idea of it ever happening still feels light years away. Let's face it, if Forest were to reach the business end of the season with a shout of making it up to the top flight, I'm sure we'd all be far too caught up in the excitement to even give a second's thought to whether or not we actually want the prize on offer.

Such is one of the great prerogatives of being a football fan – that licence we have to ride those waves of euphoria whenever they happen to come along, and ignore our inner voice of reason if it suits us to do so. Whether or not we care to admit it, we're a fickle bunch.

From a selfish perspective, Forest making a late charge for promotion would also be of enormous benefit to this book. After all, it'd enable me to quickly rewrite the ending - and give it the Hollywood finale it's painfully lacking.

In reality of course, I can't see it actually happening.

But I'm okay with that.

Indeed, having set my expectations accordingly, I find that I'm much better placed to enjoy the matchday experience for what it is these days whenever I go and watch Forest. And the fact that I only tend to head down to the City Ground every now and again has made me appreciate a lot more some of the small things you probably take for granted when you're going to every game.

The stroll to the ground from town, and the way you feel an increasing sense of purpose in your step the further you get down London Road.

The brilliant view of City Ground as you walk across Trent Bridge.

The guy with the amazing moustache who runs a stall selling Forest memorabilia in front of the boat club.

The psychotic Canada geese prowling by the back of the Trent End, who always seem slightly put out by their usually tranquil territory being invaded by 20,000 lairy people dressed in red.

The clank of the turnstiles.

The strangely alluring aroma of the chicken balti pies.

That first glimpse of the green baize as you walk up the steps.

The hair-on-back-of-neck moment just before kick-off as everyone sings along to 'Mull of Kintyre'.

The satisfying crunch of the game's first proper tackle.

The way the cries of "Come on you Reds!" ring around the ground like a Gregorian chant.

That split second when you realise the ball is on its way into the back of the opposition net.

The gleeful cheers when it's announced at half-time that Derby are losing.

The smug feeling when the away fans are wildly celebrating an equaliser, but you've spotted way before them that the linesman's flag is up.

The sound of the final whistle when the Reds have either held on for a win or a decent point.

The way fans get unofficial right of way over traffic as everyone spills out onto the streets surrounding the ground.

All in all, I think I have a healthier relationship with Forest these days than I did during my last few years as a season ticket holder.

Yes, there are still lots of things about the club, and indeed football in general that, I'd love to change.

But I'm happy now to be at a point where, if I'm going to a game, I actually spend the week looking forward to it.

Which is exactly how it should be.

Acknowledgements

So, here's the bit where I get to act like an Oscar winner – or *anyone* writing a Facebook post on New Year's Eve - and express my gratitude to a load of people. And to be fair, there are a lot of folk who have helped me with both writing this book, and also preparing to unleash it on an unsuspecting world.

First and foremost, my wife Emma for her unwavering patience and support as I spent many an hour tapping away at a laptop.

Brian Rice for writing the foreword.

My Mum for taking on the herculean job of proof reading and trying in vain to curb my flagrant overuse of exclamation marks and the word 'brilliant'.

Various people who have been part of my Forest journey for helping me remember some of the detail – in particular my Dad and my brother Al, and also Andy Best, Rachel Shires, Graham Austin and Sanjay Nijran.

Numerous other folk who took time to read bits of the book in draft form and offer encouragement and constructive feedback – most notably 'Little' Mick Fisher, Ed Baker, Paul Turp, Max Newton, James Houghton, Ian Davis, Paul and Geraldine Ellis, Marcus and Sarah Alton, Trish Riley, Mike Blundell, Ian Black, Sue Warburton, Kris Walden, Stewart Green, Mark Fletcher, Chris Groves, Darren Webster, Dave Storer and Steve Hartshorn.

The very talented Nat Bontoft for interpreting an impressively vague brief to come up with a wonderful design for the front cover. You can see more of her work on Instagram at natbontoftdesign. And there are plans to make prints available of the cover artwork of this book – keep an eye on www.facebook.com/churchofstuartpearce for full details on that.

Lots of folk too numerous to mention who helped me spread the word about the book's impending publication on social media. You know who you are!

The guys at Forza Garibaldi, who also agreed straight away when I asked them if they could help me get word out about this book to fellow Forest fans. In case you're not aware, Forza Garibaldi is a fan movement set up in recent years with the aim of improving the atmosphere at Reds games. From pre-match boat trips along the Trent to getting loads of banners made to wave around in the stands, they organise all sorts of brilliant initiatives – all of which takes a lot of time, effort and resource. And though I don't think 'The Church of Stuart Pearce and other stories' is ever likely to become a million-seller, I do like the idea of 'giving something back' – so to help Forza Garibaldi, I'll be chucking them 50p from every copy of the book sold. You can find out more about Forza Garibaldi at www.forzagaribaldi.com

Dan Donson and Anthony Cooper at Waterstones, and Mick Garton at MSR Newsgroup, for making me feel like a proper author by offering to throw launch events for the book. And Dave Jackson from BBC Radio Nottingham, for kindly agreeing to play host at the Waterstones bash.

Controversially, there's also someone from the wrong end of the A52 who I'd like to thank. Kalwinder Singh Dhindhsa is someone who I got to know through our shared love of the greatest managerial duo English football has ever seen – and he was heavily involved in the project that led to a statue of Brian Clough and Peter Taylor being erected outside Derby County's iPro stadium. Kal also happens to be an author, and his generous advice on the whole process of writing a memoir and publishing it has been invaluable.

And finally, while he didn't directly assist me in any way with anything to do with the creation of this book, I guess it's only right to give due recognition to the gentleman who's namechecked in the title.

Stuart Pearce has been an enormous inspiration to me ever since I began my Forest journey as a wide-eyed nine-year-old – and as is probably evident from the 28 chapters of this book, he's a figure who has loomed large throughout my years as a Reds fan.

In fact, Psycho is a figure who continues to loom large in my life full stop - as the lifesize cardboard cutout of the great man that led to the accidental birth of the Church of Stuart Pearce back in 2003 now lives in my downstairs toilet! Needless to say, it can be quite disconcerting for visitors to my house when they go to use the facilities and find themselves faced with the former Forest captain and manager staring impassively at them.

It's not known what Psycho's thoughts are on the fact that there's now a book that exists called *The Church of Stuart Pearce and other stories*. I did write to him in November 2017 care of West Ham United Football Club, but received no response. But I like to think he'd be quite amused.

Rich Fisher, February 2018

Printed in Great Britain
by Amazon